Biology
for IGCSE
Revised for the latest syllabus

MARY JONES

Heinemann

Heinemann Educational Publishers
Halley Court, Jordan Hill, Oxford OX2 8EJ
A Part of Harcourt Education Limited

Heinemann Publishers (Pty) Limited
PO Box 781940, Sandton 2146, Johannesburg, South Africa

OXFORD MELBOURNE AUCKLAND
JOHANNESBURG BLANTYRE GABORONE
IBADAN PORTSMOUTH (NH) USA CHICAGO

First published by Heinemann Educational Publishers in 1994

Second edition 2002

The right of Mary Jones to be identified as the author of this work has been asserted by her in accordance with the Copyright, Designs and Patents Act 1988.

British Library Cataloguing in Publication Data

A catalogue record for this book is available from the British Library.

Illustrated by Gecko Limited and Geoffrey Jones

Cover design by Gabriel Kern

Cover photograph of false-colour SEM of pollen grains by David Scharf/Science Photo Library

ISBN : 978 0 435 96878 2

Text designed and produced by Gecko Limited, Bicester, Oxon

Printed by Multivista Global Ltd

08 09 / 10 9 8

Acknowledgements

The author and publishers would like to thank the following for supplying photographs: Bill Aron/Science Photo Library (Figure 9.11); Biophoto Associates (Figures 4.3a, c, 5.9, 6.3, 6.4, 6.5, 12.4, 12.5); Dr Jeremy Burgess/Science Photo Library (Figures 8.2, 9.14); J. Allan Cash Photolibrary (Figure 10.9b); CNRI/Science Photo Library (Figure 5.2); Bruce Coleman Ltd (Figures 8.8b, c, 14.11); Nigel Dickinson/The Environmental Picture Library (Figure 15.15); Mark Edwards/Still Pictures (Figures 1.1, 4.14, 14.18, 15.3); Martin Flitman/The Environmental Picture Library (Figure 15.7); Simon Fraser, Royal Victoria Infirmary, Newcastle-upon-Tyne/ Science Photo Library (Figure 10.4); Peter Gould (Figures 3.1, 4.1, 4.15, 7.7, 7.8, 9.6, 9.9, 9.14, 9.15); Eric Grave/Science Photo Library (Figure 7.13); Robert Harding Picture Library (Figures 10.9a, 12.19); Jimmy Holmes/The Environmental Picture Library (Figure 15.5); Holt Studios International (Figures 1.15b, 6.11a, b, 6.13, 8.8a, 11.16, 12.25, 14.7, 14.13, 15.14 [above]); Dr J.B. Howells/Science Photo Library (Figure 3.10); Institut Pasteur/CNRI/Science Photo Library (Figure 9.8); Hank Morgan/Science Photo Library (Figure 12.22); Professor P. Motta/Science Photo Library (Figure 12.13); National Medical Slide Bank (Figure 4.9); Heldur Netocny/Still Pictures (Figure 4.13); NHPA (Figure 1.15c); OMIKRON/Science Photo Library (Figure 11.7); Panos Pictures (Figure 15.4); Petit Format/Institut Pasteur/ Science Photo Library (Figure 1.19); D. Phillips/Science Photo Library (Figure 12.15); Photofusion (Figure 13.9); David Scharf/Science Photo Library (Figure 12.26); James Stevenson/Science Photo Library (Figure 9.10); Martin Stott/The Environmental Picture Library (Figure 15.14 [below]); ZEFA (Figures 1.16c, 13.10a, b, 15.2, 15.11).

Note to the teacher

If you do not wish your students to have a copy of the answers to questions, you should cut out pages 295 onwards.

Contents

Introduction

This book covers all of the material that you need to know for your IGCSE Biology course. Each chapter has been written so that it precisely matches the requirements of the IGCSE syllabus.

Core and Supplement content

The content of the IGCSE Biology syllabus is divided into Core and Supplement. Everyone taking IGCSE Biology needs to know the Core material. In addition, if you are hoping to get a grade A*, A or B, then you also need to know the Supplement material. You can easily see which parts of this book contain Supplement material, because it is printed on a grey background.

Summaries

At the end of each chapter there is a summary of what has been explained in that chapter, and what you should know when you have finished working through it. These summaries closely match the content of the IGCSE Biology syllabus. You will find them especially helpful when you are revising for your examinations.

Chapter questions

In IGCSE Biology, you are not only tested on the facts that you know. You will also be expected to demonstrate that you really *understand* these facts. You may, for example, be given an examination question that at first sight looks completely unfamiliar to you. However, if you have learnt and understood what is in this book, then you will always find that you *do* have knowledge and understanding that you can use in answering that question, however unfamiliar it may look. So it is really important to check that you understand your work, and do not just learn it by heart without thinking about it. The questions that appear in each chapter will help you to do this, by making you think and use your knowledge as you go along.

Practical work

A very important part of any science course, including Biology, is practical work. There are many suggestions for practical work in this book. They will help you to develop all four of the practical skills that will be assessed as part of your IGCSE Biology examination. You will learn how to use techniques, apparatus and materials; to make and record observations and measurements; to interpret and evaluate experimental observations and data; and eventually to plan and carry out your own investigations. To help you to become confident in these skills, many of the practicals give you the chance to think quite a lot out for yourself. For example, you may be expected to design your own results chart, rather than just filling in an outline one. There are also several suggestions for you to design and carry out your own experiments. If you are unsure about some of these things early in your course your teacher will be able to help you.

Apparatus and guidelines for investigations are provided at the back of the book. Practical skills covered by each investigation are provided.

The variety of life

Biology is the study of living organisms. Living organisms have a number of characteristics that make them different from non-living things. Biologists classify living organisms into groups, to make them easier to study.

Living and non-living things ▶

If you look around you, you can probably see a number of living and non-living things. It is usually easy to tell which are alive and which are not. People, for example, are obviously alive because they move around. Plants are obviously alive because they grow.

Figure 1.1 ▶
What can you see here that is alive? What is not alive? How can you tell?

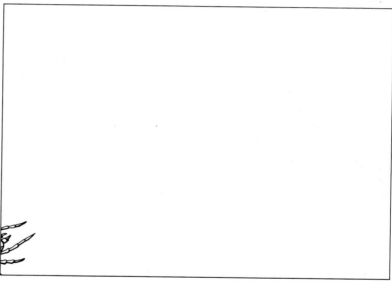

Living things are called **organisms**. Living organisms have seven characteristics that make them different from non-living things:

1 Living organisms **feed**. They need to take in substances from their surroundings. They use these substances for growth, or as a source of energy. Animals and plants feed in very different ways, as you will see in Chapters 5 and 6. Another word for feeding is **nutrition**.

2 Living organisms **respire**. This means that they break down food inside their cells, sometimes by combining it with oxygen. This releases energy from the food, and the organisms can use this energy to carry out processes 3 to 7 listed below.

3 Living organisms **move**. This is very easy to see in most animals, but it is not easy to see a plant moving! Most plants are rooted to the ground, so the whole plant cannot move. But parts of plants may move slowly. Perhaps only the contents of their cells move, so that you can only see the movement under the microscope.

4 Living organisms **excrete**. Chemical reactions take place inside the cells of an organism. Some of the substances made by these reactions are poisonous, so the organism needs to get rid of them. Getting rid of these substances is called excretion.

5 Living organisms **grow**. Some of the food they take in is used to help cells to grow, and to build new cells, so that the organism gets larger.

6 Living organisms **reproduce**. Every kind of living organism is able to make new organisms like itself.

7 Living organisms are **sensitive** to things around them. All living organisms can sense changes in their surroundings, and respond to them. The changes they sense are of many types, such as changes in temperature, light intensity, sound, day length and the presence of chemicals.

Question

1.1 The engine of a car uses petrol (gasoline). Oxygen from the air combines with the petrol, releasing energy which is used to turn the wheels of the car. Waste gases from the burnt petrol are given off in the exhaust fumes of the car.

   a Which characteristics of a car are similar to which characteristics of living organisms?

   b Explain why a car is not a living organism.

Classifying living organisms ▶

Nobody knows how many different kinds, or **species**, of living organisms there are on Earth. About 1.4 million different species have been described and named. But many biologists think that this may only be about one tenth of the species on Earth! We have almost certainly discovered most of the large land animals, but there are probably many animals living in the deep oceans which have never been seen by humans. And biologists estimate that there are certainly millions of insects and smaller animals and plants that have not yet been discovered.

To make it easier to study these organisms, biologists have sorted them into groups. This sorting is called **classification**.

Living organisms have evolved over hundreds of millions of years. (You can read about evolution in Chapter 13.) Living organisms are all related to one another. Biologists classify them by putting closely related organisms into the same group.

Question

1.2 Suggest why it is useful for biologists to classify living organisms into groups of closely related organisms. Try to think of at least two reasons.

The vertebrates

One group of organisms is the vertebrates. The vertebrates all belong to a large group, or phylum, called Chordates. The Chordates all have a stiffening rod that runs along inside the upper surface of their body. In the vertebrates, this rod has been replaced by a row of bones, the vertebral column or backbone.

All vertebrates have a tail that starts behind the anus (the opening from the digestive system). This is called a **post-anal tail**. Animals that are not vertebrates never have a post-anal tail. For example, the anus of an earthworm is right at the very end of its body.

The vertebrates are classified into smaller groups, called **classes**. Figures 1.2 to 1.6 show vertebrates from each class.

Fish are vertebrates with bodies covered by scales (Figure 1.2). Almost all fish live in water. They have fins to help them to move and balance. Fish get their oxygen from the water, using gills. Fish have a sense organ called a lateral line, which runs along each side of their body, and can sense vibrations in the water. On some fish, you can see the lateral line quite clearly.

Amphibians are vertebrates with a smooth, moist skin (Figure 1.3). The adults of some amphibians, such as salamanders, live on land. Others, such as newts, spend a lot of time in the water. But all amphibians have to go back to the water to lay their soft, jelly-like eggs. These eggs hatch into tadpoles, which gradually change into adults. Like fish, tadpoles breathe through gills, but adult amphibians breathe through their skin and through lungs. Unlike fish, amphibians have ears, and you can sometimes see their eardrums. Amphibians have four legs, or limbs.

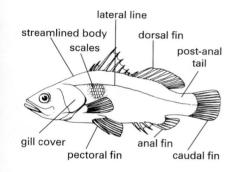

▲ **Figure 1.2**
A Nile perch, *Lates niloticus*.

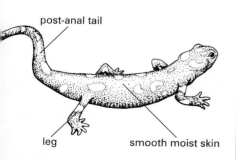

▲ **Figure 1.3**
A fire salamander, *Salamandra salamandra*.

Reptiles are vertebrates with a rough, scaly skin (Figure 1.4). Some of them, such as crocodiles, spend a lot of time in water. Others, such as lizards, live on land. All reptiles lay their eggs on land. These eggs have waterproof shells. Like frogs, reptiles have ears, but their eardrums are deep inside their heads, so that you see a hole rather than the eardrum on the surface of the head. Most reptiles have four legs, although snakes have lost theirs.

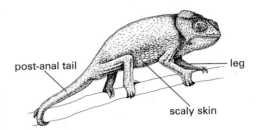

◄ **Figure 1.4**
A chameleon,
Chamaeleo chamaeleon.

Birds are very easy to recognise, because they are the only vertebrates with feathers and a beak (Figure 1.5). Birds are very closely related to reptiles, and, like reptiles, have scaly legs and holes leading to their eardrums. The front limbs of birds have become wings, and most birds can use these to fly. All birds lay their eggs on land. These eggs have much harder shells than reptiles' eggs.

Mammals are vertebrates with hair (Figure 1.6).

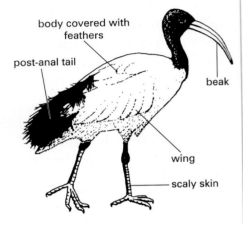

▲ **Figure 1.5**
A sacred ibis, *Threskiornis aethiopicus.*

Figure 1.6 ▶
A gnu or wildebeest,
Connochaetes taurinus.

(When many people say 'animals', they really mean 'mammals'. Be careful that you do not do this!) The eardrum of a mammal, like those of reptiles and birds, is deep inside the head, but all mammals have a pinna, or flap, on the outside of the ear. Female mammals have mammary glands, which make milk to feed their young. Mammals do not lay eggs. Mammals have teeth of different types – incisors, canines, premolars and molars – other vertebrates have only one type of tooth.

1.3 Copy out this table, and then fill in the spaces. The first row has been done for you.

	Body covering	Limbs	Ears	Eggs	Any other points
Fish	Scales	No proper limbs; fins to help with swimming and balance	No ears; they have a lateral line instead	Surrounded by soft jelly, laid in water	Almost all fish live in water
Amphibians					
Reptiles					
Birds					
Mammals					

Investigation *1.1*

Looking at vertebrates

1 Make a large, labelled drawing of one fish, one amphibian, one reptile, one bird and one mammal that lives in your country. You could use living animals, dead animals, preserved specimens or photographs. On your drawings:

- show the **scale** – that is, how much bigger or smaller your drawing is than the real animal

- label the features you can see on each animal that are characteristic of the class to which it belongs.

2 Find out about where each animal lives, and write a sentence or two about each one to explain how it is adapted to live in this environment.

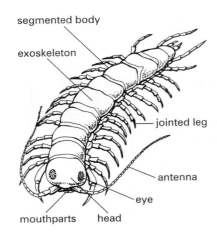

▲ Figure 1.7
A myriapod, the centipede *Lithobius*.

Arthropods

Arthropods are very common animals. There are more different species of arthropods on Earth than all other animals put together. Arthropods are invertebrates, which means that they do not have a backbone. The characteristics of arthropods are:

- They have jointed legs.

- They have a hard, outer covering over their bodies, called an exoskeleton. This protects them, supports them and has muscles attached to it to allow them to move. In terrestrial (land-living) arthropods it also stops their bodies from losing water and drying out.

- The body of an arthropod is always divided into many segments.

There are several kinds of arthropods, including **myriapods**, **insects**, **crustaceans** and **arachnids**.

Myriapods (Figure 1.7) include the centipedes and millipedes. They are arthropods whose bodies are made up of many different segments. They have many pairs of legs. They have a single pair of antennae.

Insects (Figure 1.8) are probably the group of arthropods that most people know best. Their body is clearly divided into a head, thorax and abdomen. You can usually see that the thorax is made up of three segments and the abdomen of around 10 or 11 segments. They have three pairs of legs, all attached to the thorax. Most insects have two pairs of wings, also attached to the thorax. They have a single pair of antennae.

Figure 1.8 ▶
An insect. This is a desert locust, *Schistocerca gregaria*.

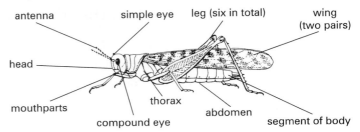

Crustaceans (Figure 1.9) include crabs, shrimps and woodlice. Their exoskeleton is usually especially strong, because it contains calcium salts that make it very hard. They have many pairs of legs – for example, a crab has five pairs. They have two pairs of antennae. Their body is made up of a combined head-and-thorax region called the cephalothorax, and also an abdomen. Each of these parts is made up of many segments.

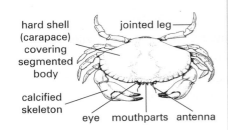

▲ Figure 1.9
A crustacean. This is an edible crab, *Cancer pagurus*.

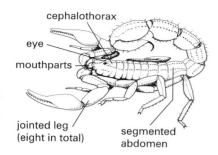

cephalothorax
eye
mouthparts
jointed leg
(eight in total)
segmented
abdomen

▲ **Figure 1.10**
An arachnid. This is a North African scorpion, *Androctonus australis*.

Arachnids (Figure 1.10) are the spiders and scorpions. Like crustaceans, their body is divided into a cephalothorax and abdomen. They have four pairs of legs and no antennae.

Questions

1.4 Draw a table (rather like the one in Question 1.3) with the four kinds of arthropods listed down the left hand side, and these features as the headings for the columns:

number of legs

how the body is divided up

number of antennae

other special features

Then fill in all the spaces in your table, to summarise the ways in which the four groups of arthropods can be identified.

1.5 The table shows the numbers of known species of organisms belonging to six different groups.

Group	Number of species
Arthropods	928 000
Other invertebrates	79 000
Vertebrates	39 000
Protista (single-celled animals)	59 000
Fungi	79 000
Plants	237 000
Total	1 421 000

a Show this information in the form of a pie chart.

b About 85% of the known species of arthropods are insects. Show this information on your pie chart.

Annelids

Annelids are worms with bodies made up of many segments or rings. Earthworms are annelids, and so are the tube worms that you may see in rock pools on a beach. Leeches are also annelids. Figure 1.11 shows an annelid.

Some annelids have an obvious head region, which may have antennae. In others, such as the earthworm, it can be difficult to tell which end is which. Annelids never have legs, but some of them do have tiny, stiff hairs called chaetae which help them to grip the surface they are travelling over.

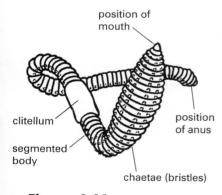

position of mouth
clitellum
position of anus
segmented body
chaetae (bristles)

▲ **Figure 1.11**
An annelid, the earthworm *Lumbricus terrestris*.

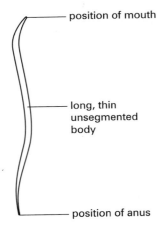

▲ Figure 1.12
A nematode, *Ascaris*.

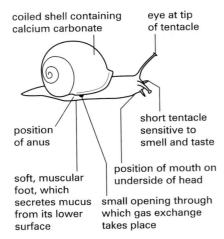

coiled shell containing calcium carbonate

eye at tip of tentacle

position of anus

short tentacle sensitive to smell and taste

soft, muscular foot, which secretes mucus from its lower surface

position of mouth on underside of head

small opening through which gas exchange takes place

▲ Figure 1.13
A mollusc, the garden snail *Helix aspersa*.

Question

1.6 Describe *one* similarity and *one* difference between arthropods and annelids.

Nematodes

Nematodes, like annelids, are worms. However, their bodies are not segmented. They usually just look like long, thin, white animals with no obvious head and no legs (Figure 1.12). Another difference from annelids is that they never have chaetae. Many nematodes live in the soil, while others are parasites, for example living in the digestive system of an animal.

Molluscs

Molluscs include slugs, snails (Figure 1.13), mussels, oysters, limpets, octopuses and squids. The name 'mollusc' means 'soft', and they all have soft bodies that are not segmented. Sometimes the body is enclosed in a hard shell made of calcium carbonate. Sometimes, as in octopuses and squids, there is a shell *inside* the soft body.

Most molluscs can move around on a soft foot that secretes slimy mucus to help them to slide along. Many of them, such as slugs and snails, have a rough tongue that they use to scrape away at leaves or other plant material that they eat. Some, such as mussels, are filter feeders, drawing water through their gills and trapping any tiny bits of food that may be floating in it. Octopuses and squids are much more mobile than most molluscs, and they can swim actively and use their long tentacles to catch other animals to eat.

Plants

So far in this chapter, all the organisms have been animals. They belong to the **animal kingdom**. However, if you look at Figure 1.14 you will see that there are four other kingdoms. We will look at one of these – the plants.

The main difference between plants and animals is the way they feed. Plants **photosynthesise** – that is, they use sunlight to make sugars from carbon dioxide and water. To do this, they need **chlorophyll**. Chlorophyll is green, so plants look green. Living organisms are made up of **cells**, as you will see in Chapter 2. The cells of plants have a **cell wall** made of **cellulose** around them, which animal cells never have.

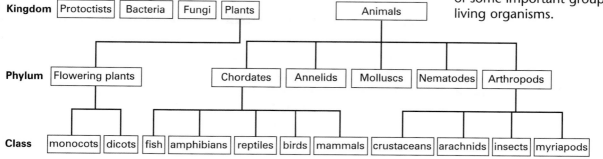

▼ Figure 1.14
A summary of the classification of some important groups of living organisms.

flower with three petals, three sepals, three stamens and three carpels

strap-shaped leaf with parallel veins

(a) The Kaffir lily, *Schizostylis.*

(b) Sorghum plants.

(c) A tulip tree, *Spathodea.*
▲ Figure 1.15

There are several phyla of plants, but the only one you need to know about at this stage is the phylum of **flowering plants**. As their name suggests, these plants have flowers! Inside the flowers, seeds develop. Most of the plants you are familiar with are flowering plants. As well as flowers, they have **roots**, **stems** and **leaves**.

The flowering plants are themselves divided up into two smaller groups, the **monocotyledonous** and **dicotyledonous** plants (monocots and dicots for short). These names refer to the number of cotyledons in their seeds (see page 207) – monocots have one cotyledon, and dicots have two. Even if you cannot inspect their seeds, you can still tell monocots and dicots apart. Monocots tend to have long, strap-shaped leaves, with veins running along the length of the leaf in parallel. Dicots often have broader leaves, with a branching pattern of veins. If the plant is flowering you have more clues, because the parts of a monocot flower (petals, stamens and so on) are always grouped in threes.

Question

1.7 Look at the photographs and drawings in Figure 1.15. Classify each plant as a monocot or a dicot.

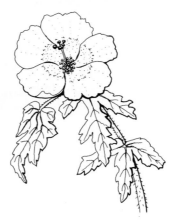

◄ Figure 1.15 (d)
Hibiscus trionum.

Figure 1.16 (a)
A mushroom.

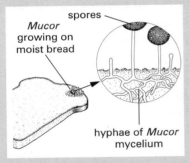

Figure 1.16 (b)
A bread mould, *Mucor*.

Fungi

In some ways, fungi are like plants. They grow rooted to the spot and do not move around. However, fungi do not photosynthesise, and do not have chlorophyll. Instead, they feed on other living or dead organisms. They do this by producing enzymes which seep out from the fungus into whatever it is growing on. The enzymes digest this food, which is then soaked up into the fungus's body. This is called **saprotrophic** feeding.

Figure 1.16 shows some different kinds of fungi. The main body of a fungus is called a **mycelium**. It is made up of many threads called **hyphae**. The hyphae grow through whatever the fungus is feeding on – perhaps a piece of bread, or through the soil. Each hypha is surrounded by a cell wall, but this is not made of cellulose like that of plant cells. Different fungi have different substances in their cell walls, but many of them have cell walls made of **chitin** – the exoskeleton of insects is also made of chitin. At certain times of year, some fungi grow a 'mushroom' above ground. This is for reproduction, which is done by producing thousands of tiny **spores**.

Yeast is a rather strange fungus. It has no hyphae and no mycelium, but lives just as single cells.

Figure 1.16 (c)
A fly agaric toadstool,
Amanita muscaria.

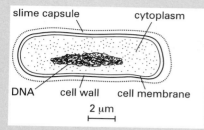

▲ Figure 1.17

A bacterium. Rod-shaped bacteria like this are called bacilli. Bacteria can also be spherical, when they are called cocci. Cocci sometimes link together to form chains. Some bacteria have a whip-like thread, called a flagellum, which they use to swim round. Notice that, although the bacterium has DNA, the DNA is not inside a nucleus as it is in an animal or plant cell.

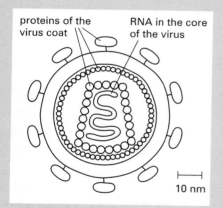

▲ Figure 1.18

A virus. This is the human immunodeficiency virus, or HIV, which causes AIDS. It is drawn as though part of its outer protein coat has been removed, so that you can see inside.

Bacteria

Bacteria are everywhere. Bacteria live in water, in soil, in food, in you . . . . Because they are so small, we tend to ignore them, but without bacteria there could be no other living things on Earth. You will see how important they are in recyling carbon and nitrogen from living things in Chapter 14.

Bacteria are single-celled organisms, as shown in Figure 1.17. Bacterial cells are *very* small, about one-thousandth the size of the cells of animals, plants or fungi. Like plants and fungi, their cells have **cell walls**, which usually contain a substance called murein. However, bacteria are different from all other kinds of living organisms because they *do not have a nucleus*.

Viruses

Viruses are very, very small. A virus is only about 100 nm across. (nm stands for nanometre. A nanometre is 1/1000000000 of a metre.) This means that a virus is about 50 times smaller than a bacterium.

Figure 1.18 shows a virus. Viruses have an outer coat made of protein, and an inner core made of nucleic acid. Nucleic acids are the hereditary material of all living things. DNA and RNA are both nucleic acids. Some viruses contain RNA, and some DNA. The virus in Figures 1.18 and 1.19 is the human immunodeficiency virus or HIV, which contains RNA.

Notice that viruses are not made of cells at all – they have no cell membrane and no cytoplasm.

Viruses cannot do most of the things other living things can do. They cannot feed, respire, move, excrete, grow, respond to their surroundings, or even reproduce – unless they are inside a living cell. Viruses live by getting inside cells, and hijacking the cell's chemicals to help them to reproduce. Figure 1.20 shows how HIV does this. Not surprisingly, the cell is usually killed when a virus reproduces inside it. Some viruses, such as HIV and those that cause colds, influenza and polio, infect human cells and cause diseases. Other viruses infect plants, or even bacteria.

As there are so many things viruses cannot do, many scientists think that they should not be classified as living things at all. Others believe that they should, because they can reproduce, even though they have to use a living cell in order to do this.

▲ **Figure 1.19**
A human immunodeficiency virus, HIV, bursts from a white blood cell. The virus is at the centre top of the picture. You can see how it has burst through the cell surface membrane of the white cell.

Figure 1.20 ▶
How a virus reproduces.
Viruses cannot reproduce on their own, but only inside another living cell. HIV reproduces inside human white blood cells. The RNA inside the virus carries instructions for making more viruses.

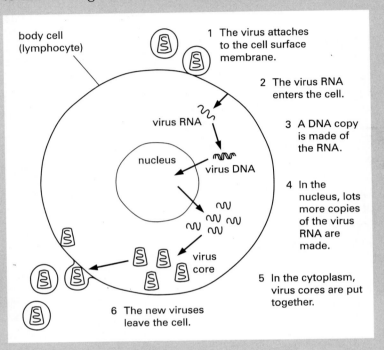

body cell (lymphocyte)

virus RNA

nucleus

virus DNA

virus core

1 The virus attaches to the cell surface membrane.

2 The virus RNA enters the cell.

3 A DNA copy is made of the RNA.

4 In the nucleus, lots more copies of the virus RNA are made.

5 In the cytoplasm, virus cores are put together.

6 The new viruses leave the cell.

Naming living organisms ▶

Each kind of living organism has a Latin name. This idea was first thought of by a Swedish scientist called Carolus Linnaeus, in 1735. He wanted to make sure that scientists all over the world could communicate about living organisms, even though they spoke different languages and so had different names for the same kind of organism. In those days, most educated people who could read and write spoke Latin, so this was the language he chose. We still use Linnaeus's naming system today.

Linnaeus gave each organism two names, so his system of naming is called the **binomial system**, and the name is called a **binomial**. An example is *Equus zebra*, which is the Latin name for a mountain zebra. The first name is the name of the genus to which zebras belong. The second name is the name of the species. Notice that the name of the **genus** is given a capital letter, and the name of the **species** is given a small letter. The name is written in italics. If you write down Latin names, you cannot really write in italics, so you should underline the name instead – <u>Equus zebra</u>.

Other animals that are very like mountain zebras are put in the same genus. Some examples are the plains zebra, *Equus burchelli*, the wild ass, *E. asinus* and the domestic horse, *E. caballus*. Notice that when you have written the name of the genus in full once, you can then use its first letter as an abbreviation.

Question

1.8 Humans belong to the genus *Homo* and the species *sapiens*. What is the binomial for a human?

Using keys

If you want to find out the name of a living organism you have found, you may be able to look it up in a book, and find a picture of it. This is often a good way of identifying organisms. But it does not always work. Perhaps your organism is a different colour from the picture, or perhaps there is no picture of it, or the picture is not good enough for you to be sure that it really shows the organism you have found.

Biologists often use **keys** to help them to identify organisms. Usually these are **dichotomous** keys. 'Dichotomous' means 'branching into *two*', and a dichotomous key works by giving you *pairs* of descriptions. Each time, you decide which of the two descriptions best fits your organism. The key then gives you another pair of choices, or tells you the name of the organism.

Figure 1.21 shows five kinds of insects. Here is a dichotomous key that could be used to identify them:

1	wings present	go to 2
	wings absent	ant
2	has one pair of wings	go to 3
	has two pairs of wings	go to 4
3	legs not as long as body	house fly
	legs longer than body	mosquito
4	wings covered with brightly coloured scales	butterfly
	wings transparent	dragonfly

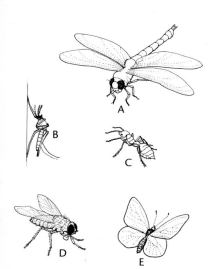

▲ **Figure 1.21**

How do we use a key like this? First, choose the insect you want to identify in Figure 1.21. To begin with, look at insect A.

Look at the first pair of descriptions in the key, and decide which one best fits insect A. Insect A has wings, so you are told to go to 2.

Again, choose the description that fits insect A. It has two pairs of wings, so you now go to 4. The wings are transparent, so insect A is a dragonfly.

Check that you could identify all these insects using the key.

Summary

- Living organisms have seven characteristics – nutrition, excretion, respiration, sensitivity, reproduction, growth and movement.

- Organisms are classified into groups. Each species has a two-word Latin name called a binomial, made up of the name of its genus and of its species.

- The five classes of vertebrates are fish, amphibians, reptiles, birds and mammals.

- The largest group of non-vertebrate animals are the arthopods, which have an exoskeleton, a segmented body and jointed legs. They include insects, crustaceans, myriapods and arachnids. Other non-vertebrates include the annelids, nematodes and molluscs.

- Plants can be classified as monocotyledonous or dicotyledonous, according to the number of cotyledons in their seeds.

- Bacteria have cells that are much smaller than those of animals and plants, and these cells have no nucleus.

- Fungi, like plants, have cell walls, but they do not photosynthesise and do not have chloroplasts.

- Viruses do not show all the characteristics of living things, and are not made of cells. They are able to reproduce, but only when inside a living cell.

- A dichotomous key is made up of pairs of questions or statements, which you lead through to the identification of an organism.

Cells, diffusion and osmosis

All living organisms except viruses are made of cells. Plant cells have some structures that are not found in animal cells. All cells have a partially permeable cell surface membrane, through which substances may pass into and out of the cell. This may take place by diffusion. Osmosis is a special type of diffusion involving water and a partially permeable membrane.

Cells ▶

The structure of an animal cell

All living organisms are made up of **cells**. Most cells are very small, and a human such as yourself contains around 1 million million cells. However, you can see cells with a microscope (Figure 2.1).

Investigation 2.1

Looking at animal cells

You need to use a microscope for this investigation. You will probably have to share a microscope with several other students, but do make your *own* slide, even if you are sharing a microscope in a group.

You will need:

- a microscope, a clean slide and a coverslip
- some animal cells, which your teacher will give to you
- a blue stain called methylene blue
- a piece of filter paper or blotting paper for cleaning your slide.

1 Set up a microscope. Make sure that you have the smallest objective lens over the stage, and the light or mirror is arranged so that you can see bright light when you look through the eyepiece.

2 Collect a clean microscope slide. Take it to your teacher, who will give you a few animal cells. You only need a very small amount of cells, and should hardly be able to see anything on your slide.

3 Using a dropper pipette, put a few drops of methylene blue onto the cells.

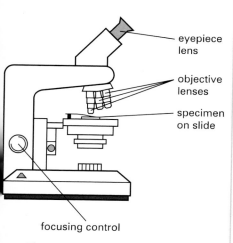

— eyepiece lens

— objective lenses

— specimen on slide

focusing control

▲ **Figure 2.1**
A microscope.

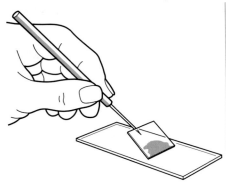

▲ Figure 2.2
How to lower a coverslip on to a slide. If you do it like this, you are less likely to trap air bubbles between the coverslip and the slide.

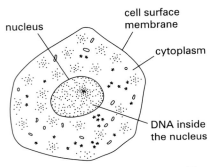

nucleus

cell surface membrane

cytoplasm

DNA inside the nucleus

magnification ×3500

▲ Figure 2.3
A section through an animal cell. This is a liver cell.

4 Very carefully, lower a coverslip onto the drop of stain and the cells. If you do this gently, as in Figure 2.2, you should not trap too many air bubbles under the coverslip. If you do, gently rub across the coverslip with the blunt end of a pencil, to try to squeeze them out.

5 If liquid has escaped from beneath the coverslip, gently remove it with filter paper, so that you will not get any methylene blue on the microscope.

6 Put your slide onto the stage of your microscope. Using the smallest objective lens, focus on the cells. When you have found them, you can try using one of the larger objective lenses.

7 Make a drawing of two or three cells, and label them. Figure 2.3 will help you.

Questions

1 Why do you think it is important to have only a very small amount of cells on your slide?

2 Why is it always a good idea to start off with the smallest objective lens when using a microscope?

3 However careful you were, you probably got a few air bubbles on your slide. What did they look like?

4 Did the methylene blue stain different parts of the cell different shades of blue? If so, explain this in the labels on your diagram – but do not colour it.

If you do investigation 2.1, you should be able to see that these animal cells have cytoplasm, a nucleus, and a cell surface membrane. All animal cells have cytoplasm and a cell surface membrane, and almost all have a nucleus, as shown in Figure 2.3. Red blood cells, however, are very unusual because they do not have a nucleus.

The structure of a plant cell

Plant cells have some structures that are never found in animal cells. These are a **cell wall**, and sometimes **chloroplasts** and a large **vacuole containing cell sap**.

Investigation *2.2*

Looking at plant cells

You will need:

• a microscope, two clean slides, two coverslips

• a piece of pondweed

• a piece of onion

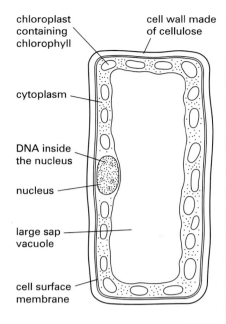

chloroplast containing chlorophyll

cell wall made of cellulose

cytoplasm

DNA inside the nucleus

nucleus

large sap vacuole

cell surface membrane

magnification ×1000

▲ **Figure 2.4**
A section through a plant cell. This is a palisade cell from a leaf.

Note

Function related to cell structure, needed for Supplement, is included in this section.

- a piece of filter paper or blotting paper to clean your slide.
1 Set up a microscope.
2 Put a drop of water onto one of your microscope slides. Take one small thread of pondweed, and place it in the water drop. Gently lower a coverslip onto it. Clean your slide.
3 Put another drop of water onto your other microscope slide. Take a small piece of one layer from the onion, and cut a square with sides of about 0.5 cm. Carefully peel the very thin, paper-like skin from the inner surface of this square. Place it in the water drop, flatten it if necessary, and then put on a coverslip. Clean your slide.
4 Look at both kinds of plant cells, one at a time, using the microscope.
5 Make labelled drawings of each kind of plant cell. Figure 2.4 will help you with your labels.

Questions

1 Were these plant cells bigger or smaller than the animal cells you looked at? How can you tell?
2 What structures were present in the pondweed, but not present in the onion cells? Can you suggest why the onion cells did not have these structures?

Structures found in all cells

All of the structures which are shown in Figures 2.3 and 2.4 have their own job or **function**.

The **cytoplasm** of a cell is like jelly. It is mostly water – about 70% in many cells – with proteins and other chemicals dissolved in it. Many chemical reactions, called **metabolic reactions**, happen in the cytoplasm.

Every cell has a cell surface membrane. This membrane controls what goes in and out of the cell. It will let some substances go through, but not others, and so it is said to be **partially permeable**. Cell surface membranes are very flexible, so they allow the cell to change shape.

Most cells have a **nucleus**. The nucleus contains a chemical called DNA. The DNA is arranged into **chromosomes**. You will not have seen chromosomes in the cells you looked at, and they are not shown in Figures 2.3 and 2.4. This is because when a cell is not dividing, the chromosomes are very long and thin, and so are invisible with a light microscope. But when a cell divides, the chromosomes get much shorter and fatter, and you can see them with a light microscope. The DNA carries coded instructions for how the cell should behave. The DNA in an organism's cells determines what kind of organism it is, and many other things about it. The DNA in your cells makes you a human, a boy or girl, with dark or light hair, and so on.

Structures found in plant cells only

As we have said, plant cells have structures that are not found in animal cells. Outside its cell surface membrane, a plant cell has a **cell wall**, made of **cellulose**. Unlike the cell surface membrane, the cell wall allows almost any kind of substances to go through it, and so it is said to be **fully permeable**. Its function is to support the plant cell and help to hold it in shape. Animal cells never have cell walls.

Many plant cells contain green structures called **chloroplasts**. Chloroplasts are green because they contain the green substance, or pigment, **chlorophyll**. Chlorophyll absorbs sunlight, and helps the chloroplasts to use this energy to make sugars. This is how a plant feeds. This way of feeding is called **photosynthesis**. Animal cells do not feed by photosynthesis, and so they never have chloroplasts.

Plant cells often contain a large, liquid-filled space, called a **vacuole**. The vacuole is surrounded by a membrane which keeps its contents separate from the cytoplasm. The liquid inside the vacuole is called **cell sap**. It is mostly water, with sugars, amino acids and other substances dissolved in it. It is a storage area for the plant cell. Animal cells often have small vacuoles, but they are hardly ever as large as the vacuole in a plant cell, and they do not contain cell sap.

Question

2.1 Make a comparison table to summarise the similarities and differences between plant and animal cells. Draw a table like this:

Structure	Is it found in animal cells?	Is it found in plant cells?	Comment

You will need six rows, one each for cell surface membrane, cytoplasm, nucleus, cell wall, chloroplasts and vacuole. Make the 'comment' column wider than the others, so that you can write plenty of information in it.

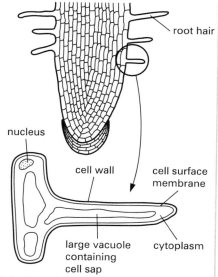

(a) A vertical section through a root tip. The outer layer of cells, a little way from the tip, forms root hairs. How does a root hair cell differ from the palisade cell in Figure 2.4? Can you explain these differences?

cell surface membrane

cytoplasm containing haemoglobin but no nucleus

cell surface membrane

cross-section

cytoplasm containing haemoglobin

(d) Red blood cells.

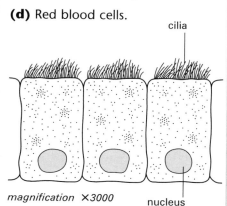

magnification ×3000

cilia

nucleus

(e) These ciliated cells make up the lining of the trachea.

▲ **Figure 2.5**
Some different tissues.

Tissues

When you peeled off the strip of cells from the inside of a piece of onion in investigation 2.2, you were peeling off part of a **tissue**. A tissue is a group of similar cells, all working together to perform the same function.

Figure 2.5 shows cells from two plant tissues and **three** animal tissues. In all of them, the cells have particular characteristics which help them to carry out their functions.

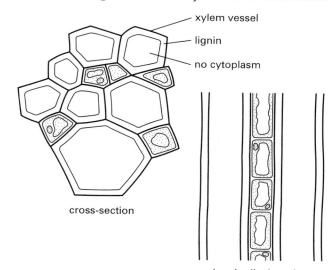

cross-section

longitudinal section

(b) Xylem tissue is made of many xylem elements, which are dead, and other kinds of living cells arranged between them.

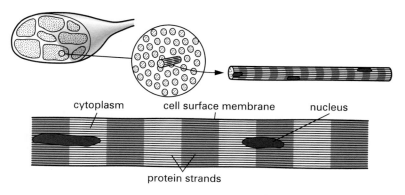

cytoplasm   cell surface membrane   nucleus

protein strands

(c) Muscle tissue is made of many muscle cells arranged to form fibres.

Root hair cells, Figure 2.5(a), are found near the tips of roots that are growing through the soil. Their functions are to help to anchor the plant in the soil, and to absorb water and inorganic ions (such as nitrates) from the soil. You can see that each root hair cell has a long thin part reaching out into the soil. This gives the cell a much larger surface area than usual. The large surface area means that a lot of water and inorganic ions can get into the cell quickly.

Xylem vessels, Figure 2.5(b), are found in the roots and stems of plants, and in their leaves. The veins in a leaf contain xylem vessels. Xylem vessels are made up of many long thin cells called elements. The elements are arranged end to end. They are very unusual cells, because they are dead! Their walls contain a very hard, strong substance called **lignin**. Wood is made of xylem vessels, which is why it is so hard and strong. There is nothing alive inside these walls – no cell surface membrane, no cytoplasm and no nucleus. All that the xylem vessels contain is water. This is one of their functions – they carry water from the roots of the plant, up through the roots and stem, and into the leaves and flowers. Their other function is to help to support the plant.

Muscle cells are found in many different animals, including humans. The cells shown in Figure 2.5(c) could be found in the biceps muscle in your arm. Like all animal cells, muscle cells have a cell surface membrane, cytoplasm and a nucleus – but each cell has many nuclei rather than just one. They look stripy because they are made up of many strands of protein arranged in a pattern. The strands of protein can slide between each other, making the cell much shorter. This is how muscles get shorter, or **contract**.

Red blood cells are smaller than most of the other cells in the human body. They have a cell surface membrane and cytoplasm, but no nucleus. The cytoplasm is full of a red protein called **haemoglobin**, which carries oxygen from your lungs to other parts of your body. Red blood cells are small so that they can squeeze through very tiny blood vessels called capillaries, taking the oxygen very close to almost every cell in your body. They are circular with a dent in the middle, which gives them a large surface area for their size. This speeds up the movement of oxygen in and out of the cell.

Ciliated cells are found lining some of the tubes inside an animal's body. The trachea and bronchi (tubes that carry air to the lungs) are lined with ciliated cells. So is the oviduct (the tube that carries an egg to the uterus in a female mammal). The cilia are tiny extensions of the cell, covered with a cell surface membrane just like the rest of the cell. The cilia can move, and all the cilia beat together in a rhythmic way so that they look rather like a field of waving grass. They help to sweep fluids along the tube. In the trachea, they help to sweep mucus up to the throat. You can read more about this on page 128.

You can read more about this on page 128.

Question

2.2 Figure 2.6 is an **annotated diagram** of a root hair cell. An annotated diagram explains something about the functions of what is drawn, as well as its structure.

Using Figure 2.5 as a starting point, make annotated diagrams of a xylem vessel, a muscle cell, a red blood cell and a ciliated cell. Your annotations should explain how the special features of the cell structure help the cell to perform its functions.

Figure 2.6 ▶
An annotated drawing of a root hair cell.

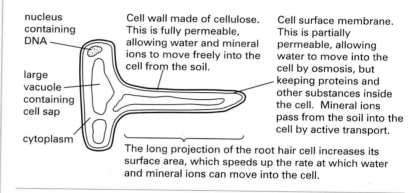

nucleus containing DNA

large vacuole containing cell sap

cytoplasm

Cell wall made of cellulose. This is fully permeable, allowing water and mineral ions to move freely into the cell from the soil.

Cell surface membrane. This is partially permeable, allowing water to move into the cell by osmosis, but keeping proteins and other substances inside the cell. Mineral ions pass from the soil into the cell by active transport.

The long projection of the root hair cell increases its surface area, which speeds up the rate at which water and mineral ions can move into the cell.

Organs

In an organism such as human or flowering plant, there are many kinds of cells, arranged into many kinds of tissues. Often, different kinds of tissues are arranged together in a particular way to make a structure called an **organ**. An organ is a group of different tissues which work together to perform particular functions.

Figure 2.7 shows a plant organ – a leaf. Leaves have many functions. The main one is to make sugars by photosynthesis. This is done by the cells inside the leaf, in tissues called the **palisade mesophyll** and **spongy mesophyll**. These cells need a supply of water, which is brought to them by **xylem vessels**. Some of the sugar which they make is taken to other parts of the plant in **phloem tubes**. The spongy mesophyll cells are arranged loosely, with air spaces in between. Thin layers of cells

Cells, diffusion and osmosis   **21**

on the top and bottom of the leaf, called the **epidermis**, let light through to the mesophyll cells, but stop too much water vapour leaving the leaf, so that it does not dry out. Small openings in the lower epidermis, called **stomata**, allow gases to move in and out of the leaf.

You can find out more about how leaves carry out their functions, and see another diagram of a leaf, in Chapters 6 and 8.

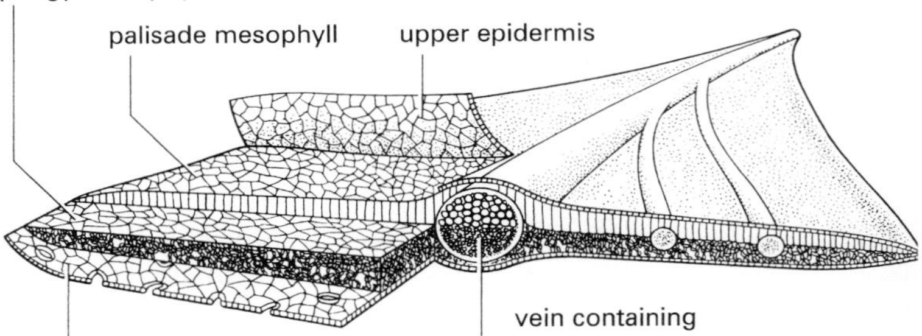

Figure 2.7 ▶
A leaf is an example of an organ. It is made up of many different tissues, arranged in layers. The epidermal tissues at the top and bottom ('epi' means 'outer', and 'dermis' means 'skin') protect the inner layers from drying out. The mesophyll ('middle leaf') tissues photosynthesise. The xylem and phloem tissues transport substances to and from the other tissues in the leaf.

spongy mesophyll
palisade mesophyll
upper epidermis
vein containing xylem tissue and phloem tissue
lower epidermis

Organ systems

Organs do not work on their own. Many organs work together to help each other to perform particular functions. For example, an eye is one of many organs that make up the **nervous system**. The lungs are part of the **gaseous exchange system**. The stomach is part of the **digestive system**.

Question

2.3 Using the index, look up the nervous system, gaseous exchange system and digestive system, and make a list of some of the organs in each of these three systems.

How substances move in and out of cells ▶

Diffusion

All substances are made up of small particles called **atoms**. In some substances, these atoms have lost or gained one or more electrons, to become **ions**. In other substances, the atoms are grouped together to form **molecules**.

Atoms, ions and molecules are always moving. In a solid, each particle has a fixed position in relation to the others, and just vibrates in this position. In a liquid, the particles move more freely around each other, but stay in fairly

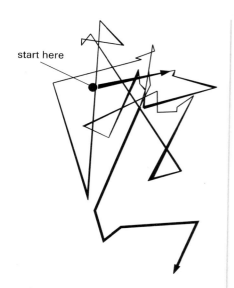

start here

▲ **Figure 2.8**
A particle in a liquid or gas moves around randomly. When it bumps into another particle, it changes direction.

close contact. In a gas, the particles are much further apart from each other, and move around very freely.

Imagine the lid being taken off a bottle of ammonia solution. Molecules of ammonia gas move out of the bottle. Each molecule moves entirely randomly – it is just as likely to go in one direction as another. The molecules bump into each other, and into other molecules in the air, such as oxygen or nitrogen molecules. When a molecule bumps into another molecule, both of them change course. Figure 2.8 shows the path one ammonia molecule might take.

When the lid of the ammonia bottle is first taken off, there are a lot of ammonia molecules inside the bottle. We say that there is a **high concentration** of ammonia inside the bottle. There are probably almost no ammonia molecules in the air on the other side of the room – here there is a **low concentration** of ammonia molecules. But as the ammonia molecules bump randomly around, some of them move erratically further and further away from the bottle. After a while, some will have moved right into the far corner of the room. The ammonia molecules have **diffused** across the room.

It is important to realise that the ammonia molecules do not head purposefully across the room from the bottle. Each molecule just bumps randomly around. It is just by chance that some of them end up a long way from the bottle. Some of them might even go back into the bottle. But, after a while, these random movements result in there being more ammonia molecules out in the room, and fewer inside the bottle. After a long time, you would probably end up with the ammonia molecules spread evenly all over the room.

The overall or **net result** of diffusion is that particles spread out evenly. They tend to spread out from a place where they are in a high concentration, to a place where they are in a low concentration. We say that they spread out down a **concentration gradient**. Diffusion can be defined as *the net movement of molecules from a region of their higher concentration to a region of their lower concentration, down a concentration gradient.*

Investigation 2.3

How quickly does ammonia diffuse?

Your teacher will probably carry out this investigation, but you can collect your own set of results. The apparatus is shown in Figure 2.9.

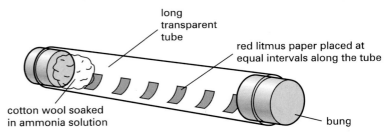

Figure 2.9 ▶
Apparatus for Investigation 2.3.

A piece of cotton wool soaked in ammonia solution is placed in one end of the tube, and quickly sealed inside with a rubber bung. (This is to stop too many ammonia molecules escaping – they do not smell very nice!) A stopwatch is started as the cotton wool goes into the tube. Ammonia turns red litmus paper blue. The time at which each piece of litmus paper turns blue is recorded.

Questions

1 Write up the method of this investigation. Include details of any problems that came up, and how these were solved.

2 Draw up a results chart to show the results of the investigation. Make sure that someone who had not seen the experiment would be able to read your results and understand exactly what they mean.

3 Draw a line graph to show these results.

4 Write a sentence summarising what the investigation has shown.

5 Discuss whether you think the results you obtained were really accurate. Suggest some possible improvements to the investigation that could make the results more valid.

6 Suggest how you could use this apparatus to test the hypothesis (suggestion) that ammonia diffuses more rapidly at high temperatures than at low temperatures. Think about how you could make your experiment a fair test.

Diffusion and living organisms

Diffusion is very important to all living organisms, including humans. You will meet several examples as you continue your Biology course. For the moment, we shall look at one example of diffusion in animals, and one in plants.

You have already seen that red blood cells have the function of transporting oxygen around your body. How does the oxygen get into and out of the red blood cells?

Your lungs are made up of hundreds of thousands of tiny air-filled sacs, called **alveoli** (Figure 2.10). Wrapped around each alveolus are tiny blood vessels called **capillaries**, through which red blood cells are carried in the blood. Oxygen molecules in the air in the alveoli move randomly around. Some of them go right through the cells making up the wall of the alveolus and the wall of the blood capillary, right through the blood plasma, and through the cell surface membrane of a red blood cell. There are usually a lot of oxygen molecules in the air in the alveoli, and not many inside the red blood cells, so the net movement of oxygen molecules is from the alveoli into the blood (although some will, of course, go the other way as well!). The oxygen moves down a concentration gradient, by diffusion.

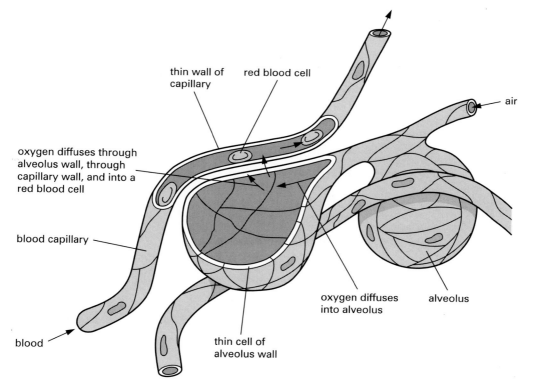

thin wall of capillary

red blood cell

air

oxygen diffuses through alveolus wall, through capillary wall, and into a red blood cell

blood capillary

oxygen diffuses into alveolus

alveolus

blood

thin cell of alveolus wall

▲ Figure 2.10
In the lungs, oxygen diffuses from an alveolus into the red blood cells.

Diffusion of gas molecules takes place in plants too. In daylight, the palisade and spongy mesophyll cells in a plant leaf photosynthesise. They use carbon dioxide and water to make sugars. These sugars may be turned into starch in the leaf. Where does the carbon dioxide come from, and how does it get to these cells?

Air contains carbon dioxide – though not very much. About 0.04% of the air is carbon dioxide. These carbon dioxide molecules bump randomly around. Some of them will go through the stomata on the underside of a leaf, into the air spaces in between the leaf cells, into a mesophyll cell and into a chloroplast. Carbon dioxide molecules arriving at a chloroplast can be made into sugar. This keeps the concentration of carbon dioxide molecules inside the chloroplasts much lower than the concentration in the air outside the leaf, so there is a concentration gradient from the air to the chloroplast. The net movement of the carbon dioxide molecules is down this concentration gradient.

Investigation 2.4

Can iodine molecules or starch molecules get through Visking tubing?

Visking tubing has very tiny, molecule-sized holes in it. Small molecules can move through these holes, but large ones cannot.

Iodine solution reacts with starch to produce a dark blue-black colour.

You will need:

- a piece of Visking tubing about 150 mm long (the exact length does not matter)
- a dropper pipette
- some cotton thread
- some starch suspension
- some iodine solution
- a small beaker.

1 Hold your piece of tubing under water and rub it for a few seconds, to soften it. You should then be able to open it out. Tie a knot in one end.

2 Using the dropper pipette, almost fill your piece of tubing with starch suspension. Tie the open end tightly, either by tying a knot in the tubing or by using a piece of cotton. Wash the outside of the tubing, to make sure there is no starch on the outside.

3 Pour some iodine solution into a small beaker.

4 Put the tubing containing starch suspension into the iodine solution. Carefully observe what happens.

5 Write up your method, results and conclusions. Try to explain what happened.

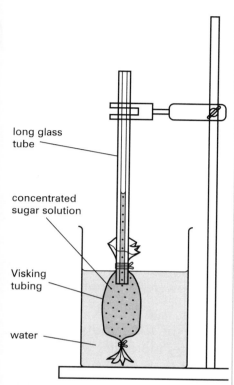

long glass tube

concentrated sugar solution

Visking tubing

water

▲ **Figure 2.11**
Apparatus for Investigation 2.5.

Investigation 2.5

Osmosis

You will need:

- a piece of Visking tubing about 150 mm long (the exact length does not matter)
- a dropper pipette
- some cotton thread
- some concentrated sugar solution
- a piece of glass tubing, at least 150 mm long
- a beaker
- a retort stand, boss and clamp
- a pen for marking on glass.

1 Hold your piece of tubing under water and rub it for a few seconds, to soften it. You should then be able to open it out. Tie a knot in one end.

2 Using the dropper pipette, almost fill your piece of tubing with concentrated sugar solution.

3 Support the long glass tube in a clamp, as shown in Figure 2.11. Hold the open end of the Visking tubing over the end of the long glass tube. Tie it on tightly with cotton. (You will need someone to help you with this.)

4 Fill the beaker with tap water. Stand it under the glass tube, so that most of the tubing filled with sugar solution is under water. Don't let the water come up to the cotton, in case you have not managed to tie it really tightly – you don't want water to get in through here.

5 Mark a line on the glass tube to show the level of the sugar solution.

6 Watch this level over the next 5 or 10 minutes. While you are watching, think about these facts:

- Sugar molecules are much bigger than water molecules.
- Visking tubing is a partially permeable membrane. It has holes in it which will let water molecules through, but are much too small to let sugar molecules through.
- In the sugar solution, water and sugar molecules are bumping about randomly; in the beaker, water molecules are bumping about randomly.

7 Write up your method, results, and conclusions. Try to explain what happened, in terms of what the water and sugar molecules were doing.

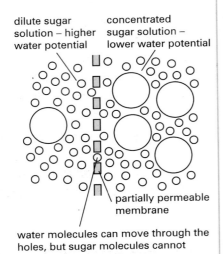

dilute sugar solution – higher water potential

concentrated sugar solution – lower water potential

partially permeable membrane

water molecules can move through the holes, but sugar molecules cannot

○ water molecule

○ sugar molecule

▲ **Figure 2.12**
How osmosis happens. The net movement of the water molecules is from the higher water potential on the left-hand side of the membrane to the lower water potential on the right.

> ### Note
> The concept of water potential gradient for Supplement is included in this section.

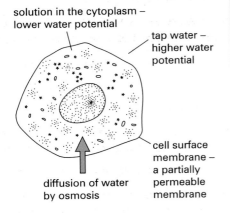

solution in the cytoplasm – lower water potential

tap water – higher water potential

cell surface membrane – a partially permeable membrane

diffusion of water by osmosis

▲ **Figure 2.13**
An animal cell in pure water.

Osmosis

Osmosis is a special sort of diffusion, involving water molecules. If you carry out investigation 2.5, you will see osmosis happening. Figure 2.12 shows how it works.

On both sides of the partially permeable membrane, molecules bounce around randomly. If sugar molecules hit the membrane, they just bounce off – they are too big to get through the holes. But if water molecules bounce into a hole in the membrane, they go through to the other side.

The water molecules on the left-hand side are freer to bounce around, because there are very few sugar molecules in the way. There are also more water molecules here. There are fewer water molecules on the right-hand side, and they cannot bounce as freely, because of all the sugar molecules. We say that there is a higher **water potential** on the left-hand side of the membrane than on the right. Concentrated solutions have a lower water potential than dilute solutions.

Because the water molecules on the left-hand side are freer to bounce around, more water molecules will bounce through a hole from left to right than from right to left. Although water molecules do bounce both ways through the holes, the *net* movement of water molecules is from left to right. *The net movement of water molecules is from a region of high water potential to a region of lower water potential.*

You should be able to see that this is really just diffusion of the water molecules. The only thing that is different from the diffusion of the ammonia molecules described on page 24 is that, this time, we have some sugar molecules involved, and also a partially permeable membrane. This sort of diffusion is called **osmosis**. *Osmosis is the net diffusion of water molecules from a region of high water potential to a region of low water potential, through a partially permeable membrane.*

Osmosis and animal cells

Figure 2.13 shows an animal cell in pure water.

The solutions inside and outside the cell are separated by the cell surface membrane. This is a partially permeable membrane. Water molecules pass easily through it, but larger molecules such as proteins cannot get through.

Inside the cell, the cytoplasm is a fairly concentrated solution of proteins and other substances in water. Outside the cell, the solution is much more dilute – it is almost pure water. The water outside the cell has a higher water potential than the water inside the cell. The net movement of water molecules is therefore from outside the cell into the cytoplasm. We can say that water moves into the cell by osmosis.

What will happen to the cell? As more and more water enters the cell, the cell swells up. After a while, it may get so big that it bursts the cell membrane. The contents of the cell will escape, and the cell will die.

Questions

2.4 Figure 2.14 shows an animal cell in a concentrated salt solution. The salt solution is more concentrated than the solution inside the cell.

    a Which has the higher water potential – the salt solution or the cytoplasm of the cell?

    b In which direction will the net movement of water molecules take place?

    c What do you think the salt molecules do?

    d Will the cell get bigger or smaller?

2.5 A scientist took a sample of human blood, and divided it between three tubes. She then added liquid to each tube, as follows:

Tube A   distilled water

Tube B   salt solution of about the same water potential as cytoplasm

Tube C   very concentrated salt solution

She mixed the contents of each tube thoroughly.
After a few minutes, she observed the following:

Tube A   a clear red solution

Tube B   a red liquid, not clear

Tube C   a red liquid, not clear

She then took a few drops from each tube, put them onto microscope slides, and looked at them under the microscope.

    a What substance makes human blood look red?

    b If you look at human blood under a microscope, you see red cells floating in a colourless liquid called plasma. Why are the cells red, while the plasma is colourless?

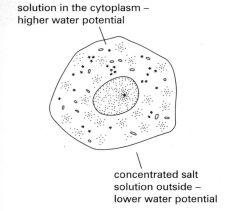

solution in the cytoplasm – higher water potential

concentrated salt solution outside – lower water potential

▲ Figure 2.14
An animal cell in a concentrated solution.

c Suggest why the contents of Tube A went clear, but the contents of Tubes B and C did not.

d Describe and explain what happened to the cells in *each* tube. Suggest what the student would have seen when she looked at a sample from each tube under the microscope.

Osmosis and plant cells

Figure 2.15 shows a plant cell in pure water.

As with the animal cell in pure water (Figure 2.13), here there is a solution with a high water potential outside the cell, and a solution with a low water potential inside. They are separated from each other by the partially permeable cell surface membrane. Just as in the animal cell, water moves by osmosis into the cell, from the higher water potential to the lower water potential.

However, this time the cell does not burst. This is because plant cells have a strong outer covering – the cell wall. As more and more water goes into the cell, the cytoplasm and vacuole get bigger and bigger, and push outwards on the cell surface membrane and the cell wall. But the cell wall will not give way. It stops the cell expanding enough to break the cell surface membrane.

A plant cell like this, as full as it can be, is very firm and rigid. It is said to be **turgid**. The cells of a well-watered plant are all turgid. This helps to keep the soft parts of a plant, such as its leaves and flower petals, firm and in shape. Turgidity helps to support a plant.

Figure 2.16 shows a plant cell in a concentrated sugar solution. Now, the solution outside the cell has a lower water potential than the solution inside it. The water molecules move by osmosis from the higher water potential to the lower one – so they move *out* of the cell.

Just as in an animal cell, this makes the contents of the cell shrink. As they lose more and more water, the cytoplasm and vacuole get smaller and smaller. They stop pushing outwards on the cell wall. Instead of being firm and stiff, the cell becomes soft. It is said to be **flaccid**.

If water keeps on going out of the cell, and the cytoplasm keeps on shrinking, the cell surface membrane will be pulled away from the cell wall. When this happens, the cell is said to be **plasmolysed.**

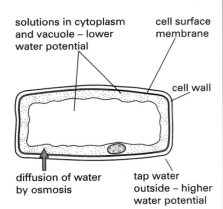

solutions in cytoplasm and vacuole – lower water potential

cell surface membrane

cell wall

diffusion of water by osmosis

tap water outside – higher water potential

▲ **Figure 2.15**
A plant cell in pure water.

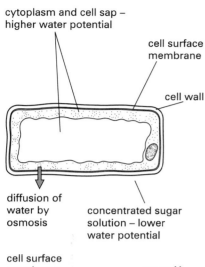

cytoplasm and cell sap – higher water potential

cell surface membrane

cell wall

diffusion of water by osmosis

concentrated sugar solution – lower water potential

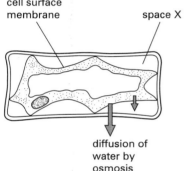

cell surface membrane

space X

diffusion of water by osmosis

▲ **Figure 2.16**
A plant cell in a concentrated solution.

Question

2.6 Look at Figure 2.16.
   a Is the cell wall of a plant cell partially permeable, or is it fully permeable? What does this mean?
   b What will be in Space X?

Investigation *2.6*

Osmosis and potato cells

You are going to investigate the effects of five different concentrations of sugar solution on pieces of potato tissue, and try to explain these effects in terms of osmosis.

You will need:

* one or two potatoes, washed and peeled
* a kitchen knife or cork borer
* some paper towels
* five different concentrations of sugar solution
* five containers
* a pen for writing on the containers
* a ruler calibrated in millimetres.

1 Look at the concentrations of the sugar solutions. Label each of the five containers with the concentration of sugar solution you are going to put in it. Pour the appropriate sugar solution into each container, leaving space to put in two pieces of potato without spilling.

2 Cut ten pieces of potato, all as close to the same size as possible. If you have a cork borer, this is quite easy; it takes a little longer with a kitchen knife.

3 Divide your ten pieces of potato into five sets of two. (You are going to put two pieces into each container.) Measure the length of each piece, and record these lengths, making sure that you write down which container they will be going into.

4 Put the appropriate pieces of potato into their containers. Make sure that each piece is not touching the other, and that they are completely covered by the solution. Leave them for at least half an hour, longer if possible.

5 While you are waiting, write up your method. Then read ahead, and draw up a suitable results chart.

6 Take out each piece of potato carefully, and measure its length. Record all the lengths in your results chart, and then calculate the changes in length. Calculate the average change in length in each solution.

7 Draw a graph of your results.

8 Write a short conclusion, and then a discussion of the results of your investigation.

Supplement

Active transport

Sometimes, a cell needs to absorb a substance that is in a very low concentration in its surroundings. For example, a plant needs to take in nitrate ions through its root hairs from the soil. But the concentration of nitrate ions dissolved in the water in the soil is usually much less than the concentration of nitrate ions in the cytoplasm of the root hair cells. If left to themselves, the nitrate ions would diffuse down their concentration gradients, passing out of the cell and into the soil solution.

The plant, however, can make the nitrate ions move in the opposite direction, up their concentration gradient. There are special proteins, called **transport proteins**, embedded in the cell surface membranes of the root hair cells. Nitrate ions from the soil combine with these proteins, and the proteins then push the nitrate ions through the membrane and into the cytoplasm of the cell. This needs energy, which comes from respiration in the cell, and it is called **active transport**. Active transport can be defined as *the movement of a substance up its concentration gradient, using energy from respiration.*

Another example of active transport is the uptake of glucose molecules from the small intestine into the blood. This is described on page 80.

Summary

- All organisms are made of cells.
- Both animal and plant cells have a cell surface membrane, cytoplasm and a nucleus.
- The cell surface membrane controls what enters and leaves the cell. Metabolic reactions take place in cytoplasm. The nucleus contains DNA in the form of chromosomes, which control the activities of the cell.

- Plant cells, but not animal cells, always have a cellulose cell wall. They often have a large, permanent vacuole filled with cell sap, and chloroplasts.
- The cell wall helps to maintain the shape of the plant cell, and prevents it from bursting if it takes in a lot of water. The sap in the vacuole is a store of sugars and other substances. Chloroplasts contain chlorophyll which absorbs sunlight, and photosynthesis takes place inside them.

- A group of similar cells working together to carry out a particular set of functions is called a tissue. Different tissues may be grouped together to form an organ, and groups of organs form systems.

- There are many types of animal cells and plant cells, each of which has a structure that is related to its function. Ciliated cells help to sweep mucus up the trachea and keep the lungs clean. Root hair cells have a large surface area for absorption of water and mineral salts. Xylem vessels transport water and help to support a plant. Muscle cells can contract to cause movement. Red blood cells contain haemoglobin and transport oxygen.

- Diffusion is the net movement of particles (atoms, ions or molecules) down a concentration gradient. Oxygen and carbon dioxide diffuse into and out of the blood of a mammal, in the alveoli of the lungs.

- Osmosis is a particular type of diffusion, in which water molecules diffuse down their concentration gradient through a partially permeable membrane.

- A solution in which there are a lot of water molecules and few solute molecules (that is, a dilute solution) is said to have a high water potential. A solution in which there are few water molecules and many solute molecules (that is, a concentrated solution) has a low water potential. In osmosis, water molecules diffuse down a water potential gradient.

- Animal and plant cells take up water by osmosis if the solution around them is more dilute than the cytoplasm. Animal cells burst. Plant cells become turgid.

- Animal and plant cells lose water by osmosis if the solution around them is more concentrated than the cytoplasm. Animal cells shrink. Plant cells become flaccid and then plasmolysed.

- Cells can take up substances even when they are less concentrated outside the cell than inside. This is done by active transport, and uses energy that the cell provides by respiration.

3 Enzymes

Enzymes are proteins which act as biological catalysts. Almost every reaction that occurs in living organisms is catalysed by an enzyme. As enzymes are proteins, they are easily damaged by high temperatures or extremes of pH.

Investigation 3.1

The effect of plant material on hydrogen peroxide

Hydrogen peroxide has the molecular formula H_2O_2. It can break down to form water and oxygen:

hydrogen peroxide $\longrightarrow$ water + oxygen

$$2H_2O_2 \longrightarrow 2H_2O + O_2$$

Left alone, this reaction happens only slowly. If a catalyst is present, it happens much faster. You can tell if the reaction is happening because the hydrogen peroxide starts to give off bubbles of oxygen.

You will need:

- three test tubes in a rack or beaker
- a dropper pipette
- some hydrogen peroxide (it is best to collect this when you need it, not before)
- a tile, a knife and a piece of fresh potato or apple
- a piece of cooked potato or apple
- some manganese(IV) oxide
- a spatula
- a wooden splint, and a flame in which to light it
- safety glasses.

Take care! Hydrogen peroxide is a powerful bleach. Wear safety glasses so that it cannot splash into your eyes. If you get any on your skin, rinse it off under cold running water.

1 Using a dropper pipette, put about 3 cm depth of hydrogen peroxide into each of your three test tubes. Stand them carefully in the rack or beaker.

2 Add a little manganese(IV) oxide to one tube. Observe and record exactly what happens.

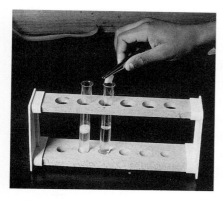

▲ Figure 3.1
Adding potato to hydrogen peroxide. Make sure that you remember to wear safety glasses!

Catalysts and enzymes ▶

3 Light a wooden splint, and blow out the flame so that the splint glows. Gently push the splint into the froth in the tube, and watch what happens.

4 Cut a few small pieces of potato or apple. Add them to the hydrogen peroxide in a second tube. Observe and record exactly what happens. Test with a glowing splint as before.

5 Repeat step 4 with a few small pieces of boiled potato or apple.

Write up your Investigation in the normal way. You should include the following points:

Method Give a detailed description of exactly how you carried out your experiment. A labelled diagram may be helpful.

Results Decide on the best way to show your results. You could write descriptions of what you saw in sentences, or you could use a results chart.

Conclusions Write a brief sentence or two about what you have found out. This could include:

• any substances you found that catalysed the breakdown of hydrogen peroxide and any that did not

• what the gas was that was given off.

Discussion This should be longer than your conclusions. In the discussion, you should:

• suggest explanations for what you observed – for example, why the pieces of fresh and boiled potato or apple had the effects you saw

• explain any possible sources of error in your investigation, and how you could have changed it to reduce these errors, and to get more information about exactly what was happening.

What is a catalyst?

A **catalyst** is a substance that speeds up the rate of a chemical reaction, but is not itself changed by the reaction. A catalyst can be used over and over again. In Investigation 3.1, you may have seen manganese(IV) oxide acting as a catalyst, speeding up the reaction in which hydrogen peroxide breaks down into water and oxygen. The manganese(IV) oxide is still there at the end of the reaction. If you added more hydrogen peroxide, the manganese(IV) oxide would help it to break down, too.

Enzymes

Living organisms have thousands of different chemical reactions called **metabolic reactions** going on inside them. Some of these reactions, such as those in respiration, photosynthesis or digestion, are described later in this book. Each of these reactions needs a catalyst to make it happen more quickly. In fact, most metabolic reactions would take place so slowly without a catalyst that they would hardly happen at all.

The catalysts in living organisms are called **enzymes**. Every kind of metabolic reaction needs a different kind of enzyme to catalyse it. This means that a living organism such as yourself contains thousands of different kinds of enzyme. Each enzyme can only catalyse one kind of metabolic reaction.

In Investigation 3.1, an enzyme from the potato or apple catalysed the breakdown of hydrogen peroxide to water and oxygen. The enzyme that does this is called **catalase**. Catalase is found in all living tissues; you could equally well have done this experiment with a piece of liver, or some yeast suspension. Inside living cells, hydrogen peroxide is often made as a by-product of other metabolic reactions. Hydrogen peroxide is a very harmful substance, so cells contain catalase to catalyse its breakdown as quickly as it is formed.

The effect of heat on enzymes

Catalase, like all enzymes, is a **protein**.

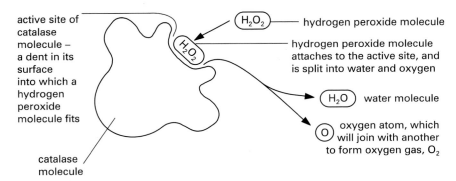

active site of catalase molecule – a dent in its surface into which a hydrogen peroxide molecule fits

catalase molecule

H_2O_2 —— hydrogen peroxide molecule

hydrogen peroxide molecule attaches to the active site, and is split into water and oxygen

H_2O water molecule

oxygen atom, which will join with another to form oxygen gas, O_2

Figure 3.2 ▲
How catalase breaks down hydrogen peroxide. The hydrogen peroxide is the substrate, and water and oxygen are the products.

Figure 3.2 shows how an enzyme works. An enzyme molecule has a dent in it called the **active site**. The substances taking part in the reaction that the enzyme catalyses fit exactly in this dent. The enzyme pulls on them a little, making them react, and then lets them go again.

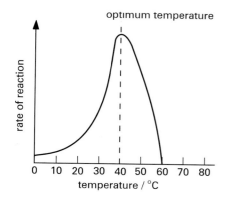

optimum temperature

rate of reaction

0 10 20 30 40 50 60 70 80
temperature / °C

▲ **Figure 3.3**
How temperature affects the rate of an enzyme-controlled reaction. Between 0°C and 40°C, increasing the temperature increases the rate of reaction. This is because the enzyme molecules and substrate molecules move around faster (they have more kinetic energy) at higher temperatures, bumping into each other more often. Above 40°C, increasing the temperature decreases the rate of reaction. This is because the enzyme molecules lose their shape at these temperatures, so the substrate no longer fits into the active site.

If the enzyme molecule loses its shape, it cannot do this, because the substances will not fit in the dent. This is why enzymes do not work if they get too hot. When the potato or apple pieces were boiled, the high temperature made the protein molecules in them lose their shape. They were **denatured**. A denatured enzyme cannot act as a catalyst.

The body temperature of a person is about 37 °C. The enzymes in our bodies work fastest at this temperature (Figure 3.3).

Question

3.1 **Amylase** is an enzyme found in human saliva. It catalyses the breakdown of starch molecules to maltose molecules.

starch $\xrightarrow{\text{amylase}}$ maltose

a Explain exactly what is meant by:
   i   catalyse
   ii enzyme.
b At what temperature do you think amylase might work fastest? Explain your answer.
c Molecules are always moving around. The higher the temperature, the faster they move. Explain why amylase breaks down starch to maltose faster at 30 °C than at 0 °C.
d Explain why amylase breaks down starch to maltose faster at 30 °C than at 80 °C.

Investigation 3.2

The effect of temperature on the rate of breakdown of protein by trypsin

Trypsin is an enzyme that catalyses the breakdown of proteins into shorter chains of amino acids, called polypeptides.

protein $\xrightarrow{\text{trypsin}}$ polypeptides

Milk contains a protein that makes it look white. When the protein is broken down to polypeptides, the liquid becomes clear. You are going to mix trypsin with milk at different temperatures, and time how long it takes for the protein to break down to polypeptides.

You will need:

• test tubes in a rack or beaker

• water baths at five different temperatures (your teacher will tell you about these)

• a measuring cylinder or syringe

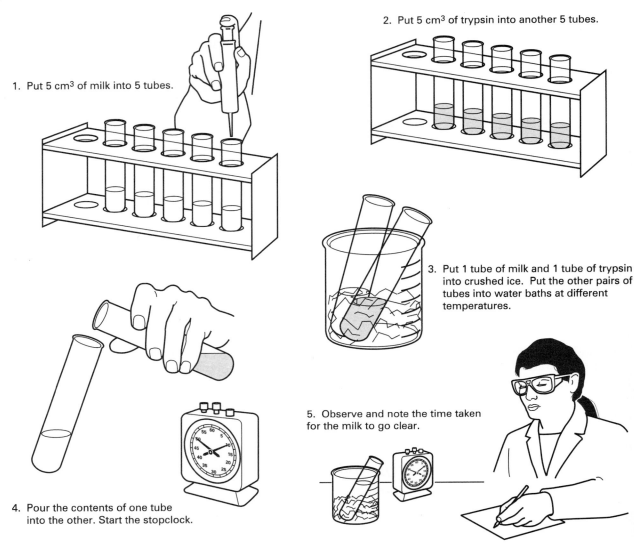

- a stopclock or a clock or watch with a second hand
- some trypsin solution
- some milk.

1. Put 5 cm³ of milk into 5 tubes.

2. Put 5 cm³ of trypsin into another 5 tubes.

3. Put 1 tube of milk and 1 tube of trypsin into crushed ice. Put the other pairs of tubes into water baths at different temperatures.

4. Pour the contents of one tube into the other. Start the stopclock.

5. Observe and note the time taken for the milk to go clear.

▲ Figure 3.4
Method for Investigation 3.2.

1 Label each of your ten tubes with your name. Find out the temperatures of the five water baths, and write each temperature on two tubes.

2 Using a measuring cylinder or syringe, put exactly 5 cm³ of milk into each of five test tubes with different temperatures written on them. Then put each tube into a water bath, according to the temperature written on the tube.

3 Clean the measuring cylinder or syringe thoroughly. Put exactly 5 cm³ of trypsin solution into the other five tubes. Stand these tubes in the correct water baths, next to the ones containing milk.

4 Leave the tubes in the water baths for five minutes, so that the milk and trypsin come to the correct temperature.

5 Start a stopclock. One at a time, pour the trypsin into the milk that is standing in the same water bath. Make sure the trypsin and milk are well mixed together. Do this for each pair of tubes.

6 Every five minutes, look at your tube to see if the milky colour is disappearing. If and when it does, record the time it took.

7 Draw a graph of your results, with temperature on the *x*-axis and time taken for milk to go clear on the *y*-axis.

8 Write up your experiment in the usual way. In your discussion, suggest explanations for any differences in the time taken for the milk to go clear at different temperatures.

The effect of pH on enzymes

pH is a measure of how acidic or alkaline a solution is. The scale runs from 1 to 14. A pH of 7 is neutral. A pH below 7 is acidic, and a pH above 7 is alkaline.

The shape and activity of enzyme molecules is affected by pH. For most enzymes, there is a small range of pH in which their molecules are exactly the right shape to catalyse their reaction (Figure 3.5). Above or below this pH, their molecules lose their shape, so the substances cannot fit into the enzyme's active site.

Investigation 3.3

The effect of pH on the breakdown of milk protein by trypsin

You are going to design and carry out this investigation yourself.

1 Using your experience from investigation 3.2, design an investigation to find out how quickly trypsin can break down milk protein at different values of pH. You will be given some liquids called **buffer solutions**, each at a different pH. Your teacher will tell you which ones are available.

Write out a detailed plan for your experiment. Think in particular about how you will make your experiment a fair test. If you want to find out what effect a different pH has, then everything else must be the same in each case, so that you can be sure that any differences you find are caused by pH, and not by something else.

2 When you have had your plan checked, do your experiment. You will probably find that, once you get started, you want to change a few details from your original design. This is a good thing to do. Make sure that you write down exactly what these changes are, and why you made them.

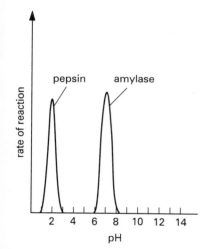

▲ **Figure 3.5**
How pH affects the rate of an enzyme-controlled reaction. Pepsin is a protein-digesting enzyme found in the stomach. There is hydrochloric acid in the stomach, and pepsin is able to work best in the low pH which this acid produces. Amylase is a starch-digesting enzyme found in the mouth, where the pH is normally between 7.0 and 7.5.

3 Write up the results and conclusion, and then a discussion. In the discussion, suggest any sources of inaccuracy in your experiment – there may be several – and make some suggestions about how you could improve it if you had more time.

Biological washing powders

Washing powders contain **detergents**. Detergents help to remove greasy dirt from clothes. They help the grease to dissolve in water, so that it can be washed off the cloth.

However, some stains on clothes are not greasy, and will not wash off with detergents. Stains like this include blood stains and egg yolk stains. These stains contain proteins, which get stuck onto the fibres of the cloth and will not wash out.

To help to get rid of these stains, some kinds of washing powder contain enzymes. They are sometimes called **biological washing powders**. They contain enzymes which break down protein molecules, rather like trypsin does. They break down the protein molecules in the stain, turning the proteins into smaller molecules. These small molecules are not coloured, so the stain disappears. Moreover, the small molecules can easily dissolve in water, and be washed away.

Question

3.2 a At what range of temperatures do you think detergents work fastest?

b At what range of temperatures do most enzymes work fastest?

c What problem does this give manufacturers and users of detergents?

d In some parts of the world, hot water wells up out of the ground. There are bacteria which can live in these hot springs. How might these bacteria be useful to manufacturers of biological detergents?

Enzymes in the food industry

Food manufacturers often use enzymes. For example, when juice is squeezed out of apples to make a drink, an enzyme called **pectinase** is usually added. Pectinase is an enzyme that breaks down the substances that hold the cell walls of the apple cells together. This makes it easier to squeeze most of the juice out. Pectinase also helps to break down the substances that make apple juice cloudy, turning it to a clear liquid which most people prefer.

Another enzyme that is often used is **lactase**. This is an enzyme that breaks down the sugar found in milk, called **lactose**, into two other sugars called **glucose** and **galactose**. This is done because, in many parts of the world, people do not have an enzyme in their alimentary canal that can break down lactose. If they drink milk with lactose in it, they may feel ill. If lactase is added to the milk, it breaks down all the lactose. The milk is then called **lactose-reduced milk**, and it is safe for people to drink even if they do not have lactase in their digestive system.

Enzymes in seed germination

A seed contains an embryo plant. It also contains a food store on which the embryo will rely while it is germinating, until it has grown leaves and can start to photosynthesise. For example, bean seeds contain a lot of starch. Starch is insoluble. When the seed begins to germinate, the enzyme **amylase** is secreted. This breaks the starch into **maltose**, which is soluble. The maltose can then be absorbed by the growing embryo, which can break it down to glucose. The seedling can then use it to supply energy for growth, and also to build up cellulose to make cell walls for the new cells that are made as the seedling grows.

Summary

- Enzymes are proteins that act as biological catalysts.
- The rate at which an enzyme-catalysed reaction takes place increases as temperature increases, until the optimum temperature is reached. Above this temperature, the enzyme molecules begin to be denatured (lose their shape) and so the reaction takes place more slowly. The temperature at which the rate of reaction is fastest is called the optimum temperature. This is about 37 °C for human enzymes, but much lower for enzymes in plants and much higher for enzymes in many bacteria.
- Most enzymes only act effectively within a narrow pH range. They are denatured at very high or very low pHs.

- Many seeds contain food stores in the form of starch, which is broken down to maltose by the enzyme amylase as the seed begins to germinate.
- Biological washing powders contain enzymes such as proteases, which help to break down molecules that have produced stains on the clothes.
- The food industry makes much use of enzymes. For example, pectinase is used to help to extract juice from fruit. Lactase is used to break down lactose into glucose and galactose.

4 Human nutrition

Nutrition means taking in all the substances we need to provide us with energy, and with the raw materials for building our bodies. Some of these substances are organic substances that have been made by plants, while others are inorganic. We need to eat a diet containing some of all of these substances in the correct proportions. If we eat too little or too much of a particular substance, we can suffer from malnutrition.

Nutrition ▶

Animal and plant nutrition

'Nutrition' means 'feeding'. The types of food that animals need are called **nutrients**. All animals, including humans, need six types of nutrients. These are:

- carbohydrates
- proteins
- fats
- vitamins
- inorganic ions
- water.

The first four nutrients in this list are **organic** substances. This means that molecules of these substances are quite large, and contain carbon.

The last two nutrients in the list are **inorganic** substances. This means that they are not made of molecules at all (in the case of inorganic ions), or they have small molecules (in the case of water), which do not contain carbon.

Organic nutrients are made by plants – you can find out how in Chapter 6. Plants make organic nutrients from inorganic substances, including carbon dioxide, water and inorganic ions. Animals are not able to make organic substances from inorganic ones. Animals, including humans, rely completely on plants for their supply of organic nutrients.

Nutrition can be defined as *the obtaining of organic substances and mineral ions from which organisms obtain their energy and their raw materials for growth and tissue repair.*

The way plants obtain their organic nutrients, by making them from inorganic ones, is called **autotrophic nutrition**. The way animals obtain their organic nutrients, by eating plants and other animals, is called **heterotrophic nutrition**.

Question

4.1 Decide whether each of these ten substances is organic or inorganic:

sugar	paper
iron	glass
wood	alcohol
water	leather
oxygen	copper sulphate

Why humans need nutrients

Why do we need to keep eating? And why does it matter just what we eat? There are really three important reasons why we need nutrients. These are:

1 We need food to give us **energy**. We need energy for many processes. These include generating heat energy to keep our bodies warm, generating kinetic energy in our muscles so that we can move, and generating chemical energy to help chemical reactions take place in our bodies. The most important nutrients for providing energy are *carbohydrates* and *fats*. *Proteins* can also provide energy.

2 We need food to provide us with **building materials** to build the cells in our bodies. The nutrients which provide the most important building materials are *proteins*, and also *fats*, *vitamins* and *minerals*.

3 We need food to provide us with chemicals that are used to help **chemical reactions** take place in our bodies. The nutrients that are most important for this are *proteins*, *vitamins*, *minerals* and *water*.

We shall look at each kind of nutrient in turn, to see what their molecules are like, what kinds of foods contain them, and what we use them for in our bodies.

Carbohydrate molecules

The carbohydrates with the smallest and simplest molecules are **sugars**. They contain just three elements – carbon, hydrogen and oxygen.

Figure 4.1b shows the structure of a molecule of the sugar **glucose**. You do not need to learn this detailed structure. You can see that the molecule is made up of a ring of carbon atoms, to which hydrogen and oxygen atoms are attached.

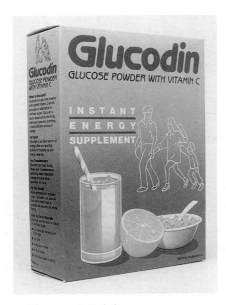

▲ **Figure 4.1 (a)**
A packet of glucose.

(b) A glucose molecule is a six-sided ring made of carbon, hydrogen and oxygen atoms.

Question

4.2 Count the numbers of carbon, hydrogen and oxygen atoms in the glucose molecule in Figure 4.1b. Can you suggest why molecules like glucose are called carbohydrates?

Glucose is a **simple sugar** (a monosaccharide) – it is made up of a single ring of carbon atoms. Other sugars, called **complex sugars** (disaccharides), are made up of two rings of carbon atoms linked together. Two glucose molecules linked together make the complex sugar **maltose**, shown in Figure 4.2.

Figure 4.2 ▶
A maltose molecule is made of two glucose molecules linked together.

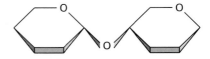

Sugar molecules can link together in very long chains, made up of thousands of rings. These big molecules are called **polysaccharides**. Three important polysaccharides are **cellulose**, which makes up the cell walls of plants, **starch**, which is stored as a food reserve in many plant cells, and **glycogen**, which is stored as a food reserve in our liver and muscle cells. Figure 4.3 shows some polysaccharides.

Figure 4.3 Polysaccharides (a) ▶
This photograph, taken using an electron microscope, and magnified about 4000 times, shows the cellulose fibres which make up the cell wall of a plant cell. Each fibre is made up of many cellulose molecules – the individual molecules are much too small to see.

(b) A cellulose molecule is a straight chain of glucose molecules.

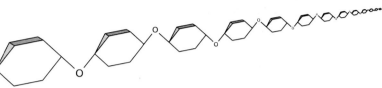

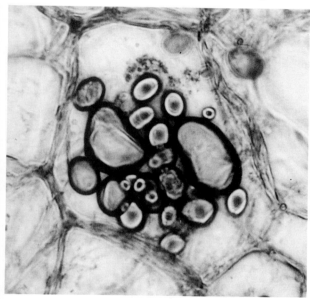

(d) A starch molecule is a spiral chain of glucose molecules.

(c) Groups of starch grains can be seen inside these cells from a potato tuber. They are magnified about 400 times. You can see starch grains like these quite easily with an ordinary school microscope.

Investigation *4.1*

Testing foods for carbohydrates

You are going to test five foods to find out which kinds of carbohydrates they contain. You will need:

- small samples of five different foods (make sure you keep them separate from each other)
- a tile or dish on which you can put the foods
- a knife or a pestle and mortar
- a spatula or other small implement for picking up pieces of food
- five boiling tubes
- a Bunsen burner, tripod, gauze and heatproof mat

- a 250 cm³ beaker
- a small amount of iodine in potassium iodide solution, and a dropper pipette
- some Benedict's solution, and a dropper pipette
- safety glasses.

Take care! You will be using very hot liquids. Wear safety glasses to stop them splashing into your eyes.

You are going to carry out two separate tests on each of the five foods. Read through the following instructions, and then design a results chart in which you can write your results and conclusions. If you are unsure about this, get your teacher to check your results chart before you begin.

Test 1 Testing for starch

Figure 4.4 ▶
How to test foods for starch.

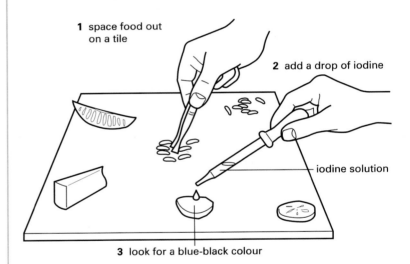

1 space food out on a tile

2 add a drop of iodine

iodine solution

3 look for a blue-black colour

The test for starch is called the **iodine test**. Starch turns iodine solution a dark blue-black colour.

1 On a clean tile or other clean surface, put small amounts of each of the five foods, keeping them completely separate from each other.

2 Using a dropper pipette, add a few drops of iodine in potassium iodide solution to each food.

3 Wait a few moments, and then write down the colour you observe in your results chart.

4 If the iodine in potassium iodide solution stays orange-brown, there is no starch in the food. If it turns dark blue-black, there is starch in the food. Record your conclusions in your results chart.

Test 2 Testing for reducing sugars

Most sugars will reduce copper sulphate solution, which is blue, to copper oxide, which is brownish red. The test for reducing sugars is called **Benedict's test**.

1 Put some water into the beaker, and boil the water on a tripod and gauze over a Bunsen burner.

2 Take a small sample of one of your five foods, and either crush it in a pestle and mortar, or cut it into tiny pieces. Put your crushed or chopped sample in a boiling tube.

3 Add enough Benedict's solution to the food to cover it. (Benedict's solution contains copper sulphate.)

4 Stand the boiling tube containing the food and Benedict's solution in the beaker of boiling water. Watch for any colour changes, and record them in your results chart.

▼ **Figure 4.5**
How to test foods for reducing sugars.

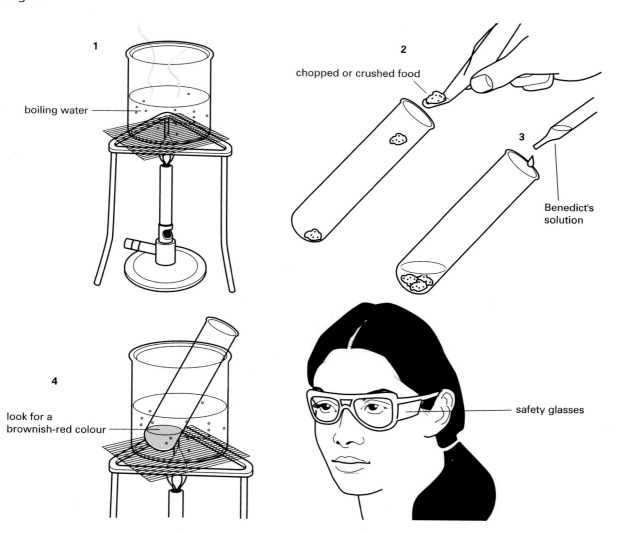

1

boiling water

2

chopped or crushed food

3

Benedict's solution

4

look for a
brownish-red colour

safety glasses

5 If the Benedict's solution stays blue, there is no reducing sugar in the food. If it changes to a rather dirty yellow-green colour, there is a small amount of reducing sugar in the food. If you see an orange or reddish-brown precipitate, there is a lot of reducing sugar in the food. Record your conclusions in your results chart.

Why we need carbohydrates

There is only one reason why we need carbohydrates in our diet. This is to provide us with **energy**.

Carbohydrates are made by plants, by the process called photosynthesis. The plants capture energy from sunlight, and lock this energy up inside the carbohydrates they make. When we eat carbohydrates, we are eating molecules in which energy is trapped, which originally came from the Sun.

The carbohydrate molecules we eat are taken to every cell in our bodies. Inside these cells, the energy in the carbohydrate molecules is released, and changed into a form which our cells can use. This process is called **respiration**, and you will find out more about it in Chapter 9.

If we eat more carbohydrates than we need, our liver cells change them into **fat**. The fat is stored in several places in our bodies, especially underneath the skin.

> **Question**
>
> **4.3 a** Using your results from Investigation 4.1 and your own knowledge, make a list of six foods that contain a lot of carbohydrate.
>
> **b** Do these foods come from animals, or from plants?
>
> **c** Suggest which foods provide the main supply of carbohydrate in North America, the Far East and Africa.

Proteins ▶

Protein molecules

A protein molecule is a long molecule, made up of many small molecules joined together. Figure 4.6 shows a protein molecule. The small molecules it is made from are called **amino acids**.

There are 20 different sorts of amino acids. By joining amino acids together in different sequences, different proteins can be made. The amino acids can be linked in an infinite number of possible orders, so there is an infinite number of possible different proteins.

Amino acids, and therefore proteins, contain five elements. These are carbon, hydrogen, oxygen, nitrogen and sulphur.

Figure 4.6 ▶

(a) Amino acid molecules. There are 20 different kinds, but only four are shown here.

(b) Amino acids can link into long chains to form protein molecules. Different sequences of amino acids make different proteins.

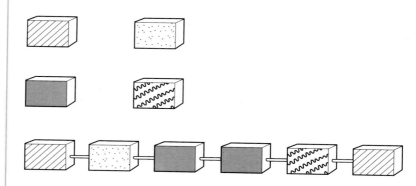

Investigation *4.2*

Testing foods for proteins

You are going to test five foods to see if they contain protein. The test you will use is called the **biuret test**. You will need:

- small samples of each of five foods
- a tile or dish on which you can put the foods
- a knife or a pestle and mortar
- a spatula or other small implement for picking up pieces of food
- five test tubes
- some potassium hydroxide solution and copper sulphate solution (or biuret reagent) and a dropper pipette
- safety glasses.

Take care! Potassium hydroxide solution is a strong alkali, so you should try not to get it onto your skin. If you do, then rinse your skin in cold water for a minute or two. Wear safety glasses to stop any chemicals going into your eyes.

Read through the instructions below, and then design a results chart in which you can write your results and conclusions.

1 Chop or crush a small sample of each of the five foods. Take care to keep them separate from one another.

2 Place a sample of one food in a test tube. Using a dropper pipette, add enough potassium hydroxide solution to cover the food. Add a little copper sulphate solution. Shake the tube to mix the food and the reagent thoroughly. Write down the colour you observe in your results chart.

3 If the mixture of food and reagent is a purple or mauve colour, then there is protein in the food. If it stays blue, then there is no protein in the food. Record your conclusions in your results chart.

Why we need proteins

When you eat proteins, your digestive system chops up the protein molecules into separate amino acids. The amino acids are taken in the blood to every cell in the body. Here, each cell uses the amino acids to make new protein molecules.

The protein molecules that the cells make have many different uses.

Some of them will be used as **building blocks** for parts of the cells. For example, **cell membranes** contain a lot of protein molecules. **Muscle** cells contain a very large number of protein molecules, which help the cells to produce movement. Bones and skin contain a protein called **collagen**. Hair and skin contain the protein **keratin**.

Some of the proteins will be **enzymes**. Enzymes help chemical reactions to take place. Every different chemical reaction that takes place inside our bodies has a different enzyme to catalyse it, so our cells have to make thousands of different enzymes.

One of the proteins made in cells from amino acids is **haemoglobin**. This is the red substance in our blood. Its function is to carry oxygen from the lungs to all the cells that need it.

Some of the proteins are **antibodies**. Antibodies attach themselves to bacteria or viruses that get into our bodies, and help to destroy them.

Some of the proteins are **hormones**. One example is the hormone **insulin**, which helps to keep the correct level of sugar in our blood. You can find out about insulin in Chapter 10.

Proteins can also be used for **energy**. This normally only happens if we have run out of carbohydrates, because there are so many other important uses for proteins – they cannot always be spared for energy production. The energy is released from the proteins in the same way that it is released from carbohydrates – that is, by respiration.

4.4 **a** Using your results from Investigation 4.2 and your own knowledge, list six foods that contain a lot of protein.

    b Do these foods come from animals, or from plants?

    c What do you think might be the main source of protein for a vegetarian (a person who does not eat food that comes from animals)?

Fats ▶

Fat molecules

A fat or oil molecule is made up of two kinds of smaller molecules. These are **glycerol** and **fatty acids**. Like carbohydrates, fat molecules contain atoms of the three elements carbon, hydrogen and oxygen. Figure 4.7 shows the structure of a fat molecule.

Figure 4.7 ▶
A fat molecule.

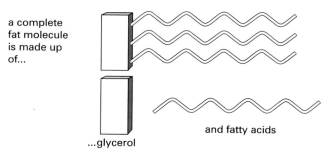

a complete fat molecule is made up of...

...glycerol

and fatty acids

Investigation 4.3

Testing foods for fats

You are going to test five foods to see if they contain fats. The test you will use is called the **ethanol test**, or the **emulsion test**.

You probably know that fats will not dissolve in water. However, they will dissolve in ethanol. In the ethanol test, you shake the food up in ethanol, so that any fat present dissolves in the ethanol. Then you pour the ethanol plus dissolved fat into some water. The fat forms tiny droplets which float around in the water, making an **emulsion**. The emulsion looks a creamy-white colour.

You will need:

- samples of five kinds of food
- a tile or dish on which you can put the foods
- a knife or pestle and mortar
- five very clean and completely dry test tubes, and five more clean tubes

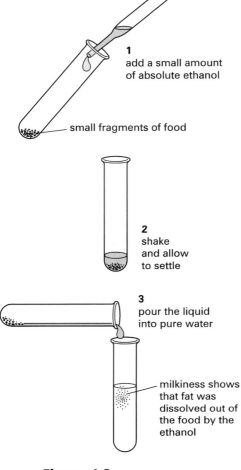

1
add a small amount
of absolute ethanol

small fragments of food

2
shake
and allow
to settle

3
pour the liquid
into pure water

milkiness shows
that fat was
dissolved out of
the food by the
ethanol

▲ **Figure 4.8**
Testing for fat.

- some absolute (pure) ethanol and a dropper pipette
- some distilled water.

Read through the instructions below, and draw up a results chart in which you can write your results and conclusions.

1 Chop or crush a small sample of each of the five kinds of food, taking care to keep them separate from one another.

2 Put one of the food samples into a dry test tube, and add a little absolute ethanol. Shake the food up in the ethanol, so that any fat in the food has a chance to dissolve. Then put the tube in a rack, and leave it to settle while you repeat this step with the other four foods.

3 Put some distilled water into another tube, and pour the ethanol from the first food sample into it. (Be careful not to pour any of the food in as well.) Write down what happens in your results chart.

4 If there was fat in the food, then the water will go milky white when you pour the ethanol into it. If there was no fat, then it will stay clear. Record your conclusions in your results chart.

Why we need fats

When you eat fat, your digestive system breaks the fat molecules up into glycerol and fatty acid molecules. These are taken to your cells, where they can be made into fat molecules again.

A lot of the fat you eat is used for **energy**. It is broken down by the process of respiration inside your cells. Any extra fat you eat can be stored for later use, often underneath the skin. Fat is especially useful for storing energy, because every gram of fat contains twice as much energy as a gram of carbohydrate or protein.

You also need fat to make **cell membranes**. The stored fat under the skin is useful as **heat insulation**; animals living in cold climates often have very thick layers of fat, called blubber, to keep heat inside their bodies. These thick fat layers are especially useful to animals like whales and seals, because they also provide **buoyancy**.

Questions

4.5 a Using your results from Investigation 4.3 and your own knowledge, make a list of six foods which contain a lot of fat.

b Do these foods come from animals, or from plants?

4.6 Draw a table with six columns, with the headings shown below.

The first row in the table has been filled in for you. You will need two more rows in the table, for proteins and for fats. Fill in these two extra rows in the table.

Nutrient	Elements contained in its molecules	Name of the smaller molecules from which it is made	Use in body	Foods that contain a lot of it	How to test for it
Carbohydrate	C, H, O	Sugars	For energy	Bread, rice, potatoes	Iodine test for starch, Benedict's test for reducing sugars

Vitamins ▶

Vitamins are organic substances that we only need in very small amounts in the diet. There are many kinds of vitamins, all of which help some of the chemical reactions inside our cells to take place. We shall look at two vitamins – **vitamin C** and **vitamin D**.

Vitamin C

This vitamin is made by plants, and is found in especially large amounts in citrus fruits and potatoes. It is sometimes called **ascorbic acid**. If you read the list of ingredients on food packets, you will find that many of them have ascorbic acid added to them. It is really added as a preservative, but it is also good for you, because it is a vitamin.

Vitamin C helps in the formation of the protein **collagen**. It helps the amino acids in collagen to be put together in just the right way. Collagen is an important part of skin, bones and the walls of blood vessels, so without vitamin C we cannot build new skin if it is damaged, and the walls of our blood vessels become weak. Vitamin C therefore helps wounds to heal, and keeps blood vessels strong.

A person who does not eat enough vitamin C may suffer from the disease **scurvy**. Scurvy is an example of a **deficiency disease**, because it is caused by a lack or deficiency of something in the diet. People with scurvy often have skin covered with bruises and ulcers, where

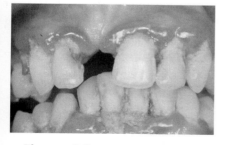

▲ **Figure 4.9**
One of the symptoms of scurvy is very weak gums, which recede from the teeth. Scurvy is easily cured by adding vitamin C to the diet.

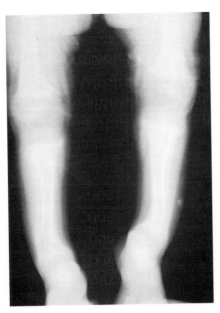

▲ Figure 4.10
Rickets causes bones to be soft. This X-ray shows the lower leg bones of a child with rickets. You can see how the bones are bent and deformed.

Inorganic ions ▶

blood capillaries have broken and where their skin has failed to heal. Their gums become soft and bleed easily. In really bad scurvy, the gums may be so badly affected that the teeth fall out.

The amounts of vitamin C in fresh fruits and vegetables gradually get less if the food is stored for a long time. If the food is cooked by boiling in water, a lot of the vitamin C washes out of the food and into the water. To make sure you have plenty of vitamin C in your diet, you should try to eat fresh fruit and vegetables.

Vitamin D

Vitamin D is made by most plants. Animals can make vitamin D as well, and it is found in fatty foods made by animals, such as fish oils, egg yolks and milk. Humans can make vitamin D in their skin cells, but only when sunlight falls onto the skin.

Vitamin D is needed to help us to absorb calcium from the food we eat, and we use calcium for making **teeth** and **bones**. Without vitamin D, even if we eat plenty of calcium, not enough calcium goes into growing bones, so the bones are not as hard as they should be. They bend too easily, and may grow into a permanently bent shape. This is called **rickets**.

Inorganic ions are sometimes called minerals. Humans need very many different ones, but most are only required in very small amounts. Two inorganic ions that we need in larger quantities are **iron** and **calcium**.

Iron

This inorganic ion is needed for making **haemoglobin**. Haemoglobin is the red molecule, or pigment, found inside red blood cells. It joins up with oxygen molecules in the lungs, and then is carried around the body in the blood to other cells that need oxygen for respiration. Here the haemoglobin lets go of the oxygen, and is carried back to the lungs to pick up some more.

Each haemoglobin molecule contains iron ions. If we do not have enough iron, we cannot make as much haemoglobin as we need, so our blood cannot carry as much oxygen as it should. Cells are not supplied with oxygen as quickly as they should be, and so cannot respire very quickly. Respiration releases energy from glucose; if our cells cannot respire, then we do not have enough energy. This deficiency disease is called **anaemia**. People with anaemia feel tired very easily.

Foods that contain a lot of iron include red meat, especially liver. Green leafy vegetables also contain iron.

Calcium

Calcium ions are needed to make bones and teeth. It is calcium salts that make bones and teeth so hard. Calcium is also needed to help blood to clot.

A shortage of calcium in the diet can lead to weak bones and teeth, and slow blood clotting. As with a lack of vitamin D, lack of calcium can cause the disease rickets.

One of the best foods for providing calcium is milk. Hard water, that is water from areas with limestone in the soil and rocks, also contains calcium.

Question

4.7 Draw up a table with four columns, with the following headings:

Nutrient	Use in body	Deficiency symptoms	Food that contains it
Vitamin C			

You will need three more rows in the table – for vitamin D, iron and calcium. Fill in the rest of the table, using the information on pages 53 to 55.

Water ▶

An adult human contains about 40 litres of water. Why do we have so much water in our bodies?

Water has many functions. First, it is a **solvent**. The cytoplasm of cells is a jelly-like solution of proteins and other chemicals. In the cytoplasm, these chemicals take part in many reactions, called **metabolic reactions**. These reactions can only take place in water. If a person loses too much water, the metabolic reactions may stop, and the person will die.

Water is used as a solvent to help to **transport** substances around the body. Blood plasma is mostly water, with many substances dissolved in it. These dissolved substances include amino acids, vitamins, glucose, inorganic ions, hormones and antibodies. Red and white blood cells float in the plasma. If there is not enough water in blood plasma, it becomes too thick, which makes it difficult for every cell to be supplied with the nutrients and oxygen it needs.

Water also takes part in many **reactions** in the body. For example, you will see in Chapter 5 that water is needed to react with large molecules such as starch, to break them down into smaller molecules in the digestive system.

The evaporation of water from skin helps to **cool** us down. When we are too hot, sweat glands in the skin take water from the blood, and secrete it onto the surface of the skin. The water turns to water vapour. As it evaporates, it takes heat from the skin.

Question

4.8 **a** From what you know of plants, which of the functions of water described above do you think apply to plants as well as to animals?

b There is an important metabolic reaction that happens in plants, but not in animals, which uses water as a reactant. What is this reaction?

Fibre ▶

As well as the six groups of nutrients so far described in this chapter – carbohydrates, proteins, fats, vitamins, inorganic ions and water – we also need **fibre (roughage)** in our diet. However, fibre is not really a nutrient, because we do not take it into our cells and use it. Fibre just goes in at one end of the alimentary canal, and comes out at the other.

This is why fibre is so important in the diet. Fibre is mostly cellulose, from the cell walls of plant cells. Cellulose is a polysaccharide, like starch. However, we have no enzymes that can break cellulose into the smaller sugar molecules from which it is made. As you will see in Chapter 5, this means that it cannot be absorbed from the alimentary canal into the blood. The cellulose remains inside the alimentary canal.

The presence of cellulose fibre inside the alimentary canal stimulates its muscles to squeeze the food along, by a process called **peristalsis** (see Figure 5.7 on page 76). With no fibre, this only happens slowly. Fibre stimulates food to move quickly through the alimentary canal. Insufficient fibre can lead to constipation.

There is some evidence that having plenty of fibre in the diet can reduce the risk of cancer in the alimentary canal. This might be because cancer can be started off by certain chemicals in food. If the food stays in the alimentary canal for a long time, then these chemicals have more chance of damaging cells in the wall of the canal. If there is plenty of fibre in the food, then not only does it move faster through the alimentary canal, but the dangerous chemicals may stay stuck to the fibre, so that they do not damage the cells in the wall of the canal.

A balanced diet ▶

A **balanced diet** is one that contains some of all the six kinds of nutrients, including all the different vitamins and inorganic ions, plus fibre. These nutrients should be in reasonable proportions, i.e. not too much or too little of each one. The total energy content of the food eaten each day should be about the same as the total energy the person uses in one day.

Energy in food

You may remember that the foods that provide us with energy are **carbohydrates**, **fats** and **proteins**. Energy is measured in **kilojoules, kJ**. Table 4.1 shows the amount of energy in 100 g of several different foods.

Table 4.1 ▶

Food	Energy per 100g / kJ
Pure carbohydrate	1600
Pure fat	3700
Pure protein	1700
Banana	330
Beef	200
Bread	230
Butter	750
Carrots	75
Chicken	120
Fish	100
Milk	65
Peas	70
Potato	90
Rice, boiled	120

4.9 Look at Table 4.1.

   a Beef contains protein and fat. Suggest why the amount of energy in 100 g of beef is so much less than the amount of energy in 100 g of pure fat or pure protein.

   b In Table 4.1, butter has much more energy per 100 g than any of the other foods. Suggest why this is so.

   c Suggest why chicken has less energy per gram than beef.

The number of kilojoules of energy a person needs in their diet depends on the number of kilojoules of energy they use each day. This in turn depends on many things, including their sex, and the job they do. Figure 4.11 shows the recommended energy intake each day for several different groups of people.

Figure 4.11 ▶
Recommended daily energy intakes for different people.

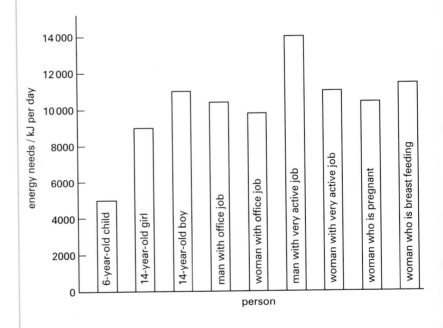

Question

4.10 Look at Figure 4.11.

   a Suggest why a 14-year-old needs more energy per day than a 6-year-old.

   b Suggest why a 14-year-old boy needs more energy per day than a man with an office job.

   c Suggest why a pregnant woman does not need more energy per day than a woman with an active job.

   d Suggest why a woman who is breast feeding needs more energy per day than she did when she was pregnant.

Nutrients in a balanced diet

Table 4.2 shows the recommended amounts of four nutrients for seven different people. You can see that these vary with age and sex. A pregnant woman needs more iron in her diet, because she has to make haemoglobin both for herself and her baby. Similarly, she needs extra calcium to help to build the baby's bones and teeth.

Person	Protein / g	Vitamin C / mg	Iron / mg	Calcium / mg
1-year-old	30	20	7	600
6-year-old	43	20	10	600
14-year-old boy	66	25	12	700
14-year-old girl	53	25	13	700
30-year-old man	70	30	10	500
30-year-old woman	55	30	12	500
Pregnant woman	60	60	14	1200

▲ **Table 4.2**

Malnutrition

Malnutrition means not eating a balanced diet. This may mean not eating enough food, or eating too much, or eating too much or too little of a particular nutrient.

Starvation is the result of not eating enough food over a long period of time. A starving person uses more energy each day than they take in as food. The body has to use its own stores to keep itself alive, and so loses a lot of weight. Any protein in the diet gets used to provide energy, instead of making the other important things such as muscles. Muscles become small and weak. Bones cannot grow.

Deficiency diseases are the result of not eating enough of one particular kind of nutrient. You have already seen the deficiency diseases resulting from not having enough vitamin C, vitamin D, iron or calcium in the diet. In some parts of the world, people do not have enough protein in the diet. This can result in the disease **kwashiorkor**.

Obesity is a condition that can result from eating too much over a long period of time. The energy taken in as food is much more than the person needs, so a lot of fat is stored. The person is very overweight. Obesity can increase the risk of suffering from several different diseases, including heart disease (page 100) and diabetes.

Constipation may be caused by a lack of fibre or liquids in the diet.

Supplement

The problems of world food supplies

Figure 4.12 shows some areas in the world where not enough food is grown to feed the people who live there.

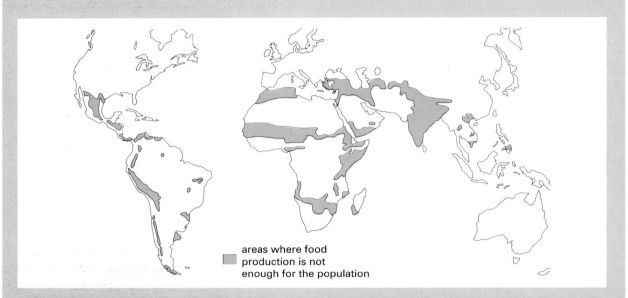

areas where food production is not enough for the population

Figure 4.12

There are many reasons for this. They include:

- **Climate** – in many of these places, there is not enough rainfall to allow crops to grow well.

- **Poor soil** – soil may be very short of inorganic ions, such as nitrate, which plants need for healthy growth.

- **Desertification** – some parts of the world which used to have good soils and enough rainfall now have poor, thin soil and less rain, because the people living there have removed most of the vegetation, perhaps by grazing too many animals on it, or by cutting down trees for fuel.

- **Natural disasters**, such as flooding, happen regularly in some parts of the world, such as Bangladesh.

▲ Figure 4.13
In a village near Baidoa, in Somalia, a mother and child wait for a meal. Famine, caused by a combination of war and drought in this area, resulted in many people suffering from undernourishment. Aid workers provided porridge, made from bean and maize flour, sugar and oil, to these people, which provided them with protein, fat and carbohydrate.

- **Lack of money** – if people do not have money to buy fertilisers, pesticides or machinery, then it is very difficult for them to grow enough crops.

- **Wars** – in regions where people are fighting each other, it may be impossible to grow crops.

- **Urbanisation** – in developing countries, many people want to move away from the countryside to the towns, because they think they will have a better life there. This leaves fewer people in the countryside to grow crops.

- **Increasing population** – in many developing countries, the population is increasing much faster than food production can grow.

Worldwide, it is quite possible to grow enough food to feed all the people on Earth, even if the population carries on increasing. However, it is not easy to distribute food from the countries that have plenty to those that do not have enough.

Questions

4.11 You will need to spend some time on this question. You will need to obtain information from different places. Try newspapers, magazines and books in your school library. Geography books may be more helpful than biology books.

Choose one particular part of the world in which many people do not get enough to eat.

Find out what you can about the crops the people grow, and how they grow them. Find out also about the problems they have in growing their crops.

4.12 Choose two or three of the following statements. Decide whether you agree or disagree with them, and give some reasons for each of your decisions.

- Rich countries should give much more food to poor countries.

- People in developing countries should not be given food, but should be given help in growing their own food.

▲ Figure 4.14
Farming in mountainous regions is very difficult, because the soil is often shallow, and slopes are steep. People have to work hard to grow enough to eat. This family, in Bolivia, is harvesting potatoes. They are subsistence farmers, which means that they grow enough food to feed themselves, rather than selling it to make money.

- If people have overgrazed their land and cut down trees, then it is their own fault that they do not have enough food.
- If we can slow down the growth in the world population, then fewer people will die of starvation.

Food additives

A **food additive** is a substance that is added to a food product during its manufacture. Food additives have many different functions. They include:

- **preservatives**, which keep the food fresh and prevent decay
- **flavourings** and **colourings**, which add to the taste and visual appeal of a food
- **antioxidants**, which stop components of the food combining with oxygen. This can cause discoloration (such as browning in apples) or spoil the taste
- **stabilisers**, which stop a food such as ice cream separating out into watery and fatty components.

Many of these additives are naturally occurring substances, and some are positively good for you. For example, one of the most common food additives is ascorbic acid (vitamin C) which is added as an antioxidant. Many flavourings and colourings are also natural products, as are most stabilisers.

However, some people are concerned that a few commonly used additives may be harmful to health. In some children, for example, it is thought an orange food colouring, which is sometimes used to colour soft drinks or sweets, may cause behaviour problems. Some preservatives are also thought to carry a slight risk to health.

Figure 4.15 ▶
Which substances on this label are food additives?

> **INGREDIENTS (greatest first):**
> Wheat Flour, Water, Vegetable and Hydrogenated Vegetable Oils (contains Emulsifier E471), Minced Beef, Concentrated Tomato Purée, Onion, Sliced Mushrooms (contains Acid E330, Antioxidant E300), Tomatoes, Ham (contains E450, Antioxidant E301, Preservative E250), Modified Starch, Red Wine, Beef Bouillon (Hydrolysed Vegetable Protein, Maltodextrin, Salt, Flavourings, Onion Powder, Dextrose, Yeast Extract, Spices), Carrots, Garlic Purée (contains Acid E330), Stabiliser E461, Salt, Herbs, Sugar, Spices, Concentrated Lemon Juice (contains Preservative E220). Minimum 10.5% meat.

Food preservatives

Food preservatives are very useful additives. Without them, many foods would have to be eaten very quickly after manufacture. The use of food preservatives means that foods can be kept for longer, which makes it cheaper for manufacturers and shops to transport and store them. This makes the foods cheaper than if preservatives were not used. It also greatly reduces the risk of people getting food poisoning from bacteria which might otherwise grow in the food.

Commonly used food preservatives include **sulphur dioxide** or **sulphite**, which kills bacteria and is often added to processed meats. It also prevents yeast growing in fruit juices, stored fruits and dried vegetables.

Nitrite is added to some meat products, to stop bacteria growing. However, nitrite does have a slight risk of harming health. Nitrite has been used as a food preservative for hundreds of years, in making brine to 'cure' meat. It is now known that nitrites can combine with other substances in food to form chemicals called **nitrosamines**. Nitrosamines are known to cause cancer in animals, when fed in large amounts. Despite this, nitrites are still used in foods for human consumption. This is because it is believed that the benefits of nitrite as a food preservative outweigh the slight risk to health. There is no evidence that the very small amounts of nitrosamines found in food have ever harmed a human. Moreover, most of the nitrites in our diet do not come from preservatives, but from vegetables, in which they are found naturally. Also, without nitrite as a preservative, there would be many more instances of fatal food poisoning caused by the bacterium *Clostridium botulinum*, which can breed in cans of meat.

Question

4.13 a Collect labels from a range of food packages, including cans, packets and other types of packaging. What additives are listed on the labels? Try to find out why these additives are included in the food product.

b Make a survey of people's attitudes to food additives. You could design a questionnaire. You could find out if people know why additives are added to food, what these additives are, and if they are worried about how they might affect their health.

Using microorganisms to make food

For thousands of years, humans have used micro-organisms to make food. **Yeast**, a fungus, has been used to produce alcoholic drinks from grain and fruit, and to make bread. **Bacteria** have been used to make yoghurt and cheese from milk. Recently, other kinds of fungus have been used to make a food product called **mycoprotein**.

Investigation 4.4

Which milk makes the best yoghurt?

You are going to use two different types of milk to make yoghurt. If you make your yoghurt in a laboratory, it is not safe to taste it. You will have to use some other method of deciding how good your yoghurt is.

Yoghurt is made by bacteria, called *Lactobacillus,* acting on milk. The bacteria produce enzymes which change the sugar in the milk into lactic acid. The easiest way to get some of these bacteria is from some bought natural yoghurt.

You will need:

- a small amount of natural yoghurt containing bacteria
- about 10 cm^3 of two different sorts of milk
- some cling film
- two clean boiling tubes and a rack or beaker
- a warm place to leave the tubes, or a water bath at about 40 °C
- a clean syringe, pipette or measuring cylinder to measure 10 cm^3
- a pH meter, or some Universal Indicator solution
- a way of labelling your boiling tubes.

1 Measure 10 cm^3 of one type of milk into one of your boiling tubes, and 10 cm^3 of the second type into the second tube. Label each tube.

2 Add approximately 1 cm^3 of natural yoghurt to each tube. Stir gently.

3 Cover each tube with cling film. Put them in a warm place or a water bath.

4 Look at your yoghurt after an hour or so, and again at intervals for up to five hours. Record its appearance. Take small samples and measure their pH. (If you have a pH meter, you can simply put this into the tube of yoghurt.)

Investigation 4.5

Making bread

Bread flour contains starch and a protein called gluten. When yeast is added to wet flour, the yeast produces enzymes which break down the starch into sugar. The yeast then respires, using the sugar to produce carbon dioxide. (You can find out more about this on page 133.) The carbon dioxide forms bubbles in the wet flour, which make the bread rise. The gluten forms strong, stretchy fibres, which trap the bubbles and give the bread a good texture.

Below is a recipe for making bread dough. Use this recipe to test one of the following hypotheses.

- Bread rises faster at warm temperatures than at cold temperatures.
- Bread made with flour containing a lot of gluten (often sold as 'strong' flour) rises more than bread made with flour containing only a little gluten.
- Flour containing the added flour improver ascorbic acid rises better than flour without improvers.
- Bread dough containing a lot of salt is less stretchy than dough containing no salt.

Recipe

For the basic bread recipe, you will need:

- a little sugar
- a little dried yeast
- two 250 cm^3 beakers
- about 75 g of flour
- a 100 cm^3 measuring cylinder

1 Add about 1 g of sugar to about 50 cm³ of warm water in a beaker. Stir in about 1 g of dried yeast. Leave for a few minutes for the yeast to become active. It should form a bubbly 'scum' on top of the liquid.

2 Measure about 75 g of flour into another beaker. Add the yeast liquid, and mix thoroughly. Stir to form a stiff dough. If it is wet and sticky, add a little more flour. If it is dry and hard, add a little more warm water. Take the dough out of the beaker, and pull and stretch it around with your hands until it forms a stretchy ball.

3 Put your dough into a 100 cm³ measuring cylinder. Record the volume of the dough.

4 Leave the dough in a warm place. Record its volume at intervals.

Mycoprotein

'Myco' means 'fungus', and mycoprotein is a food made from a fungus. It is sometimes called **single-cell protein**, or SCP for short.

People began to experiment with making high-protein foods from microorganisms in the 1950s and 1960s. They wanted to do this to provide protein cheaply for people in parts of the world where food was in short supply. Many different microorganisms were tried, including single-celled plants. However, people did not want to buy or eat them. Many people were suspicious of these new foods, often because they were afraid of the idea of eating microorganisms. (Perhaps they did not realise that yoghurt and cheese are made using microorganisms!) The appearance and taste of many of the foods were not attractive. Quite a few of these SCP foods are no longer sold as food for people, but are quite widely used as foods for animals.

However, one kind of SCP has become a widely marketed food for people. This is a food made from a fungus. In Britain, a food called Quorn, a mycoprotein, is made from the fungus *Fusarium*. The fungus is grown on waste from flour making. A similar process in Finland uses a fungus called *Paecilomyces*, grown on waste from the wood and paper industry. The hyphae of the fungus are processed to make threads, rather like the fibres found in meat. The fungus makes a food that is high in protein and carbohydrate, but very low in fat.

Question

4.14 Summarise the advantages of using SCP such as mycoprotein instead of meat, as high-protein foods.

Summary

- The diet of humans and other animals needs to include carbohydrates, fats, proteins, vitamins, inorganic ions, water and fibre (roughage).

- Carbohydrate molecules contain the elements carbon, hydrogen and oxygen. They include starch and sugars. Carbohydrates are broken down inside cells in the process of respiration, which releases energy from them. Iodine solution turns black in the presence of starch. Benedict's solution produces a brick red precipitate when heated with reducing sugars.

- Protein molecules are made up of many amino acids linked in a long chain. They contain carbon, hydrogen, oxygen and nitrogen. They can be respired to release energy, or used for building many parts of the body, including cell membranes, bones, skin and blood. They are also needed for making enzymes and antibodies. Proteins produce a purple colour when mixed with biuret reagent.

- Fat molecules also contain carbon, hydrogen and oxygen. They too can be respired to release energy. They can also be used to make cell surface membranes, for insulation and for buoyancy. Fats can be detected by the ethanol test.

- Vitamin C is found in fresh fruit and vegetables, especially citrus fruits, and is needed for the formation of strong skin and blood vessels. Lack of vitamin C causes scurvy.

- Vitamin D is found in dairy products, and can also be made in the skin when sunshine falls onto it. It is needed for the formation of strong bones and teeth. Lack of vitamin D causes rickets.

- Iron is found in meat, eggs and some dark green vegetables such as spinach. It is needed for making haemoglobin. A lack of iron causes anaemia.

- Calcium is found in dairy products, and is needed for the formation of strong bones and teeth.

- Fibre consists of cellulose and lignin from plant cell walls. It cannot be digested or absorbed, and helps to keep the alimentary canal working well and prevents constipation.

- A balanced diet contains some of each type of nutrient in the correct proportions, and the right amount of energy. People of different genders, ages and occupations need differing amounts of energy in their diets.

- Enough food is produced in the world to feed everybody, but it is not distributed evenly and many people do not have enough food and suffer from malnutrition or starvation.

- Additives can be added to foods before sale, to increase shelf life and increase palatability.

- Bacteria can be used to turn milk into yoghurt. Yeast produces carbon dioxide which helps bread to rise. Fungi can be used to make mycoprotein.

Digestion and absorption

The food we eat travels through a single long tube, running all the way from the mouth to the anus. This tube is the alimentary canal. To get to body cells, food molecules must pass through the walls of this canal, and into the blood. Only small molecules can do this, so large molecules in the food are broken down to small ones in the process called digestion. This process is carried out by enzymes.

The alimentary canal ▶

The organs of the alimentary canal

Figure 5.1 shows the human alimentary canal. This is a long tube, wide in some parts and narrow in others, which leads all the way from the mouth to the anus. The tube is about 7m long – it can fit inside a person because parts of it are coiled round and round.

Figure 5.1 ▶
The human digestive system.

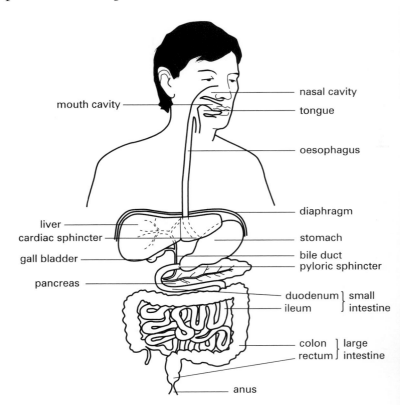

mouth cavity

nasal cavity

tongue

oesophagus

diaphragm

liver
cardiac sphincter

stomach

gall bladder

bile duct
pyloric sphincter

pancreas

duodenum ⎤ small
ileum ⎦ intestine

colon ⎤ large
rectum ⎦ intestine

anus

In fact, the alimentary canal varies in length, because some parts of it, especially the small intestine, have muscles in the wall which make the tube wriggle around as food passes through.

On Figure 5.1, follow the path the food takes. It enters the **mouth**, and then travels through the **oesophagus**. This takes it past a 'gateway' called the **cardiac sphincter** and into the **stomach**. It may stay here for a while, before passing out through another gateway, the **pyloric sphincter**, into the **small intestine**. This is called 'small' because it is quite narrow, but is actually much the longest section of the alimentary canal. The food travels round and round the coils of the small intestine, and enters the **large intestine**, which goes up, across and down. The remains of the food eventually leave the alimentary canal through the **anus**.

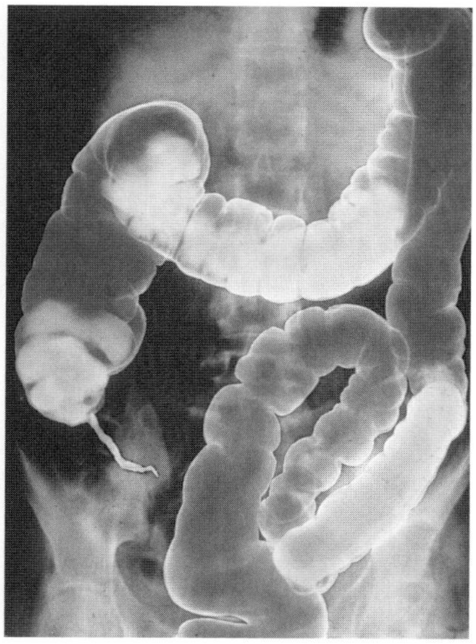

The length of time that this journey takes varies from person to person, and from day to day. On average, it takes about 10 hours for the food to reach the large intestine. It may then quite quickly pass from here through the anus, or it may wait in the large intestine for more than a day. The speed with which it passes through partly depends on the amount of fibre in the food.

The remains of food which eventually pass out of the anus are rather different from the food that goes into the mouth! What happens to it in between, and why?

Breaking down the food

The alimentary canal, as you have seen, is a tube passing right through the body. The food inside it is separated from the rest of the body by the walls of the alimentary canal. Before the food can get into the blood, or into any of the body cells, it must pass through these walls. This is called **absorption**.

The walls are made of living cells. These cells will only allow small molecules to pass through them. Big molecules, such as proteins or polysaccharides (starch, for example) cannot get through.

This means that the big molecules in the food we eat have to be broken down to small ones before they can be absorbed. First, large lumps of food are broken down into smaller pieces. This is called **mechanical digestion**, and is done by teeth, and muscles in the stomach wall. Then the big molecules in the pieces of

▲ Figure 5.2
This X-ray shows the large intestine. Towards the centre left of the picture, you can see a small thread-like structure, which is the appendix. Leading upwards from here, on the left, is the first part of the colon, which then runs across the top, and down the right-hand side, with a few twists and turns on the way. The rectum can be seen at the bottom of the photograph. The vertebral column is faintly visible in the background.

food are broken into smaller ones. **Enzymes** do this. This process is called **chemical digestion**.

Mechanical digestion ▶

Teeth

Figure 5.3 shows the four kinds of human teeth. At the front of the mouth are the **incisors**. These help to bite off pieces of food to take into the mouth. On either side of them are **canines**, which are more pointed than incisors. Human use their canines rather like incisors, but in some animals they are long and pointed, and are used for killing prey. ('Canine' means 'dog tooth'.) Behind these are the **premolars** and **molars**, which are used for chewing food. Chewing breaks up the food into very small pieces, mixing it with saliva. This makes it easier to swallow and gives us a chance to taste it. It also increases its surface area, so that enzymes in the mouth and further on in the alimentary canal have a better chance of getting at every bit of the food.

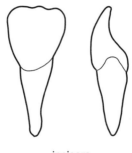
incisors

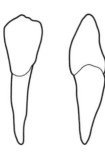
canines

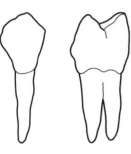
premolars

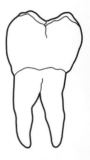
molar

▲ **Figure 5.3**
Human teeth.

Figure 5.4 shows a tooth cut in half. The outer layer is made of the hardest substance in the human body – **enamel**. Beneath this is a layer of **dentine**, which contains living cells, surrounded by material containing calcium salts. In the centre of the tooth is the **pulp cavity**, containing blood vessels and nerves. The blood vessels bring oxygen and nutrients to supply the living cells in the tooth.

The part of the tooth above the gum is called the **crown**, and the part buried in the gum is the **root**. The root goes right down into the jawbone, where it is held in place by fibres. These allow slight movement, so that not too much strain is put on the tooth when you bite on something hard. Instead of enamel, the root of the tooth is covered with a substance called **cement**.

Figure 5.4 ▶
Section through a human molar.

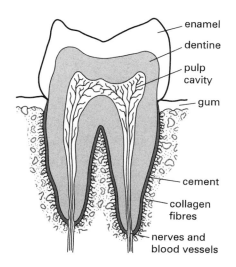

enamel

dentine

pulp cavity

gum

cement

collagen fibres

nerves and blood vessels

Investigation 5.1

Human teeth

1 Using a mirror, identify your *incisors*, *canines* and *premolars/molars*. How many of each do you have? Do you have the same number on the top and bottom jaw?

2 Take a bite from a piece of firm food such as a maize cob, an apple or some meat, and chew it. Concentrate on exactly how you use your teeth. What is the function of **a** your incisors, **b** your canines and **c** your premolars and molars?

Tooth decay

Although enamel is extremely hard, it is quite easily dissolved by acids. This is how **tooth decay** happens.

We all have bacteria living in our mouths. No matter how carefully you brush your teeth, or use mouthwashes, you can never get rid of all the bacteria. When you chew food, some of it will be left on your teeth. The bacteria feed on these food remains. The mixture of bacteria and the food remains on the teeth is called **plaque**.

If the food is sugary, the bacteria produce **acid**. The acid begins to dissolve the enamel. Eventually, the acid may make a hole right through the enamel and into the dentine.

How can this be prevented? There are many things which you can do to reduce the chances of tooth decay. These include:

● Don't eat too many sugary foods. If you do eat them, then try to do so just once or twice a day, rather than sucking, chewing or drinking sweet things all through the day.

- Clean your teeth regularly. This helps to remove the plaque from the teeth. Dental floss or tooth picks help to remove food and plaque from between the teeth.

- Use toothpaste containing fluoride. Fluoride is absorbed by the teeth, and helps them to resist attack by acid.

- If possible, visit a dentist regularly – perhaps once a year. She or he will be able to treat any decay on your teeth quickly, before it gets too bad.

Supplement

Question

5.1 In the 1930s, it was realised that people who lived in places where there were quite large amounts of fluoride in the water had less tooth decay than other people. Where fluoride levels are especially high, there is virtually no tooth decay, although the teeth frequently develop patches of dark colour. In some countries, fluoride is now added to the water supply. Figure 5.5 shows the results of a study in the USA investigating the relationship between the amount of fluoride in the public water supply and the amount of tooth decay in children.

▼ **Figure 5.5**
Dental decay and the fluoride content of tap water.

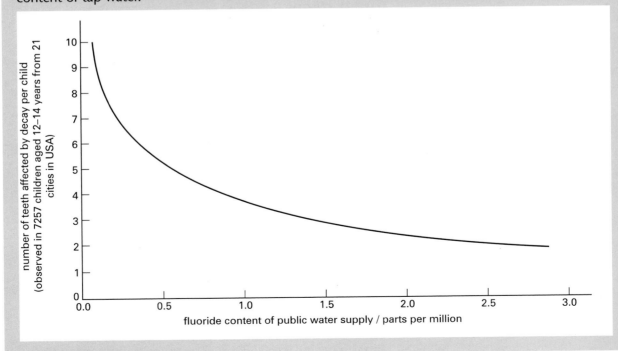

a Describe the effect fluoride has on the incidence of tooth decay.

b Do you think fluoride should be added to the water supply in all parts of the world? Explain your answer.

c Suggest *two* reasons why, despite the evidence shown on the graph, many people do not like the idea of having fluoride added to their water supply.

d If fluoride is not added to the water supply, how else might people supply their teeth with fluoride?

Chemical digestion ▶

Enzymes and digestion

Figure 5.6 shows the three different kinds of enzymes involved in digestion.

▼ **Figure 5.6 (a)**
How carbohydrate is digested.

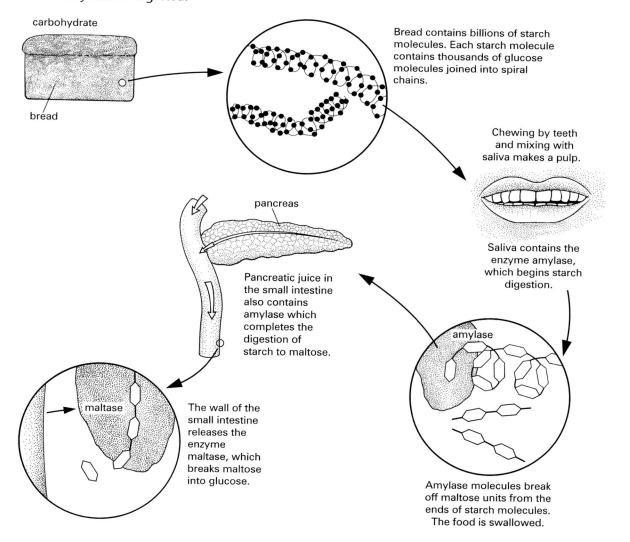

carbohydrate

bread

Bread contains billions of starch molecules. Each starch molecule contains thousands of glucose molecules joined into spiral chains.

Chewing by teeth and mixing with saliva makes a pulp.

pancreas

Pancreatic juice in the small intestine also contains amylase which completes the digestion of starch to maltose.

Saliva contains the enzyme amylase, which begins starch digestion.

amylase

maltase

The wall of the small intestine releases the enzyme maltase, which breaks maltose into glucose.

Amylase molecules break off maltose units from the ends of starch molecules. The food is swallowed.

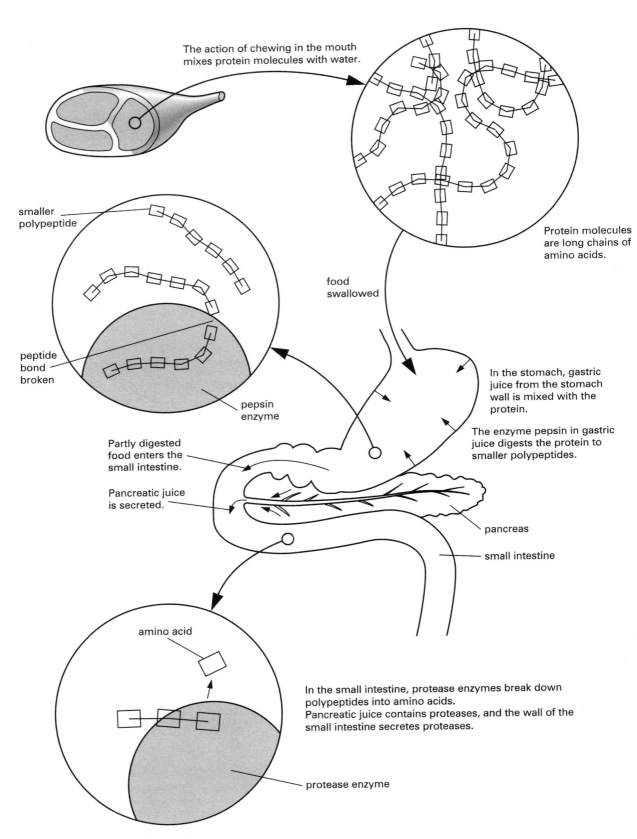

The action of chewing in the mouth mixes protein molecules with water.

Protein molecules are long chains of amino acids.

smaller polypeptide

peptide bond broken

pepsin enzyme

food swallowed

In the stomach, gastric juice from the stomach wall is mixed with the protein.

The enzyme pepsin in gastric juice digests the protein to smaller polypeptides.

Partly digested food enters the small intestine.

Pancreatic juice is secreted.

pancreas

small intestine

amino acid

In the small intestine, protease enzymes break down polypeptides into amino acids.
Pancreatic juice contains proteases, and the wall of the small intestine secretes proteases.

protease enzyme

(b) How protein is digested.

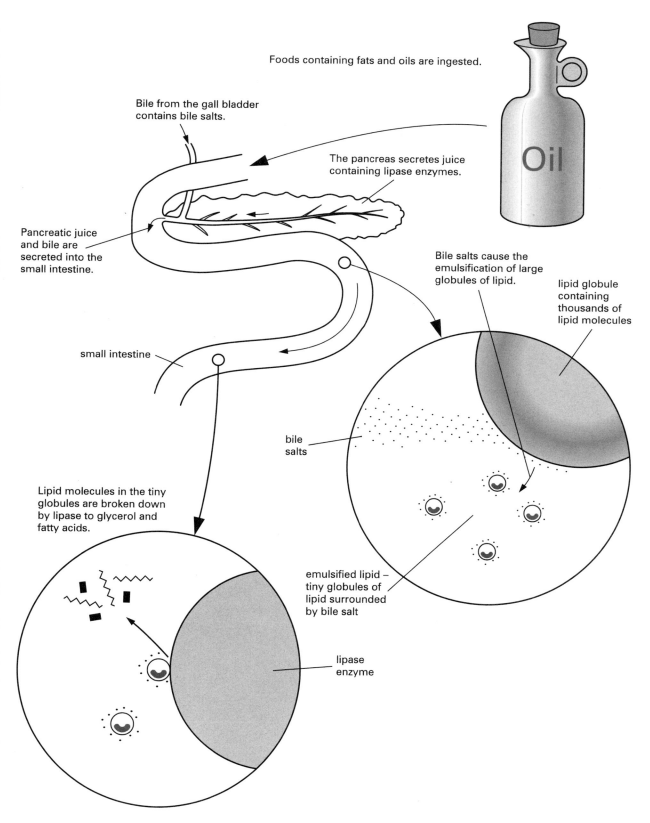

Foods containing fats and oils are ingested.

Bile from the gall bladder contains bile salts.

The pancreas secretes juice containing lipase enzymes.

Pancreatic juice and bile are secreted into the small intestine.

Bile salts cause the emulsification of large globules of lipid.

lipid globule containing thousands of lipid molecules

small intestine

bile salts

Lipid molecules in the tiny globules are broken down by lipase to glycerol and fatty acids.

emulsified lipid – tiny globules of lipid surrounded by bile salt

lipase enzyme

(c) How fat is digested.

- **Carbohydrases** digest carbohydrates. **Amylase** is a starch-digesting enzyme, which breaks starch molecules into the two-unit molecules of **maltose**. Maltose is then broken down to **glucose** by the enzyme **maltase**.

- **Proteases** digest proteins. First, the protein molecules are broken into shorter lengths, called **polypeptides**. The polypeptides are then broken down into their individual **amino acids**.

- **Lipases** digest fats. The fat molecules are broken down into **fatty acids** and **glycerol**.

As the food passes along the alimentary canal, these enzymes are mixed with it. Different enzymes work in different parts of the alimentary canal. Muscles in the walls of the alimentary canal help to churn the food and enzymes inside it around, so that they get well mixed up. We shall follow the path taken by the food, and look at what happens to it in each part of the alimentary canal. The food is moved along the alimentary canal by **peristalsis** as shown in Figure 5.7.

Figure 5.7 ▶
Food is pushed through the alimentary canal by a process called **peristalsis**. Circular muscles in the wall of the alimentary canal contract behind the food, squeezing in on it and pushing it forward. The circular muscles just ahead of the food relax, making it easy for the alimentary canal to be pushed wider as the food passes through.

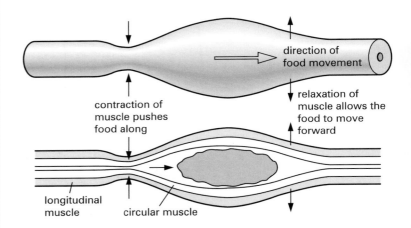

The mouth

The correct biological name for taking food into the mouth is **ingestion** – not to be confused with indigestion! We ingest food using the teeth, lips and tongue.

Inside the mouth, **saliva** is mixed with the food. Saliva is a watery liquid made in the salivary glands. It contains the carbohydrase enzyme **amylase**. The amylase begins to break starch in the food into **maltose**. If you chew for a long time on a piece of bread, you can begin to taste the sweet maltose produced from the starch in the bread. Saliva also contains the slippery substance **mucus**. In fact, mucus is made along the whole length of the alimentary canal; its function is to help the food to slide along easily.

While the food is in the mouth, teeth chew the food. Chewing breaks the food down into smaller pieces (but not into smaller *molecules* – this has to be done by enzymes), increasing its surface area and so making it easier for enzymes to get at every bit of it.

The chewed food, mixed with saliva, is then swallowed. It goes into the oesophagus, which passes it swiftly into the stomach.

The stomach

People sometimes use the word 'stomach' to mean the lower part of the body, between the ribs and the hip bones. The proper name for this part of the body is the **abdomen**. The stomach is really a widened out part of the digestive system. It lies just below the ribs, on the left-hand side of the body.

The stomach has a volume of up to 5 litres. It isn't always as big as this – it has muscles and elastic tissue in its walls which allow it to change its size and shape.

At each end of the stomach, there are rings of muscle around the tubes that enter and leave it, shown in Figure 5.8. These are called **sphincter muscles**. When

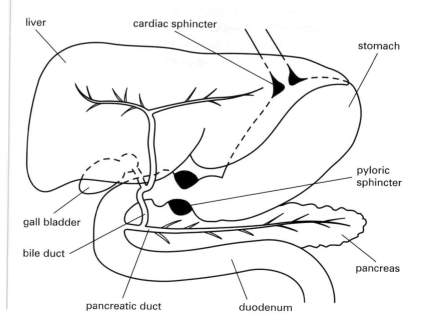

Figure 5.8 ▶
A more detailed view of the stomach, liver and pancreas.

they contract, they close off the tube. When you swallow food, the **cardiac sphincter** muscle relaxes, allowing the food into the stomach, and then contracts. If the **pyloric sphincter** also contracts, then the food is trapped in the stomach. It is often held in the stomach for several hours. While it is there, a fluid is secreted by the cells in the stomach lining. The fluid is called **gastric juice** (which means 'stomach juice'), and contains **hydrochloric acid** and a protease enzyme called **pepsin**.

Hydrochloric acid is a strong acid, and can damage living cells very badly. So can pepsin – cells contain a lot of protein, and pepsin could digest this protein and kill the cells. To protect the cells lining the stomach from these two dangerous substances, there is a thick layer of mucus covering the whole of the inner surface of the stomach wall. Nevertheless, sometimes so much acid is secreted that it begins to eat through this wall. It leaves a raw, sore patch called an **ulcer**.

The purpose of having hydrochloric acid in the stomach is to kill bacteria in the food. All food, however clean, contains bacteria. Some of these might be harmful, and the acid in the stomach helps to destroy them.

Pepsin begins to break down protein molecules into smaller chains called polypeptides. Unlike most enzymes, it works best at a very low pH – it has to, because of the hydrochloric acid.

While the food is in the stomach, the muscles in the stomach walls contract and relax rhythmically, churning the food around and mixing it up with the hydrochloric acid and pepsin. After an hour or so, the food is almost liquid.

Question

5.2 Suggest reasons for each of the following:

 a People who do not make much gastric juice are more likely to suffer from food poisoning than other people.

 b It is known that excitement or anger increases the amount of gastric juices secreted. People with stressful lives are more likely to suffer from stomach ulcers than other people.

The small intestine

The food leaving the stomach enters the **small intestine**. Here, juices from two glands are poured onto it. These glands are the **liver** and the **pancreas**.

Bile is the juice from the liver. The liver makes bile all the time, and it is stored in the **gall bladder** until needed. When food from the stomach enters the small intestine, bile is squirted along the **bile duct** (Figure 5.8) and mixes with the food in the small intestine.

Bile is a watery, greenish liquid. It helps with digestion of fats. Fats are difficult to digest, because they are not soluble in water. This makes it difficult for lipase (the fat-digesting enzyme) to get at them. Bile contains **salts**, which help to form the fat into tiny droplets that can float in liquid. This is called **emulsification**, and it makes it easier for the fat to be digested, and to be absorbed.

Pancreatic juice is the juice from the pancreas. It flows along the **pancreatic duct** into the small intestine. Pancreatic juice contains **sodium hydrogencarbonate**, and also several enzymes.

Sodium hydrogencarbonate helps to neutralise the acidic food that has entered the small intestine from the stomach. This is important because the enzymes that digest food in the small intestine will not work in acidic conditions. It also helps to stop the acid from the stomach damaging the walls of the small intestine.

The enzymes in pancreatic juice include all three kinds of digestive enzymes – **carbohydrase**, **protease** and **lipase**. The carbohydrase is **amylase**, which, just like the amylase in saliva, breaks down starch to maltose. The protease is called **trypsin**, and breaks down proteins to polypeptides. **Lipase** breaks down fats to fatty acids and glycerol.

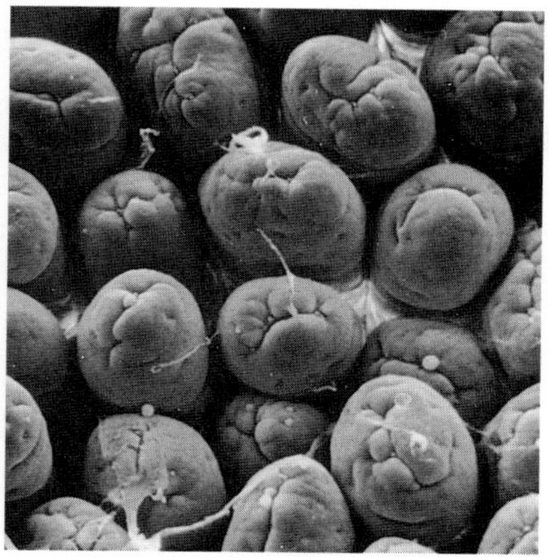

▲ Figure 5.9
The inner surface of the small intestine, magnified about 200 times, showing some of the thousands of villi.

Absorption ▶

Absorption in the small intestine

Figure 5.9 shows part of the wall of the small intestine. It is covered with very small, wriggling, finger-like projections called **villi**. Each villus is about 1 mm long.

The cells on the surface of the villi have two jobs to do. First, they produce enzymes which finish the digestion of the food. Any remaining complex sugars, such as maltose, are broken down to simple sugars, such as glucose. Polypeptides are broken down to amino acids.

Second, the villi **absorb** the digested food. Simple sugars, amino acids, fatty acids and glycerol, vitamins and inorganic ions are all absorbed into the villi so that they can pass into the blood and be transported to the cells that need them.

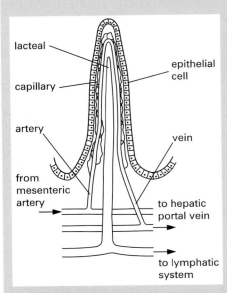

Figure 5.10
A vertical section through a villus.

Figure 5.10 shows a section through a villus. Inside it are **blood capillaries** and a **lacteal**. The sugars, amino acids, vitamins and inorganic ions are absorbed into the blood capillaries. The fatty acids and glycerol are absorbed into the lacteal. (You will find out much more about blood capillaries and lacteals in Chapter 7.)

The structure of the villi is designed to help this absorption happen quickly and efficiently. Features of the villi which help with this are:

- Their tiny size – this means that the food molecules only have a very small distance to travel from the inside of the intestine to the blood capillaries and lacteals.

- The large number of them – there can be as many as 40 villi on just one square millimetre of the intestine wall. This greatly increases the surface area across which absorption can happen.

- Their muscles – villi have muscles inside them, which can make the villi squirm around, so bringing them into contact with much more food inside the intestine than if they kept still.

The large intestine

After the food has been through the small intestine, it passes into the **large intestine**. There may not be very much food left by now, because much of it will have been absorbed into the blood. All that is left is fibre and water.

As the food is moved along the first part of the large intestine, called the **colon**, water and salts pass through its walls and into the blood. What is left – mostly fibre, mixed with mucus and cells that have rubbed off the walls of the alimentary canal as the food passed through it – carries on into the **rectum**. It may stay here for a while, before being passed out through the **anus** as **faeces**. The removal of faeces from the body is called **egestion**.

5.3 Copy and complete this table. The first row has been done for you.

Part of alimentary canal	Juices secreted	What the juices contain	What is digested	Any other points
Mouth	Saliva	Water, mucus, amylase	Starch is digested to maltose by amylase	Teeth grind food into smaller pieces, increasing the surface area for enzymes to act on
Stomach				
Small intestine				
Large intestine: Colon Rectum				

Assimilation

Assimilation means using the molecules that have been absorbed from food, and making them part of the body.

When the small food molecules have been absorbed into the blood, they are taken to the **liver**. They travel along a blood vessel called the **hepatic portal vein**.

One of the liver's functions is to 'sort out' these molecules. Some will be allowed to continue in the blood, and be carried all around the body to cells that need them. Some will be stored in the liver, to be used later. Some will be changed into something else, and then either allowed into the blood, or stored (Figure 5.11).

For example, if a lot of glucose has been absorbed into the blood in the small intestine, the liver will change some of it into **glycogen**, and store it in the liver cells. Some glucose will also be changed into **fat**, which is stored as an energy reserve in various parts of the body.

Amino acids from the absorbed food may be built up into **protein** molecules inside liver cells. Some amino acids will travel round the body in the blood. They will be taken into cells all over the body, which will also use them to make proteins. If you have more amino acids than you need, the liver will break them down to form **urea**. You can find out more about this in Chapter 10.

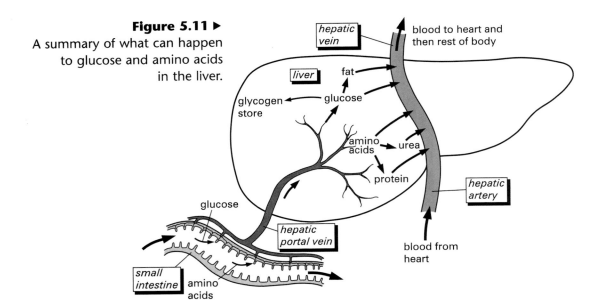

Figure 5.11 ▶

A summary of what can happen to glucose and amino acids in the liver.

Summary

- The alimentary canal is a long tube leading from mouth to anus, in which food is digested and absorbed. Food is pushed through it by peristalsis. Mucus is secreted to allow the food to slide through easily, and to protect the cells in the wall of the canal.

- Digestion involves the breakdown of large pieces of food to small ones by the teeth and stomach muscles, followed by the breakdown of large molecules to small ones by enzymes. This is necessary as only small molecules can be absorbed through the wall of the small intestine into the blood.

- Humans have four types of teeth – incisors, canines, premolars and molars. Tooth decay happens when acids in the mouth, produced by bacteria, dissolve away part of the enamel covering of a tooth. Regular cleaning can help to prevent this from happening.

- Fluoride helps to strengthen enamel and help it resist decay, and is sometimes added to drinking water.

- Starch is first broken down by amylase to maltose. This happens in the mouth and small intestine. The maltose is then broken down to glucose by the enzyme maltase.

- Proteins are broken down to amino acids by proteases. These include pepsin in the stomach and trypsin in the duodenum.

- Fats are broken down to fatty acids and glycerol by lipases. Bile salts help to emulsify fats so that it is easier for lipase to digest them.

- The small intestine is well adapted for absorption. It has many folds, and also thousands of tiny villi, which greatly increase the surface area across which absorption can take place.

- Each villus contains capillaries which carry away amino acids and glucose, and a lacteal which takes away fatty acids and glycerol.

- The remaining material passing into the colon consists of fibre and mucus. It forms faeces, which are passed into the rectum and out of the body through the anus. This is called egestion.

- The products of digestion are taken to the liver in the hepatic portal vein. Eventually, these nutrients are taken into cells, either in the liver or elsewhere. This is called assimilation.

Nutrition in plants

Plants feed by photosynthesis. They use carbon dioxide from the air and water from the soil to make carbohydrates. This process requires an energy input – the energy comes from sunlight, and is absorbed by the green pigment chlorophyll. The carbohydrates can then be made into other substances such as proteins or chlorophyll, by adding nitrate or magnesium ions to them.

Photosynthesis ▶

How plants feed

Plants feed in a very different way from animals. In Chapter 4, you saw that animals need six types of nutrients – carbohydrates, proteins, fats, vitamins, inorganic ions and water. Plants need only two of these – **inorganic ions** and **water**. They make all the other nutrients themselves. They do, however, need one substance that animals do not need. This substance is **carbon dioxide**.

You may remember that carbohydrates, proteins, fats and vitamins are all **organic** substances, while water and inorganic ions are **inorganic**. Carbon dioxide is also inorganic. Plants, therefore, need only inorganic nutrients. They can make all the organic substances themselves.

'Photosynthesis' means 'making with light'. The word describes the way in which plants use light energy to make water and carbon dioxide combine together to form sugar (a carbohydrate) and oxygen (Figure 6.1). The light energy is captured by the green pigment (colour) called **chlorophyll**. The word and molecular equations for photosynthesis are:

carbon dioxide + water $\xrightarrow{\text{sunlight}}$ sugar + oxygen

$6CO_2 + 6H_2O \longrightarrow C_6H_{12}O_6 + 6O_2$

Carbon dioxide and water are the **raw materials**. Sugar and oxygen are the **products**.

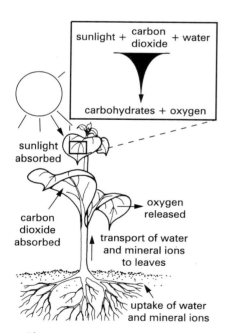

▲ Figure 6.1
Plants use water from the soil, carbon dioxide from the air and energy from sunlight, to make carbohydrates and oxygen. They can use mineral ions from the soil to convert the carbohydrates into other substances, such as proteins.

The structure of a leaf

Most photosynthesis takes place in leaves. Leaves are the sugar factories of a plant. Inside leaves, energy from sunlight is captured by chlorophyll, and used to make carbon dioxide and water combine together to form sugar and oxygen.

Figures 6.2 and 6.3 show the structure of a leaf.

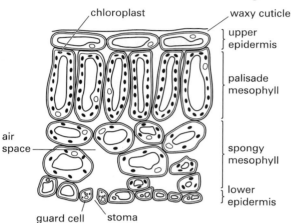

▲ **Figure 6.2**
The structure of a leaf. A leaf is to made up of several **different layers of** cells.

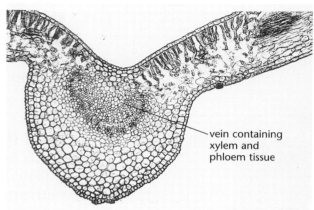

▲ **Figure 6.3**
A section through a privet leaf, magnified about 80 times. Can you pick out all the layers labelled in Figure 6.2?

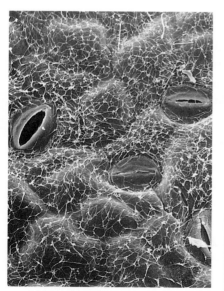

▲ **Figure 6.4**
A surface view of the underside of a rose leaf, showing some stomata. You can clearly see the sausage-shaped guard cells, which control how much each stoma opens.

Although leaves are very thin, they are actually made up of several layers of cells, as you saw in Chapter 2. The top and bottom of the leaf are covered with a layer of fairly thin cells called the epidermis. The **epidermis**, especially on the top of the leaf, is often covered with a layer of **wax**, called the **cuticle**. The centre of the leaf, or **mesophyll** ('middle leaf') contains two layers. The one nearest the top of the leaf is made up of tall, rectangular cells called the **palisade layer**. (A palisade is a kind of fence, and the person who named this layer must have thought that these cells looked rather like planks of wood in a fence!) Beneath the palisade layer is the **spongy layer**, which, like a sponge, has many **air spaces** between the cells.

There are two other important features of the leaf. First, in the lower epidermis, there are gaps here and there called **stomata**. These gaps are surrounded by two **guard cells**, which can change shape to open or close the space between them. Figure 6.4 shows the guard cells around stomata. The second feature is the **veins** or **vascular bundles** in the mesophyll layer. These contain xylem vessels, which bring water to the leaf, and phloem tubes, which take away substances that the leaf cells make. You can find out more about xylem and phloem in Chapter 8.

Photosynthesis in a leaf

Photosynthesis happens inside the mesophyll cells, especially the palisade cells, and also the guard cells, of leaves. If you look carefully at Figure 6.2, you will see that these cells all have **chloroplasts** inside them. Chloroplasts contain **chlorophyll**, which captures light energy. Photosynthesis happens inside chloroplasts.

Figure 6.5 shows a picture of a chloroplast taken with an electron microscope. The stripes are membranes, on which the chlorophyll molecules (which are too small to see) are kept. The large 'blobs' are starch grains. Chloroplasts often turn some of the sugar they make into starch, as this is a good way to store it.

Chloroplasts can move around inside cells. On a dull day, they may all move to the end of the cell nearest the top edge of the leaf, to get as much as sunlight as possible. On a very bright day, they may spread out more.

Chloroplasts need a good supply of raw materials – water and carbon dioxide – and also of sunlight, if they are to carry out photosynthesis efficiently. The next three sections look at how the structure of a leaf makes sure that the chloroplasts get the best 'delivery service' possible.

Carbon dioxide supply

Land plants get their carbon dioxide from the air. There is not very much carbon dioxide in the air – only about 0.04% – and, as you will see later, this often slows down photosynthesis.

As the chloroplasts in the mesophyll cells carry out photosynthesis, they use up carbon dioxide. This makes the concentration of carbon dioxide in and around them even lower than that in the air. There is therefore a **concentration gradient** for carbon dioxide, resulting in net diffusion of carbon dioxide into the leaf. Carbon dioxide molecules diffuse through the stomata, through the air spaces between the spongy cells, through the cell walls, cell membranes and cytoplasm of the spongy and palisade cells, and into the chloroplasts.

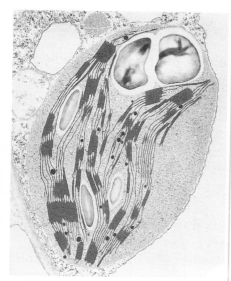

▲ **Figure 6.5**
A chloroplast. Five starch grains can be seen inside it. You can also see the neatly arranged membranes, which are where the chlorophyll is attached.

6.1 Look at Figure 6.2 on page 84. Describe *three* features of the leaf which help to provide an efficient supply of carbon dioxide to the chloroplasts in the mesophyll cells.

Water supply

Plants get their water from the soil. It is taken up by root hairs and moves across the root into the xylem vessels. In these vessels it flows up through the root and stem to the leaves. Inside the leaf, the water moves out of the xylem vessels, and some of it goes into the chloroplasts in the mesophyll cells. You can find out more about this in Chapter 8.

Sunlight supply

Sunlight usually falls on the upper surface of leaves. It passes through the thin layer of epidermis cells, and into the mesophyll cells. As the palisade cells are nearer to the top of the leaf than the spongy cells, the palisade cells get more sunlight, and therefore tend to photosynthesise faster than the spongy cells.

Question

6.2 Look at Figure 6.2 on page 84, and also at some living leaves. Describe as many features as you can which help the chloroplasts in the mesophyll cells to get as much as sunlight as possible.

Investigation *6.1*

Oxygen production by a water plant

From the photosynthesis equation on page 83, you can see that plants produce oxygen when they photosynthesise. This is easiest to see in a water plant, as the oxygen gas forms bubbles which you can see and trap. You will need:

- a healthy water plant
- a glass beaker
- some pond, stream, river or tap water
- a test tube
- a retort stand, boss and clamp to support the test tube
- a wooden splint.

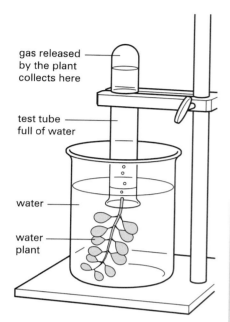

gas released by the plant collects here

test tube full of water

water

water plant

▲ Figure 6.6
Apparatus for Investigation 6.1.

1 Find a place to work where there is sunlight, or where you can shine a light onto your plant.

2 Fill the beaker with water. Follow your teacher's instructions on what to do with the water plant, and then put it into the beaker of water.

3 Set up your retort stand, boss and clamp, and check that they are in the correct position to hold the test tube as shown in Figure 6.6.

4 Take the test tube out, and fill it right to the top with water. Put your thumb over the top, hold it very close to the beaker of water, and then tip it upside down so that its open end is under water, and there is no air in the tube. (This can be tricky – keep trying until you get it right.) Carefully move it into position in the clamp, and clamp it there.

5 Move the plant into position so that any oxygen it releases will rise into the tube. Leave it for half an hour or so.

6 After half an hour, check to see if any gas has collected in the tube. Decide how much longer you will need to leave it to collect about half a tube full of gas. If possible, leave it for at least this length of time before moving on to step **7**.

7 Light a splint, and blow out the flame so that it is glowing. Take the tube out of the clamp, keeping your thumb over the end, and then gently let the water out. Carefully put the glowing splint up into the tube, making sure you do not get it wet, and look to see if it glows any more brightly as you do so. If it does, this shows that the gas you have collected is oxygen.

Questions

1 Explain why a water plant was used, rather than a land plant, in this experiment.

2 Suggest why pond, stream or river water would be better to use in this investigation than tap water.

3 When you tested the gas collected in step **7**:

   a What other gases would you expect to have been in the tube, as well as oxygen?

   b Why was it important not to get the splint wet?

4 Describe, in detail, exactly how you could modify this experiment to test one of the following hypotheses:

   • Photosynthesis happens faster at high light intensities than at low light intensities.

   • Photosynthesis happens faster in red light than in green light.

   • Photosynthesis happens faster when plenty of carbon dioxide is available than when it is in short supply. (You could provide your water plant with carbon dioxide by adding some sodium hydrogencarbonate to the water.)

- Photosynthesis happens faster at high temperatures than at low temperatures.

Investigation 6.2

Do leaves need light and chlorophyll to make starch?

The first substance plants make when they photosynthesise is sugar. They may turn quite a lot of this sugar into starch, which they can store. Before you begin this investigation, answer the following questions.

1 How do you test for starch? What colour would you expect to see if starch is present?

2 Exactly where is the starch which is stored in a leaf? (Look back at Figure 6.5.)

3 Can starch get through cell membranes?

You will need:

First session

- a healthy variegated (green and white) plant, growing in a pot, which has been in a dark place for several days so that is has used up all its starch stores

- some black paper, scissors and paperclips or a stapler.

Second session

- the plant from the first session
- a Bunsen burner, tripod, gauze and heat-proof mat
- a 250 cm^3 beaker
- a boiling tube
- forceps or other implement for handling a soft, wet leaf
- a white tile or other surface
- some iodine solution and a dropper pipette
- some ethanol (do not collect this until you get to step **5**).

1 Choose a healthy green and white leaf on the plant – do not take it off! Cut a piece of black paper big enough to fold around the leaf and cover most of it. Cut a shape from the paper, and then fasten it onto the leaf, as shown in Figure 6.7. Leave the plant in a sunny place for a few days.

2 Remove the leaf from the plant. Remove the paper from the leaf.

3 Boil some water in a beaker. When it is properly boiling, put in your leaf. Leave it for about 3 minutes (or as advised by your teacher).

▲ **Figure 6.7**
Method for Investigation 6.2.

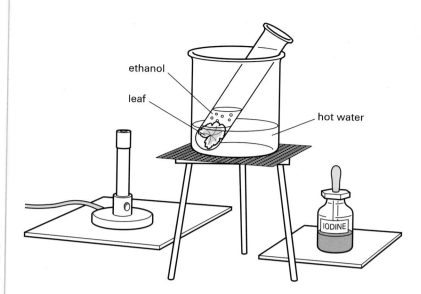

Figure 6.8 ▶
Steps 5 and 6 in Investigation 6.2.
Make sure you turn out the Bunsen
burner before using the ethanol.

4 Take the leaf out of the beaker (be gentle, as it will now be very soft) and put it onto a tile. Turn off the Bunsen burner.

5 Collect some ethanol in a boiling tube, filling the tube half full. Put the leaf into the ethanol, pushing it down gently. Stand the boiling tube in the beaker of hot water, as shown in Figure 6.8.

6 Leave the leaf in the ethanol until most of the green colour has come out. Then gently remove it from the ethanol, taking care because the ethanol will have made it brittle.

7 Dip the leaf into water, to soften it. Then gently spread it out on the tile.

8 Put some iodine solution all over it using a dropper pipette. Leave it for a few minutes, to give the iodine solution time to penetrate the leaf cells. Record your results by means of a labelled drawing.

Questions

1 Did the covered and uncovered parts of the leaf look any different when you took off the black paper?

2 Explain why the leaf was boiled.

3 Suggest why the chlorophyll was removed from the leaf.

4 What do your results tell you about the effects of
   a light and **b** chlorophyll on photosynthesis?

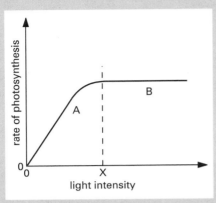

▲ Figure 6.9
The effect of light intensity on the rate of photosynthesis.

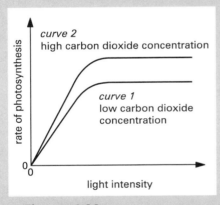

▲ Figure 6.10
The effect of light intensity on the rate of photosynthesis at different carbon dioxide concentrations.

Limiting factors

Figure 6.9 shows the results of an experiment in which the rate of photosynthesis of a plant was measured at different light intensities. You can see that when there is no light there is no photosynthesis. As the light intensity is increased, the rate of photosynthesis also increases. This is what we would expect. Light provides the energy needed for photosynthesis, so more light should mean more photosynthesis.

However, once the light intensity has reached a certain level (point X on the graph), giving the plant even more light has no effect. The extra light cannot be used by the plant. It is photosynthesising as fast as it can.

What is preventing the plant from photosynthesising any faster? There are many possibilities. One reason could be that it is short of carbon dioxide. We could check whether this is so by giving the plant more carbon dioxide, and doing the experiment all over again. If we got the results shown by curve 2 in Figure 6.10, then we know that carbon dioxide was in short supply in the first experiment (curve 1).

Both the amount of light, and the amount of carbon dioxide, affect the rate of photosynthesis. If either of these is in short supply, the rate of photosynthesis is limited.

Look back at Figure 6.9. You can see that, at relatively low light intensities, over the range labelled A, you can make the plant photosynthesise more quickly by giving it more light. This shows that over this range the amount of light was limiting the rate of photosynthesis. We say that light was the **limiting factor**.

Over range B, however, light is *not* the limiting factor. Even if you give the plant more light, it cannot photosynthesise any faster. However, if you give it more *carbon dioxide*, as shown in curve 2 on Figure 6.10, then the plant does photosynthesise faster. So the amount of carbon dioxide was limiting the rate of photosynthesis. Carbon dioxide was the limiting factor.

Supplement

▲ **Figure 6.11**
(a) Chinese cabbage being cultivated in Thailand.

(b) Barley growing in Switzerland. What do you think might be the limiting factors for growth of crops in these two environments?

Questions

6.3 Suggest *one* factor, other than light intensity or carbon dioxide availability, that could limit the rate of photosynthesis. How could you check that you are right?

6.4 Figure 6.12 shows the rate of photosynthesis of a tomato plant at different carbon dioxide concentrations.

Figure 6.12 ▶
Rate of photosynthesis of a tomato plant at varying carbon dioxide concentrations.

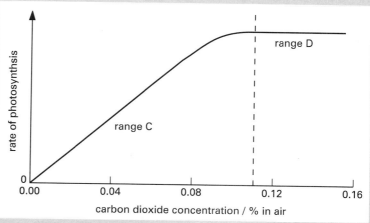

a What is the limiting factor over range C? Explain how you arrived at your answer.

b Suggest what could be the limiting factor over range D. How could you confirm your answer experimentally?

In temperate countries, crops such as tomatoes are often grown in glasshouses. Growers do this because:

- they can control the temperature at which their plants grow

- they can provide artificial lighting
- they can provide extra carbon dioxide in the air in the glasshouse.

By doing this, the growers can increase the rate of photosynthesis of their plants, and so increase crop production.

  c Suggest why it is useful to be able to control the temperature at which plants are growing.

  d A grower has asked you to advise her on whether she should provide artificial lighting, extra carbon dioxide, or both to her tomatoes in a glasshouse. What experiments would you carry out in order to answer her question? What other information would you need?

Changing sugars into other nutrients ▶

Inorganic ions needed by plants

So far in this chapter, we have looked at the way plants make sugars and starch. These are both carbohydrates. They contain carbon, hydrogen and oxygen.

Plants can use the carbohydrates they make by photosynthesis to make **proteins**. Proteins, like carbohydrates, contain carbon, hydrogen and oxygen – but they also contain a lot of **nitrogen** and a little **sulphur**. So, to make proteins, plants need to add nitrogen and sulphur to them. Sulphur is usually in plentiful supply, and plants only need a little of it. But they need nitrogen in much larger quantities.

Although there is a lot of nitrogen gas in the air, plants cannot use it. (You can find out more about this in Chapter 14.) Plants get their nitrogen from **inorganic ions** in the soil. The most important ones are **nitrate ions**, NO_3^-. Plants take up the nitrate ions through their root hairs.

If a plant is short of nitrate ions, then it cannot make proteins. Growers may add **fertilisers** containing nitrate ions to the soil in which their plants are growing. This does increase the growth of the plants, but it can also cause environmental problems; you can find out more about this in Chapter 14.

Another inorganic ion taken up by plants from the soil is **magnesium**. This is needed to make the green pigment **chlorophyll**.

Figure 6.13 ▶
The wheat on the left of this experimental plot has been grown using nitrate fertiliser, while that in the strip on the right has had no fertiliser added. What differences can you see between the plants in the two parts of the plot?

Supplement

Proteins are needed to make cell membranes and cytoplasm, so if the plant does not have enough nitrate ions it cannot make new cells and does not grow properly. Because enzymes are proteins, a plant that is short of nitrogen cannot make enzymes, so its metabolic reactions cannot take place efficiently.

If a plant is short of magnesium ions, it becomes a yellowish colour, instead of green. It cannot photosynthesise effectively, and so does not grow properly.

Summary

- Green plants make carbohydrates from water and carbon dioxide, using energy from sunlight. This process is called photosynthesis, and happens inside chloroplasts in the mesophyll cells of leaves.

- The word equation for photosynthesis is:
  carbon dioxide + water → glucose + oxygen

- The large surface area of a leaf helps it to absorb sunlight and carbon dioxide. Carbon dioxide enters the leaf by diffusion, through stomata which are mostly on the lower surface. It diffuses through air spaces in the spongy mesophyll layer, then through the cell walls and membranes and into the chloroplasts.

- Water is brought to the photosynthesising cells in xylem vessels. The glucose that is made is often changed into sucrose, and carried away from the leaf in phloem vessels. Some of the glucose may be changed into starch and stored inside the chloroplasts in the leaf.

- When testing a leaf for starch, it must first be boiled to break down the cells, and then placed in hot alcohol to dissolve out the chlorophyll.

After washing in water, iodine solution is added; if it turns blue-black then starch is present.

- Any factor that is limiting the rate of photosynthesis is called a limiting factor. This could be light, or it could be carbon dioxide. If the value of a limiting factor is increased, then photosynthesis can take place more rapidly. If crops are grown in glasshouses, then the growers can provide extra light or extra carbon dioxide, to speed up photosynthesis and get a better yield. The temperature can also be kept at the optimum level.

- Plants need inorganic ions, which they absorb from the soil through root hairs, often by active transport. Magnesium is needed for the manufacture of chlorophyll; if it is in short supply, leaves become yellow. Nitrate is needed for the manufacture of proteins; if it is in short supply, it grows slowly and looks stunted. Growers often add fertilisers to the soil to provide crop plants with extra inorganic ions.

Transport in animals

Large animals need transport systems to carry oxygen and nutrients to all the cells in their bodies, and to take away waste products such as carbon dioxide. Mammals, such as humans, have a circulatory system that does this. Blood is pumped through a network of blood vessels by the heart.

The human circulatory system ▶

The double circulatory system

Figure 7.1 shows the basic design of the human circulatory system. The **heart** pumps blood into two large **arteries**. One artery, the **pulmonary artery**, takes blood to the lungs, while the other, the **aorta**, takes it to all the other parts of the body. The blood from the lungs goes back to the heart in the **pulmonary vein**. The blood from the rest of the body goes back to the heart in the **vena cava**. The blood leaves one side of the heart and returns to the opposite side, and is pumped out again.

Figure 7.1 ▶
Plan of the human circulatory system. It is drawn as though the person is facing you, so the left side of the body is on the right side of the diagram. RA = right atrium, LA = left atrium, LV = left ventricle and RV = right ventricle.

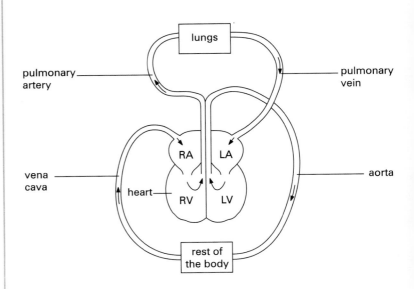

If you follow the pathway round, you will see that the blood has to go through the heart *twice* on one complete journey around the system. For this reason, the system is called the **double circulatory system**.

When the blood is in the lungs, it picks up oxygen. When it is in other parts of the body, it gives up oxygen to the cells that need it. Blood with a lot of oxygen in it is called **oxygenated blood**. Blood that has given up its oxygen is called **deoxygenated blood**.

Question

7.1 Make a copy of Figure 7.1. Shade all the oxygenated blood red, and the deoxygenated blood blue. (Where the blood loses its oxygen, you could show it gradually changing from red to blue. Where it picks up oxygen, you could show it gradually changing from blue to red.)

The heart

Figure 7.2 shows a human heart. The heart of an adult man weighs about 300 g. It can hold about 250 cm^3 of blood.

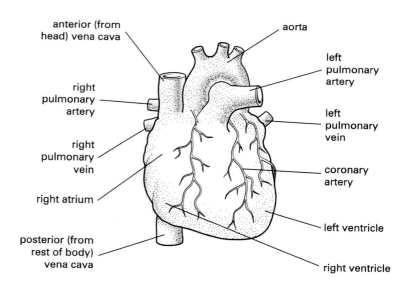

anterior (from head) vena cava

aorta

left pulmonary artery

right pulmonary artery

left pulmonary vein

right pulmonary vein

coronary artery

right atrium

left ventricle

posterior (from rest of body) vena cava

right ventricle

Figure 7.2 ▶
The external appearance of a human heart.

The heart is made of **cardiac muscle**. This muscle contracts and relaxes, without stopping, from about 4 weeks after conception (fertilisation) until death. If you lived to the age of 70 years, and your heart were to beat, on average, 60 times a minute, then it would have performed 2 207 520 000 beats!

To keep up this activity, the cardiac muscle needs a constant supply of **glucose** and **oxygen**. These are used to release energy by respiration, a process described in Chapter 9.

The glucose and oxygen are supplied to the heart muscle by the blood. The muscle lining the chambers inside the heart has plenty of blood next to it all the time. However, in places the heart muscle is up to a centimetre thick, so the muscle near the outside of the heart needs its own blood supply. This is provided through the **coronary arteries**, which you can see in Figure 7.2.

Figure 7.3 shows a heart cut in half vertically (from top to bottom). The right and left sides of the heart are separated by a **septum**. The blood cannot get through this. To get from one side of the heart to the other, the blood goes out of the heart, round half of the circulatory system, and then back in again.

Figure 7.3 ▶
A vertical section through a human heart.

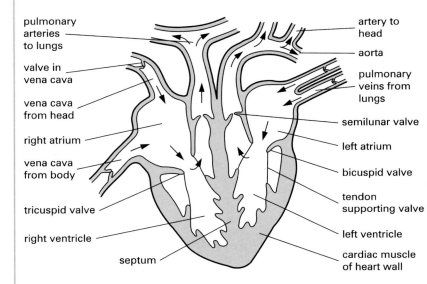

Each side of the heart has two chambers. The ones at the top are called **atria**. The ones at the bottom are called **ventricles**.

Question

7.2 Compare Figure 7.3 with Figure 7.1.

    a Which two chambers of the heart contain oxygenated blood, and which contain deoxygenated blood?

    b Into which chambers does blood flow when it first enters the heart?

    c From which chambers does blood flow when it leaves the heart?

Heartbeat

We will follow what happens to the blood, and what the heart does, as blood passes through the heart. Figure 7.4 shows the sequence of events.

First, the whole heart relaxes. This stage is called **diastole**. During diastole, blood trickles into the left and right atria, from the pulmonary vein and the vena cava.

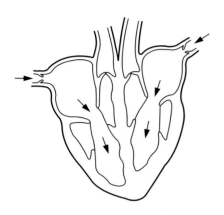

1 All the muscles relax. Blood flows into the atria and ventricles from the veins, through the open atrioventricular valves (the tricuspid and bicuspid valves).

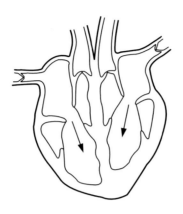

2 The muscles of the atria contract. Blood from the atria is pushed into the ventricles. The valves in the veins close.

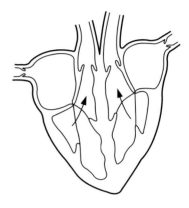

3 The muscles of the ventricles contract. This forces the atrioventricular valves shut. The arterial valves (the semilunar valves) open as the blood is forced into the arteries.

▲ **Figure 7.4**
How the heart beats.

After about 0.1 seconds, the muscles in the walls of the atria contract. When muscles contract, they get shorter, so this makes the walls squeeze in on the blood. This stage is called **atrial systole**. The blood is pushed down into the ventricles. It cannot go back the way it came, into the veins, because there are valves in the veins which stop it flowing backwards. However, the valves between the atria and the ventricles are made so that they open when the blood is pushed downwards. Figure 7.5 shows how they do this.

After another 0.1 seconds, the muscles in the walls of the ventricles contract. This is called **ventricular systole**. They squeeze inwards on the blood, and force it up into the pulmonary artery and the aorta. The valves between the atria and the ventricles slam shut when the blood pushes up against them, so the blood cannot go back into the atria. The valves in the aorta and pulmonary artery, however, are designed to open when the blood is pushed up against them. The blood shoots up into these two big arteries, and begins its journey around the body.

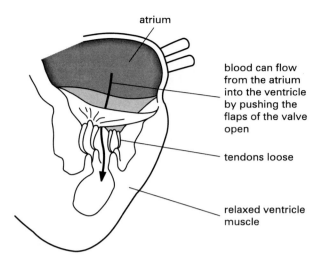

atrium

blood can flow from the atrium into the ventricle by pushing the flaps of the valve open

tendons loose

relaxed ventricle muscle

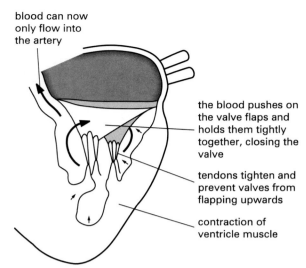

blood can now only flow into the artery

the blood pushes on the valve flaps and holds them tightly together, closing the valve

tendons tighten and prevent valves from flapping upwards

contraction of ventricle muscle

▲ **Figure 7.5** How the heart valves work.
(a) With the ventricle muscle relaxed, blood can pass down the atrium to the ventricle.

(b) With the ventricle muscle contracted, blood cannot pass from the ventricle to the atrium, and so leaves the heart via the artery.

Question

7.3 Figure 7.6 shows how the pressure in the ventricles and atria of a human heart changes during a single heartbeat.
a How long does one heartbeat last?
b How many heartbeats will there be in one minute?
c Explain the shape of the curve for
  i pressure in ventricles
  ii pressure in atria.

Figure 7.6 ▶
Pressure changes in ventricles and atria during one heartbeat. The contraction of the atria and ventricles increases the pressure inside them. From about 0.2 s to 0.4 s, the pressure inside the atria increases, even though they are relaxed. This is because blood is flowing into them from the vena cava and pulmonary vein.

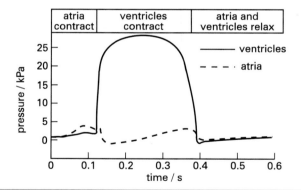

Investigation 7.1

Listening to a heart beating

You do not need any apparatus for this investigation. However, you could use a stethoscope if there is one available.

1 Listen to a friend's heartbeat, either by putting your ear on their body near to the heart, or by using a stethoscope.

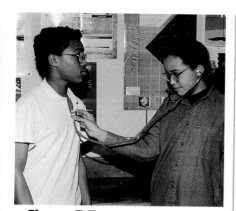

▲ Figure 7.7
Using a stethoscope to listen to a heartbeat. Move the stethoscope around until you can hear the heartbeat clearly, and then hold it very still.

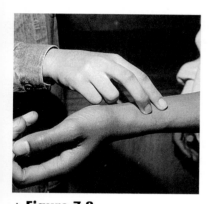

▲ Figure 7.8
Taking a pulse. You may find it easier if the subject rests their arm on the bench.

2 Describe what you can hear. The rhythmic sounds are made by the valves. These sounds are often called 'lub' and 'dup'. Which do you think is the atrio-ventricular valves slamming shut, and which is the arterial valves slamming shut? How can you work it out?

3 Get your partner to take a deep breath while you listen to his or her heart. Does this make any difference to the pattern of sounds you can hear?

4 Write up your experiment in the usual way.

Investigation 7.2

The effect of exercise on heart beat

You do not need any apparatus for this investigation. You can do this investigation on your own, or with a partner.

Before you begin this investigation, read through it carefully and then draw a results chart in which you can write down your results.

You are going to record your pulse rate in beats per minute. To save time, however, you will not count your pulse for a whole minute each time. Instead, you will count it for half a minute, and then multiply by two. You can use the second half of the minute to do this multiplication, and to write your result into your chart.

1 Find your pulse. Figure 7.8 shows you how to do this. Sit quietly for a few minutes until you feel really relaxed.

2 Start a stopclock, or watch a clock with a second hand. Count your pulse for 30 seconds. Record this in your chart. Repeat two more times, so that you have three results in your chart.

3 Stand up. Repeat step **2**, so that you have three more results in your chart.

4 Do some exercise, as advised by your teacher. As soon as you have finished, sit down and record your pulse rate as in step **2**. Keep recording your pulse rate until it has returned to normal. This might take quite a long time, so you might have lots of results to write in your chart.

5 Draw a line graph of your results. If you are not sure how to do this, ask your teacher to help you.

6 Write up your experiment in the usual way.

7.4 a The thicker the muscle, the greater the force it can produce when it contracts. Suggest why:

  i the walls of the ventricles are much thicker than the walls of the atria.

  ii the wall of the left ventricle is much thicker than the wall of the right ventricle.

b Sometimes the valves between the atria and the ventricles get damaged, so that when they are pushed upwards they do not completely close together. How might this affect blood flow? How might this affect a person?

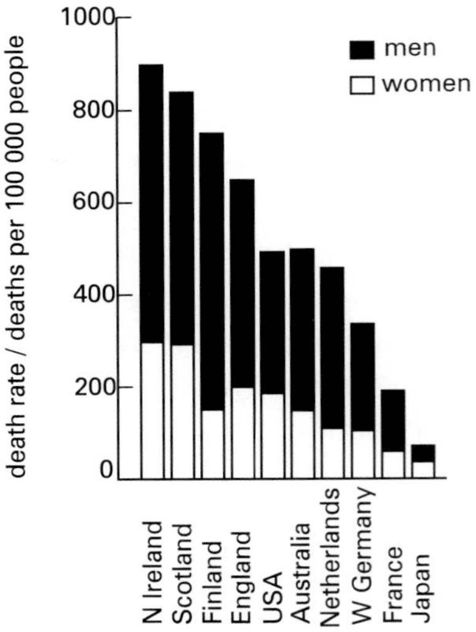

Heart attacks

In many parts of the world, heart attacks are one of the major causes of death. Figure 7.9 shows the importance of heart attacks in several different countries.

A **heart attack** happens when one of the coronary arteries gets blocked. This is often because of a build-up of deposits on the inner wall of the artery. The deposits make the space through which the blood flows very narrow. Eventually, the blood may not be able to get through at all. This stops glucose and oxygen getting to the heart muscle, so it stops beating.

A person's diet can affect their chances of having a heart attack. Diets containing a large amount of animal fat, or a large amount of salt, may increase the likelihood of heart attacks. Smoking also increases these chances, as does stress.

People can reduce their chances of having a heart attack by:

- not smoking

- taking regular exercise

- trying to reduce stress in their lives

- eating a diet that does not contain too much animal fat or salt.

▲ Figure 7.9
Death rates from heart attacks in different countries. The differences are partly caused by differences in diet and lifestyle.

Blood vessels ▶

Arteries

The blood vessels that carry blood away from the heart are called **arteries**. Figure 7.10 (a) shows a section across an artery.

When blood is forced out of the heart, it is at a very high pressure. The arteries therefore need thick, strong walls, to be able to withstand this pressure. The walls are also able to stretch. This allows them to 'give' as the blood is forced through.

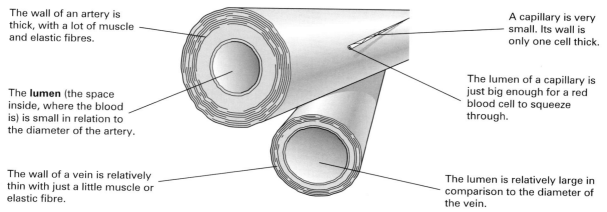

The wall of an artery is thick, with a lot of muscle and elastic fibres.

The **lumen** (the space inside, where the blood is) is small in relation to the diameter of the artery.

The wall of a vein is relatively thin with just a little muscle or elastic fibre.

A capillary is very small. Its wall is only one cell thick.

The lumen of a capillary is just big enough for a red blood cell to squeeze through.

The lumen is relatively large in comparison to the diameter of the vein.

▲ **Figure 7.10(a)**
An artery, vein and capillary.

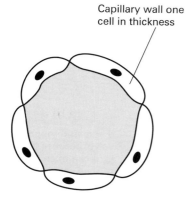

Capillary wall one cell in thickness

▲ **Figure 7.10(b)**
Section across a capillary, drawn to a larger scale than the scale used for Figure 7.10(a).

Each time the ventricles contract, blood is forced into the arteries, pushing outwards on their walls. As the ventricles relax, the blood pressure in the arteries is reduced, and the walls of the arteries spring inwards again. This is what you feel when you take your **pulse**. The rate of your pulse is the rate of your heartbeat.

Question

7.5 Look back at Figure 7.1 on page 94. How does the pulmonary artery differ from all the other arteries in the body?

Capillaries

The arteries deliver blood to all the tissues in the body. When they arrive at the tissue, the arteries divide to form very narrow vessels called **capillaries**.

The function of capillaries is to take the blood as close as possible to the cells in the tissues, so that substances can be exchanged between the blood and the cells.

Some capillaries are so narrow that red blood cells can only just squeeze through them. Red blood cells carry oxygen. The narrow capillaries make sure that the oxygen the red blood cells are carrying is taken as close as possible to the cells in the tissue. The oxygen can quickly diffuse from the red blood cells into the cells that need it. This is helped by the fact that the walls of capillaries are only one cell thick.

Other substances that diffuse from the blood into the cells include glucose, amino acids, inorganic ions, vitamins and water. Carbon dioxide diffuses from the cells into the blood.

You can find out more about how materials are exchanged between the blood in capillaries and the cells in tissues on page 106.

Veins

Capillaries gradually join up to form larger vessels called **veins**. Veins carry blood back to the heart.

When blood leaves the heart and goes into the arteries, it is at a high pressure, because it has been forced out of the heart by the contracting ventricles. As it enters the tiny capillaries, it loses a lot of this pressure. By the time it flows into the veins, it is at a low pressure.

This means that blood tends to flow quite slowly through the veins. Blood in your feet, for example, has very little pressure to push it back up through your legs and body towards your heart.

To help the blood along, the veins from your feet run between the muscles in your legs. When you contract these muscles to move your legs, they squeeze in on the veins. Figure 7.11 shows how they do this.

Figure 7.11 ▶
Longitudinal section through a vein, to show the valves.

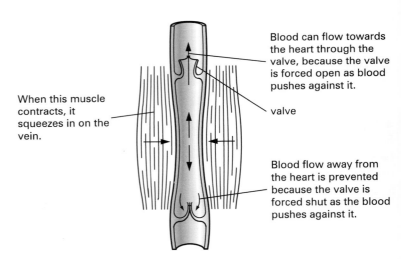

When this muscle contracts, it squeezes in on the vein.

Blood can flow towards the heart through the valve, because the valve is forced open as blood pushes against it.

valve

Blood flow away from the heart is prevented because the valve is forced shut as the blood pushes against it.

The veins have **valves** in them, which only let blood move *towards* the heart, not away from it. When your leg muscles squeeze the blood in the veins, it is squeezed upwards through the valves. When the leg muscles relax, the blood cannot drop down again.

7.6 Copy and complete the table below, summarising the differences between arteries, veins and capillaries. In each case, apart from the first line, say why these features are present.

Feature	Arteries	Veins	Capillaries
What is their function?			
How thick are their walls?			
Do the walls contain elastic fibres?			
How wide are the vessels?			
Do they contain valves?			

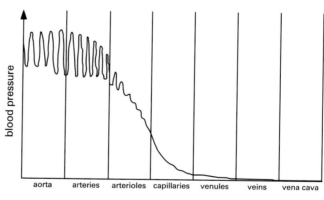

part of the circulatory system

▲ **Figure 7.12**

Blood pressure in different parts of the circulatory system.

7.7 Figure 7.12 shows the pressure of the blood in different kinds of blood vessels as it goes around the body.

    a Explain why the blood pressure in arteries is greater than the blood pressure in veins.

    b Explain why the blood pressure in arteries increases and decreases, while the blood pressure in veins is steady and does not fluctuate.

Blood ▶

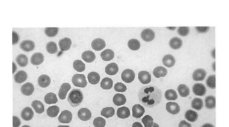

▲ Figure 7.13
Human blood, as it appears through a microscope. Most of the cells are red cells, but you can also see two white cells. One is a lymphocyte and one a phagocyte – which is which?

The components of blood

Blood is made up of several different kinds of cells floating in a liquid. The liquid is called **plasma**.

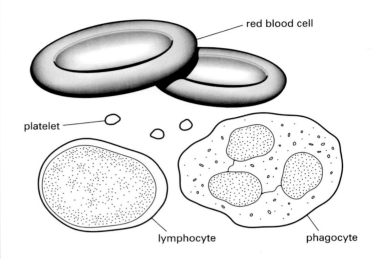

▲ Figure 7.14
Blood cells.

Figure 7.13 is a photograph of some human blood and Figure 7.14 shows the different types of blood cells. Most of the cells in the photograph are **red blood cells**. These are some of the smallest cells in the human body. They are round, with a dent in each side as though someone had pinched them between a finger and thumb. This shape is described as a **biconcave disc**.

The function of red cells is to transport oxygen around the body. To enable them to do this, they are full of the red pigment **haemoglobin**. As the blood passes through the lungs, oxygen diffuses into the red blood cells and combines with the haemoglobin to form **oxyhaemoglobin**. As the blood passes through capillaries in the tissues, the oxyhaemoglobin gives up its oxygen to become haemoglobin again. The oxygen diffuses out of the red blood cells and into the tissue cells.

Haemoglobin is blueish-purple. Oxyhaemoglobin is red. The blood therefore changes colour as it flows around the body.

7.8 **a** What colour will the blood be in most veins?

    b What colour will the blood be in most arteries?

    c Name *one* artery and *one* vein in which the blood will be a different colour from your answers to **a** and **b**.

The other cells in the photograph are **white blood cells**. They are part of the body's defence system against invaders. Some of them, called **phagocytes**, crawl actively around and eat any harmful bacteria that may have got into the body. Phagocytes can squeeze out of capillaries (which have tiny gaps in their walls) and get into almost every part of the body. Other white blood cells are **lymphocytes**. They make chemicals called **antibodies**, which attack and destroy bacteria and viruses.

There are also tiny fragments of cells in the blood, called **platelets**. They help blood to clot. You can find out more about this on page 108.

The blood plasma is a pale yellow liquid. It is mostly water, but it has many different substances dissolved in it. These include glucose, amino acids, inorganic ions such as sodium and chloride, hormones, carbon dioxide and urea. The blood plasma carries these substances from place to place in the body.

Question

7.9 **a** Suggest how the shape of red blood cells helps them with their job of transporting oxygen.

    b Suggest why it is useful for red blood cells to be much smaller than most other human cells.

    c Iron is needed to make haemoglobin. People who do not have very much iron in their diet may suffer from anaemia, when they may be a paler colour, and feel very tired. Explain why this is so.

Tissue fluid

Figure 7.15 shows some blood capillaries. They are inside a tissue. (As you saw in Chapter 2, a tissue is a group of similar cells.)

Blood capillaries have tiny holes between the cells in their walls. The blood plasma leaks out through these holes and fills up the spaces between the cells in the tissue. It is then called **tissue fluid**.

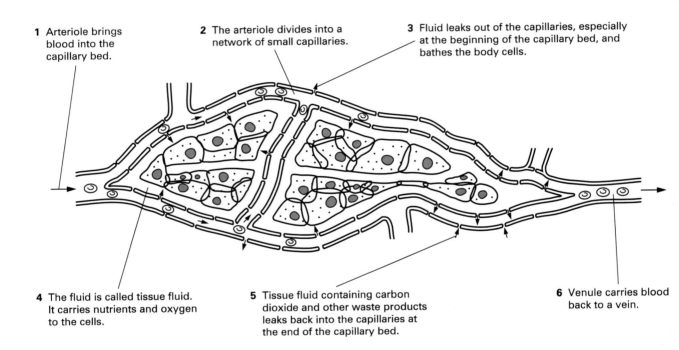

1 Arteriole brings blood into the capillary bed.

2 The arteriole divides into a network of small capillaries.

3 Fluid leaks out of the capillaries, especially at the beginning of the capillary bed, and bathes the body cells.

4 The fluid is called tissue fluid. It carries nutrients and oxygen to the cells.

5 Tissue fluid containing carbon dioxide and other waste products leaks back into the capillaries at the end of the capillary bed.

6 Venule carries blood back to a vein.

▲ **Figure 7.15**
How tissue fluid forms.

Some of the white blood cells can also squeeze through the holes, so they get into the tissue fluid. Red blood cells, however, although they are small, cannot change their shape. They cannot get through the holes, so they stay in the blood. Tissue fluid does not contain red blood cells.

As substances diffuse between the blood and the cells in the tissue, they pass through the tissue fluid.

The lymphatic system

Some of the fluid that leaks out of blood capillaries returns to the blood in the capillary bed. Some does not, and it must eventually be returned to the blood. This is done by **lymph vessels**.

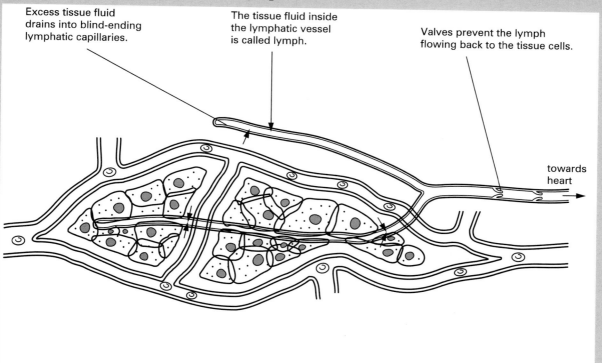

Excess tissue fluid drains into blind-ending lymphatic capillaries.

The tissue fluid inside the lymphatic vessel is called lymph.

Valves prevent the lymph flowing back to the tissue cells.

towards heart

▲ **Figure 7.16**
How lymphatic vessels collect tissue fluid. The gaps in the capillary walls are not shown in this diagram.

Figure 7.16 shows how the tissue fluid is collected and returned to the blood. In the tissue, there are tiny blind-ending vessels called **lymphatic capillaries**. Tissue fluid moves into these. Once it is inside the lymphatic capillaries, the fluid is called **lymph**. The lymphatic capillaries gradually join up to form larger lymph vessels. These take the lymph to the large veins that run just below the collarbone, called the **subclavian veins**. The lymph flows into the blood in these veins.

There is no pump to push lymph around the lymph vessels. The lymph is made to move through them in the same way as blood is made to move through veins. The lymph vessels pass through muscles, which squeeze in on the lymph vessels when they contract. Valves in the lymph vessels make sure that the lymph can only be pushed one way.

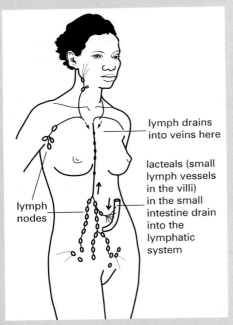

▲ Figure 7.17
Some of the main lymphatic vessels in the human body. The lymph is eventually emptied back into the veins.

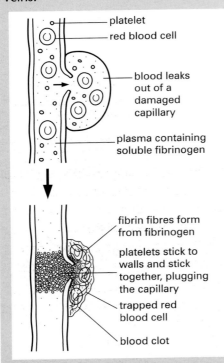

platelet
red blood cell
blood leaks out of a damaged capillary
plasma containing soluble fibrinogen

fibrin fibres form from fibrinogen
platelets stick to walls and stick together, plugging the capillary
trapped red blood cell
blood clot

◄ Figure 7.18
Formation of a blood clot.

Figure 7.17 shows some of the main lymph vessels in the body. You can see that, in places, the lymph vessels pass through **lymph nodes**. Inside lymph nodes, the white blood cells called **lymphocytes** collect. The lymphocytes make antibodies to destroy bacteria and viruses. If you have an infection, some of the lymphocytes may multiply, so that more antibodies can be made.

In Chapter 5, you saw how fatty acids and glycerol pass into the lacteals in the villi of the small intestine. There is lymph inside the lacteals, and the lymph carries the fatty acids and glycerol around the body.

Question

7.10 a In what ways is lymph similar to blood?
  b In what ways is lymph different from blood?

Blood clotting

When you cut yourself, your blood clots. It does this to stop too much blood flowing out of the cut. It also stops bacteria getting into the wound.

What makes blood clot? When a blood vessel is cut or damaged, its walls – which are normally smooth – become rough. Platelets bump into these rough walls. The damaged cells in the walls, and the platelets, react to this by producing a protein.

Blood plasma always contains a soluble protein called **fibrinogen**. The protein produced by the platelets makes the fibrinogen turn into **fibrin**. Fibrin is *not* soluble. It forms long fibres which precipitate out of the blood plasma. The fibres get tangled with each other, and with the red and white blood cells in the blood. This forms a **clot** (Figure 7.18). The clot eventually dries to form a scab.

The immune system

The **immune system** defends us against organisms that can cause disease. Organisms that can cause disease are called **pathogens**. They include bacteria and viruses.

When a bacterium enters the body, the white blood cells will attempt to destroy it. The first ones to go into action are often the **phagocytes**. If you cut yourself, for example, phagocytes will collect at the wound. They will take in and digest any bacteria they find there. Figure 7.19 shows the process by which they do this. It is called **phagocytosis**.

▼ **Figure 7.19**
How a phagocyte destroys bacteria.

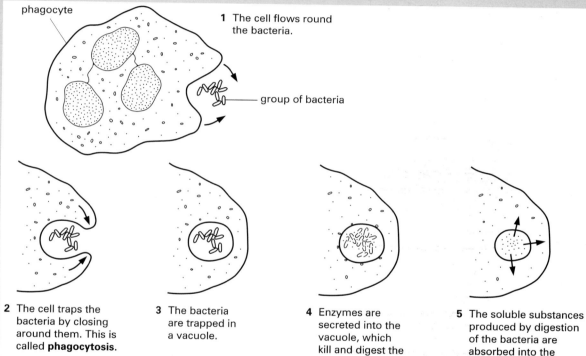

phagocyte

1 The cell flows round the bacteria.

group of bacteria

2 The cell traps the bacteria by closing around them. This is called **phagocytosis**.

3 The bacteria are trapped in a vacuole.

4 Enzymes are secreted into the vacuole, which kill and digest the bacteria.

5 The soluble substances produced by digestion of the bacteria are absorbed into the phagocyte's cytoplasm.

Lymphocytes attack pathogens in a different way. They produce chemicals called **antibodies** which help to kill pathogens. You have thousands of different kinds of lymphocytes in your body. Each kind of lymphocyte makes just one kind of antibody – so you can make thousands of different antibodies.

All cells have molecules on the outside called **antigens**. Cells of different organisms have different antigens. Your own lymphocytes know and recognise the antigens on your cells. But if cells, for example bacteria, with *different* antigens get into your body, your lymphocytes

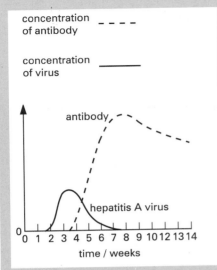

concentration
of antibody ----

concentration
of virus _____

antibody

hepatitis A virus

0 1 2 3 4 5 6 7 8 9 10 12 13 14
time / weeks

▲ Figure 7.20
The immune response. Invasion of
the body by foreign organisms,
such as bacteria or viruses, alerts
lymphocytes to produce
antibodies. It takes time for these
to be produced in sufficient
amounts to destroy the invaders.
The level of antibody in the blood
stays high for some time after the
infection has been dealt with.

react to them by producing an appropriate antibody,
which will destroy the invading cells.

If this is the first time this particular sort of bacterium
has entered your body, you will only have a few of the
lymphocytes that produce the right antibody to attack
it. These particular lymphocytes respond to the bacterium
not only by making the antibody, but also by dividing
to make thousands more lymphocytes like themselves.
After a few days, all these lymphocytes will be producing
the antibody, and will destroy the bacteria.

If this kind of bacterium enters your body again, you
will already have lots of this sort of lymphocyte. They
will be able to make a lot of antibody very quickly,
killing the bacteria before they have time to make you
ill. You are said to be **immune** to this illness.

Something similar happens if someone is given a
transplant. The lymphocytes in the recipient's body
react to the antigens on the 'foreign' cells by producing
antibodies. The antibodies destroy the cells in the
transplanted organ. This is called **rejection**. To prevent
rejection, doctors try to take the organ to be transplanted
from someone who has very similar antigens to those
on the recipient's cells. This often means a close relative,
such as a parent, brother or sister. Another way of
preventing rejection is to give the recipient **immuno-
suppressant drugs**. These drugs stop the recipient's
lymphocytes making antigens.

Questions

7.11 **a** Explain the difference between an antigen and an
antibody.

b Explain why, if you have had a disease once, you
probably will not get it again.

c Influenza ('flu') is a disease caused by a virus. The
viruses that cause influenza keep changing, so that the
viruses that are around one year have different
antigens from those that are around in another year.
Explain why people can get influenza more than once.

d Tuberculosis is a disease caused by a bacterium. The bacterium which causes tuberculosis is very common, and it is estimated that one third of the world's population is infected with this bacterium. However, most of these people do not suffer from tuberculosis. Suggest why this is so.

e In the disease AIDS, some of the lymphocytes are damaged so that they cannot make antibodies. As AIDS spreads in many countries, tuberculosis is become increasingly common. Suggest why this is so.

f To stop someone getting tuberculosis, they can be injected with some bacteria which have been weakened, so that they cannot cause the disease. This is called **vaccination**. Explain how vaccination could make someone immune to tuberculosis.

Summary

- Humans have a double circulatory system, in which blood travels from the heart to the lungs and back to the heart, and then to the rest of the body and back to the heart again.

- The heart has four chambers. Blood enters the atria, and leaves from the ventricles. The right side of the heart contains deoxygenated blood, while the left side contains oxygenated blood.

- Valves between the atria and ventricles, and in the entrances to the pulmonary artery and aorta, prevent backflow of blood.

- Coronary arteries supply the heart muscle with oxygen. If they become blocked, a heart attack may result. The risk of this can be reduced by taking regular exercise, not becoming overweight, not smoking and trying to reduce stress.

- Arteries have thick elastic walls and carry blood away from the heart. Veins have thinner walls, contain valves, and carry blood towards the heart. Capillaries are very small and take blood close to every cell in the body.

- Blood consists of a liquid called plasma, and red and white blood cells. Red cells transport oxygen. White cells help to fight against disease. If a blood vessel is broken, the blood clots to seal the wound.

- Tissue fluid forms because plasma leaks out of capillaries.

- Tissue fluid drains into lymphatic vessels, which carry it back into the circulatory system. White blood cells called lymphocytes are produced inside lymph nodes.

- White blood cells are part of the immune system. Some white cells destroy bacteria and viruses by phagocytosis. Lymphocytes produce antibodies. The immune system attempts to destroy foreign cells, such as transplanted organs.

8 Chapter

Transport in plants

Plants, like animals, have a system of vessels to carry fluids from one part to another. However, the fluids in plants are not at all like blood – they do not contain cells, nor do they transport oxygen. Plants do not have a pump like the heart. Plants have two separate transport systems – xylem vessels carry water and inorganic ions from the roots to the leaves, while phloem sieve tubes carry substances made by photosynthesis from the leaves to the roots and to other parts of the plant.

The transport of water ▶

Plant cells need water for many reasons. These include:

- Water helps to keep cells turgid, so that soft parts of the plant, such as leaves and flower petals, are held in shape (see page 30).

- Water is a solvent; substances need to be dissolved in water inside cells so that metabolic reactions can take place (see page 55).

- Water is needed for photosynthesis (see page 83).

Plants get their water from the soil. The water is taken up by **root hairs**. It then travels across the root to the centre, and up the plant through long tubes called **xylem vessels** which take it all the way to the leaves. In the leaves, some of the water evaporates, turning into water vapour. The water vapour diffuses out of the plant's leaves, through the stomata, into the air, in a process called **transpiration**. The movement of the water along this pathway, from soil to air, is sometimes called the **transpiration stream** (see Figure 8.1 opposite).

The uptake of water into root hairs

Figure 8.2 is a photograph of the tip of a root. The threads growing out from it are **root hairs**. Each root hair is part of a single cell. Figure 8.3 shows a section of a root and the root hairs.

Root hairs are very delicate and easily damaged. As the root grows through the soil, it keeps producing new root hairs, just behind its tip, to replace the old ones

Figure 8.1 ▶
The transpiration stream. Start at the bottom and work up!

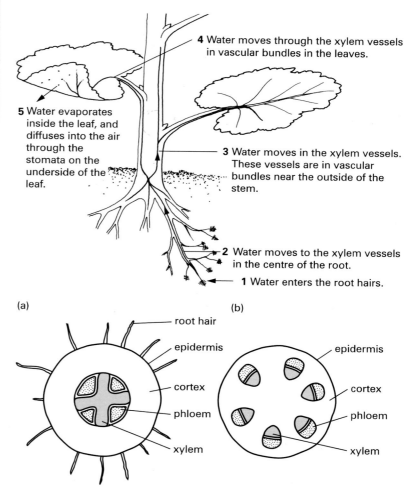

4 Water moves through the xylem vessels in vascular bundles in the leaves.

5 Water evaporates inside the leaf, and diffuses into the air through the stomata on the underside of the leaf.

3 Water moves in the xylem vessels. These vessels are in vascular bundles near the outside of the stem.

2 Water moves to the xylem vessels in the centre of the root.

1 Water enters the root hairs.

▲ Figure 8.2
A radish seedling, showing root hairs. Notice that the root hairs do not grow right at the tip of the root.

(a)

(b)

- root hair
- epidermis
- cortex
- phloem
- xylem

- epidermis
- cortex
- phloem
- xylem

▲ Figure 8.3
Transverse sections across **(a)** a root and **(b)** a stem.

that have been destroyed. Most root hairs probably live for less than a day.

Root hairs grow in between the soil particles. Water from the spaces in the soil moves into the root hairs by osmosis. It does this because the soil water has a higher water potential than the cytoplasm in the root hair cell (see page 28). The cell surface membrane of the root hair cell, like all cell surface membranes, is partially permeable. It lets water molecules into the cell, but will not let the molecules inside the cell, such as proteins, get out. The root hairs greatly increase the surface area of the root, which speeds up the rate at which water can be taken into the plant. Root hairs also take up mineral salts. This is described on page 32.

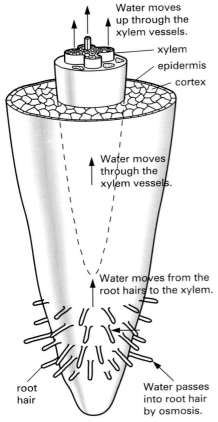

▲ Figure 8.4
The pathway followed by water, as it passes from the soil into the xylem vessels in a root.

Question

8.1 Fertilisers often contain ammonium nitrate, which is soluble in water. If you put too much fertiliser around the roots of a plant, you can kill it. Can you explain this?

Across the root

Figure 8.4 shows the structure of a root. You can see the root hairs on the outside. In the middle of the root are **xylem vessels**. These are long tubes that run straight up the root. From the root hairs, the water travels across the root towards these xylem vessels in the centre.

The part of the root between the root hairs and the xylem vessels is called the **cortex**. The cortex contains 'ordinary' plant cells – they are very like the typical plant cell on page 17, except that they do not have any chloroplasts. As the water moves towards the centre of the root, some of it goes into the cytoplasm of the cortex cells and then out of them again, moving from cell to cell across the root. A lot of the water, however, does not go inside the cytoplasm of the cortex cells at all. Instead, it just soaks through the cell walls, rather like moving through blotting paper.

Xylem vessels

Figure 8.5 shows a xylem vessel. Xylem vessels are made of long, hollow, dead cells placed end to end to form a continuous tube. They have small holes in their sides

Xylem vessels are long tubes containing no cytoplasm. Water and dissolved ions pass freely through them.

Figure 8.5 ▶
Xylem vessel.

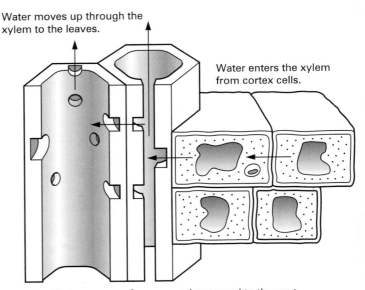

Water moves up through the xylem to the leaves.

Water enters the xylem from cortex cells.

Water can pass from one xylem vessel to the next through thinner areas of the vessels, called pits.

called **pits**. When the water from the root hairs arrives in the centre of the root, it goes into the xylem vessels through these pits.

The water then moves up the xylem vessels, which take it up through the root and stem and into the leaves. To understand what makes the water move up like this, we must look at what happens to it in the leaves.

Transpiration

Figure 8.6 shows part of a leaf. The cell walls of the mesophyll cells are always wet. Water **evaporates** from these cells, so that the air spaces inside the leaf are full of water vapour. The water vapour diffuses out of the air spaces, through the stomata, into the air, in the process of **transpiration**.

Figure 8.6 ▶
Transpiration.

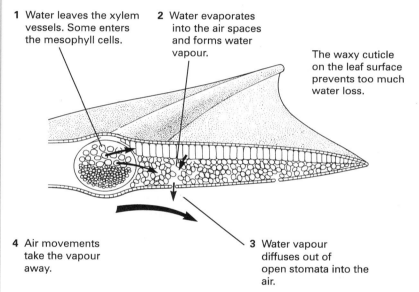

1 Water leaves the xylem vessels. Some enters the mesophyll cells.

2 Water evaporates into the air spaces and forms water vapour.

The waxy cuticle on the leaf surface prevents too much water loss.

4 Air movements take the vapour away.

3 Water vapour diffuses out of open stomata into the air.

The loss of water from the leaves reduces the water pressure at the tops of the xylem vessels. This is rather like sucking on a straw. If you reduce the pressure on the liquid at the top of the straw, the pressure at the base pushes the liquid upwards. This is why water moves up xylem vessels. Transpiration reduces the pressure at the top of the xylem vessel so that it becomes less than the pressure at the base. The water therefore moves upwards.

A plant transpires about 98% of all the water it absorbs. Only about 2% is used in photosynthesis. The quantities of water that can move through a plant in this way can be enormous. In a tropical rainforest, up to 75% of the water falling as rain will be taken up by trees and transpired back into the atmosphere from which it came.

8.2 a If the trees in an area of tropical rainforest were all cut down, what would happen to the rainwater that fell on the ground?

b What effect do you think this might have on the humidity (wetness) of the atmosphere?

8.3 For each of the following pairs of conditions, suggest which one will produce the fastest rate of transpiration, and explain your answer.

a hot weather or cold weather

b a dry atmosphere or a humid atmosphere

c a still day or a windy day

d bright sunshine or dull weather.

(Remember that, when plants are photosynthesising, they need to allow carbon dioxide into their leaves.)

Supplement

Why water moves up through a plant

You may have met the term **water potential** in Chapter 2. The water potential of a substance is a measure of how much water there is in it, and how easily the water molecules can move around. A substance containing a lot of water has a high water potential. A substance containing little water has a low water potential. Water moves from areas with a high water potential into areas with a low water potential.

Water moves up the plant because of a difference in water potential between the soil and the air. There is a **water potential gradient** from the soil to the air.

If the air does not contain very much water vapour, it has a *low* water potential. The air spaces in the leaf contain a lot of water vapour, so they have a *high* water potential. Therefore the water vapour diffuses out of the leaf into the air.

This reduces the water potential in the air spaces in the leaf. The water potential in the cell walls of the mesophyll cells is much greater. Water therefore moves from the cell walls into the air spaces.

As the water evaporates from the cell walls, the water potential in the cell walls is reduced. The water in the xylem vessels has a high water potential. Therefore water moves from the xylem vessels into the cell walls of the mesophyll cells.

This reduces the pressure at the top of the xylem vessel. The pressure at the top of the vessel is less than the pressure at the bottom. This difference in pressure causes water to move up the xylem, all the way from the roots right to the top of the plant.

(a)

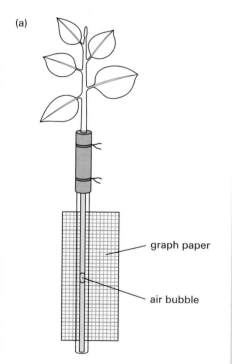

graph paper

air bubble

(b)

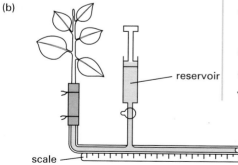

reservoir

scale

▲ **Figure 8.7**
Two types of potometer.

Investigation 8.1

Measuring the rate of water uptake

Anything that affects the rate at which water vapour diffuses out of a plant's leaves will affect the rate at which the plant takes up water. It is not easy to measure water uptake by a whole plant, so you are going to use a leafy shoot. Normally, water would enter the plant through its root hairs. In your shoot, water will go straight into the xylem vessels in the plant's stem.

The apparatus you will use is called a **potometer**. 'Poto' means 'water', and 'meter' means 'measurer'. A potometer measures how much water a plant takes up.

Figure 8.7 shows two sorts of potometers. Although the one shown in part (b) looks much more complicated than the one in part (a), its only real advantage is that it is easier to refill it with water. You can get perfectly good results with the simpler potometer.

You will need:

- a potometer
- a freshly cut leafy shoot, with a stem that will fit tightly into your potometer
- a stopwatch, or a clock or watch with a second hand
- some petroleum jelly.

You may also be able to use a fan.

1 Fill your potometer with water. Your teacher will explain how to do this. Make sure there are no air bubbles.

2 Make sure that the end of your leafy shoot is cleanly cut. Push the shoot into your potometer, so that no air can get in or out. Make sure that the cut end of the shoot is not covered by an air bubble – the water needs to be able to get into it easily.

3 Leave your apparatus for 5 or 10 minutes, to give the shoot a chance to settle down. (You could be drawing your apparatus while you wait.)

4 Mark the position of the air/water meniscus (see Figure 8.7) in your potometer. Start a stopwatch. Every two minutes, record the position of the meniscus. Keep doing this either for 15 minutes, or until the meniscus gets to the end of the capillary tube.

5 Draw a line graph of your results.

6 Write up your experiment in the usual way.

7 Describe, in detail, how you could use a potometer to test one of the following statements:

- The rate of transpiration is greater in light than in darkness.
- The rate of transpiration is greater in moving air than in still air.
- The rate of transpiration is greater in dry air than in humid air.
- Most stomata are on the lower surfaces of leaves.

Supplement

Controlling the rate of transpiration

Plants that live in dry environments, such as a desert, cannot afford to lose too much water by transpiration. If a plant loses more water than it takes in, then the water content of its cells decreases. The cells lose their turgor and become flaccid. The plant's leaves become floppy. The plant wilts. If even more water is lost, the plant may die.

Plants which live in places where there is not very much water often have shapes which cut down the rate of transpiration. Some examples of these plants are shown in Figure 8.8.

▲ **Figure 8.8**
Plants adapted for growth in arid environments.
(a) Sisal in Tanzania   **(b)** Cactus in Mexico   **(c)** Baobab in Namibia.

Question

8.4 For each of the plants shown in Figure 8.8 explain how the shape of its leaves, stem and its growth form will help it to survive in a hot, dry environment.

Investigation 8.2

Adaptations of plants to their environment

You are going to look at several different plants, which grow in different environments. Your teacher will give you some information about the environment in which each of the plants grows.

Make large, clear diagrams of all, or parts of, at least two different plants. Annotate your diagrams to explain how the shapes and forms of the leaves, stems and/or roots of the plants are adapted for the environment in which the plant lives.

Translocation ▶

The xylem vessels are not the only transport system in a plant. There is another system of tubes, called **phloem tubes** or **sieve tubes**. The phloem tubes usually run alongside the xylem vessels. Together, they form **vascular bundles** or **veins**.

Photosynthesis in the leaves produces glucose. All the cells in the plant need glucose for respiration (see

Chapter 9). The cells in the roots cannot make their own glucose, because they have no light. Glucose made in the leaves is changed into the complex sugar **sucrose**. Sucrose is carried in the phloem to all parts of the plant, including the roots. **Amino acids** are also carried in the phloem tubes. The transport of substances in the phloem tubes is called **translocation** (see Figure 8.9).

Figure 8.9 ▶
Translocation.

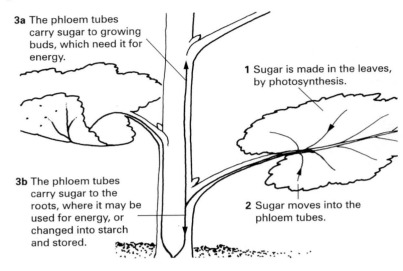

3a The phloem tubes carry sugar to growing buds, which need it for energy.

1 Sugar is made in the leaves, by photosynthesis.

3b The phloem tubes carry sugar to the roots, where it may be used for energy, or changed into starch and stored.

2 Sugar moves into the phloem tubes.

Question

8.5 **a** Why do all the cells in a plant need amino acids?

b The phloem tubes of a tree trunk are just underneath the bark. If a complete ring of bark, and the phloem underneath it, is removed from a tree trunk, the tree slowly dies. Suggest why this happens.

Supplement

Systemic pesticides

Insects and fungi can cause great damage to plant crops. Growers often spray their crops with **pesticides**, which are chemicals that kill pests.

Some pesticides are **contact pesticides**. These pesticides have to be sprayed directly onto the pest. Many insects and other pests may be missed when these pesticides are sprayed onto the plant, as they may be underneath the leaves.

Some pesticides are **systemic pesticides**. These are absorbed by the plant, and taken into its phloem tubes.

The pesticide is transported in the phloem to all parts of the plant. Any pest feeding on the plant will take in the pesticide. Systemic pesticides have a much better chance of reaching and killing all the pests on the plant than contact pesticides do.

Great care has to be taken when using any kind of pesticide. Many farmers are now trying to use fewer pesticides, because they are expensive, and can harm the environment. You can find out more about this in Chapter 15.

Summary

- Water is absorbed into the root hairs of a plant by osmosis. It passes across the root from cell to cell, also by osmosis. At the centre of the root it enters xylem vessels, which transport it up through the stem and into the leaves.

- Xylem vessels are made from dead, hollow cells with lignified walls, laid end to end.

- Water seeps out of the mesophyll cells in the leaf, and evaporates into the air spaces from the wet cell walls. The water vapour then diffuses out of the leaf through the stomata. This process is called transpiration.

- The loss of water from the leaves by transpiration creates a 'pull' from above. It does this by reducing the water potential in the leaves. The water potential in the roots is high. Water therefore moves down this water potential gradient from the roots towards the leaves, flowing through the xylem vessels.

- Transpiration happens most rapidly in warm, dry, windy conditions.

- If water is lost from a plant more quickly than it is taken up by the roots, then the cells lose water and become flaccid. This causes the plant to wilt.

- Plants that are adapted to live successfully in dry environments are called xerophytes. Adaptations include hairs on the leaves to trap a layer of moist air; thick waxy cuticles to waterproof the leaves; and thick, swollen leaves or stems to reduce the surface area to volume ratio and to store water.

- Sucrose and amino acids are transported from places where they are made, such as leaves, to regions where they are needed for respiration or growth. This is called translocation, and it takes place through phloem sieve tubes.

- Systemic pesticides, for example systemic insecticides, can be absorbed by a plant, and then transported through all parts of it in the phloem vessels. This means that an insect feeding on the plant will take in insecticide when it feeds, and be killed.

Respiration

All living cells need energy. They obtain useful energy by breaking down glucose and other organic molecules, in a chemical reaction called respiration. Respiration happens inside every living cell. If oxygen is used to break down the glucose, the process is called aerobic respiration. If oxygen is not used, it is called anaerobic respiration.

Aerobic respiration ▶

Obtaining energy from food

Everyone knows that we need to eat so that we will have energy to do things. We use energy to move around, and for our heart to beat. We use it to keep our bodies warm and to send nervous impulses from one part of the body to another. All of the energy to do these things comes from the food we eat.

One kind of food we use for energy is **glucose**. When you eat starchy food, enzymes in your alimentary canal break down the long starch molecules into small glucose molecules. When the glucose molecules get to your small intestine, they move through the walls of the intestine and into the blood. The blood takes them all around the body. Every cell has a constant delivery of glucose, brought by the blood.

The glucose goes right into each cell in your body. Inside the cells, the glucose molecules are combined with oxygen. They are changed into carbon dioxide and water. This chemical reaction is called **aerobic respiration**. The equation for aerobic respiration is:

glucose + oxygen → carbon dioxide + water + energy

$$C_6H_{12}O_6 + 6O_2 \rightarrow 6CO_2 + 6H_2O + energy$$

Aerobic respiration releases energy from glucose. (Other molecules, such as amino acids or fatty acids, are also broken down by aerobic respiration to release energy, but we will concentrate on glucose in this chapter.) Releasing energy is the purpose of respiration. *Respiration is the breakdown of glucose to release energy which cells can use.*

Investigation 9.1

Releasing energy from a peanut

Peanuts are a good 'energy food'. When you eat a peanut, the 'peanut molecules' are digested and then absorbed into your blood. They are taken to your cells, where respiration takes place. The 'peanut molecules' are combined with oxygen, and the energy from them is released.

In this investigation, you are going to make the 'peanut molecules' combine with oxygen and release energy. This process is similar to respiration.

You will need:

- a peanut
- a mounted needle
- access to a Bunsen burner
- a retort stand, clamp and boss
- a syringe, graduated pipette or measuring cylinder
- a thermometer
- a boiling tube
- access to a balance for weighing your peanut.

1 Weigh your peanut and record its mass in grams.

2 Measure out 40 cm³ of water. Fix the boiling tube into the clamp, as shown in Figure 9.1, and pour the water into the boiling tube.

3 Take the temperature of the water, and record it.

4 Carefully spear the peanut on the mounted needle. Set light to the peanut by holding it in the Bunsen flame. When it is burning, hold it under the tube of water. Hold it as close as you can without putting out the flame. Keep it there until it completely stops burning.

5 Record the final temperature of the water.

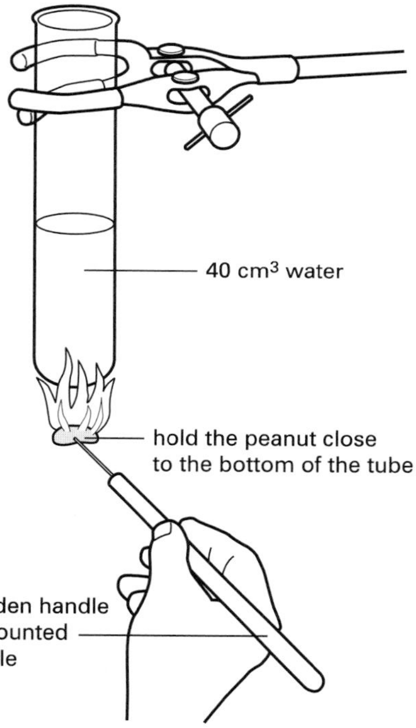

▲ Figure 9.1
Method for investigation 9.1.

Labels in figure: 40 cm³ water; hold the peanut close to the bottom of the tube; wooden handle of mounted needle

Questions

1 Energy is measured in joules. One joule, or 1 J, is only a very small amount of energy. It takes 4.2 J to raise the temperature of 1 cm³ of water by 1°C. Using this fact, and the change in temperature you have recorded, you can work out how much energy was used to heat up your 40 cm³ of water. Try to work this out for yourself. Ask for help if you are not sure.

2 The amount of energy you have worked out in question 1 came from one peanut. You know the mass of your peanut, so you can work out how much energy would come from *one*

gram of peanut. Try to work this out for yourself. Ask for help if you are not sure.

3 Food scientists have calculated that, on average, one gram of peanut contains 23 000 J of energy. This value is probably much larger than the one you have calculated. Suggest why this is so. You should be able to think of at least four different reasons.

4 Suggest what changes you could make to your apparatus, in order to get a more accurate value for the amount of energy in a peanut.

Gaseous exchange ▶

Respiration needs oxygen. Each living cell in your body needs a constant supply of oxygen, so that it can release energy from glucose.

We get the oxygen we need from the air. We take air into our lungs by **breathing**. In the lungs, some of the oxygen in the air goes into the blood, and carbon dioxide in the blood goes into the air. This is called **gaseous exchange**.

Figure 9.2 shows the structure of the human lungs. Air goes into the lungs through the mouth or nose, down the **trachea**, and into the right and left **bronchi**. The bronchi branch into smaller tubes called **bronchioles**,

Figure 9.2 ▶
The human gaseous exchange system.

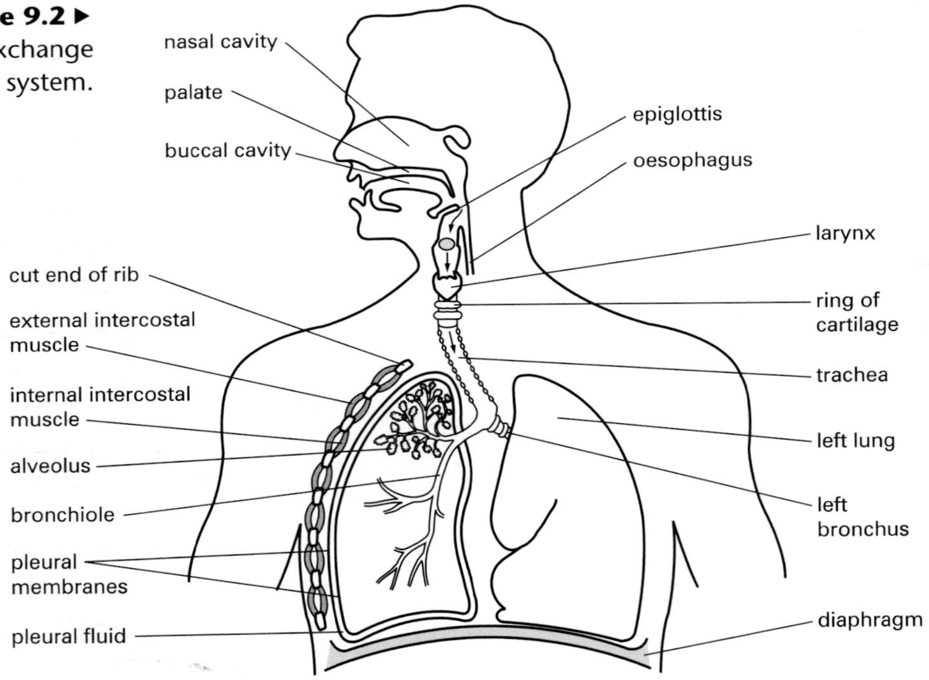

- nasal cavity
- palate
- buccal cavity
- epiglottis
- oesophagus
- larynx
- ring of cartilage
- trachea
- left lung
- left bronchus
- diaphragm
- cut end of rib
- external intercostal muscle
- internal intercostal muscle
- alveolus
- bronchiole
- pleural membranes
- pleural fluid

Figure 9.3 ▶

Gaseous exchange between air
and the blood.

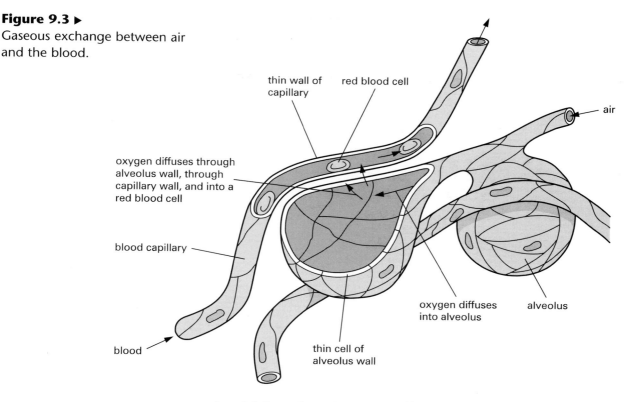

which end as tiny sacs called **alveoli**. Each alveolus is
about 0.25 mm in diameter, and each lung contains
several million alveoli. The total surface area of all the
alveoli in your two lungs is about 70 m^2. Each alveolus
has blood capillaries wrapped closely around it.

Figure 9.3 shows a section through an alveolus and a
blood capillary. The cells that make up the walls of both
the alveolus and the capillary are very thin. The
thickness of both layers together is only about
0.001 mm. This is the distance that separates the air in
your lungs from your blood.

Blood is brought to these capillaries along the
pulmonary artery. This blood is deoxygenated. The
haemoglobin inside the red blood cells is not carrying
oxygen. The concentration of oxygen in the air inside
the alveoli is greater than the concentration of oxygen
in the blood. Oxygen therefore diffuses from the alveoli
into the blood, down a concentration gradient. It moves
into the red blood cells, and combines with
haemoglobin to form oxyhaemoglobin. The blood flows
away along the **pulmonary vein**.

At the same time as oxygen diffuses from the alveoli into
the blood, carbon dioxide diffuses in the other direction.

9.1 a Where does the blood in the pulmonary artery come from? Why is it deoxygenated?

b Where does the blood in the pulmonary vein go to?

9.2 Figure 9.4 shows the gills of a fish. Fish get their oxygen from the water, which contains dissolved oxygen.

Human alveoli and fish gills are two examples of **gaseous exchange surfaces**.

a Make a list of at least three similarities between these two gaseous exchange surfaces.

b For each of these similarities, explain why all gaseous exchange surfaces need these features.

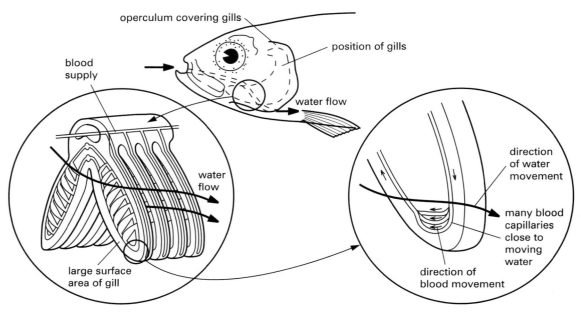

▲ Figure 9.4
Structure of the gills of a fish.

Investigation 9.2

Comparing inspired and expired air

The air you breathe in is called **inspired air**. The air you breathe out is called **expired air**. You are going to compare how much carbon dioxide they contain, how warm they are, and how much moisture they contain.

You will need:

- the apparatus shown in Figure 9.5, or as provided by your teacher

- some hydrogencarbonate indicator solution (you could use limewater instead)

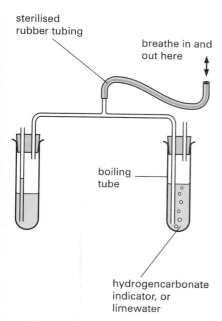

▲ Figure 9.5
Apparatus for investigation 9.2.

▲ Figure 9.6
Breathing onto a thermometer.
Don't put it into your mouth!

- a thermometer
- some dry cobalt chloride paper.

Carbon dioxide

1 Set up the apparatus shown in Figure 9.5, or as provided by your teacher. Pour equal amounts of hydrogencarbonate indicator solution into each tube. You need enough to cover the ends of the long tubes, but not the ends of the short tubes. Hydrogencarbonate indicator solution is orange-red when it contains a small amount of carbon dioxide, and yellow when it contains a larger amount of carbon dioxide.

2 Breathe *gently* in and out of the tube shown in Figure 9.5. If you blow too hard, you will blow the solution out of the tubes. Be very careful not to suck too hard, or you will get a mouthful of hydrogencarbonate indicator solution. Record:

- in which tubes bubbles appear when you breathe in, and when you breathe out
- in which tube the colour of the indicator first changes from orange to yellow.

Temperature

3 Hold the thermometer in the air around you. Record the temperature.

4 Hold the thermometer near to *but not inside* your mouth (see Figure 9.6). (You are taking the temperature of the air, not of your body.) Breathe out onto the thermometer for a few minutes. Record the temperature.

Moisture content

Cobalt chloride paper is blue when dry and pink when wet.

5 Using forceps, take a piece of dry cobalt chloride paper and hold it in the air around you for a few minutes. Record the colour.

6 Using forceps again, take a second piece of dry cobalt chloride paper. Hold it near to *but not inside* your mouth. Breathe onto it for a few minutes. Record the colour.

7 Write up your experiment in the usual way. You may like to record your results and conclusions as a table.

Table 9.1 ►
The composition of inspired and expired air.

	Inspired air	**Expired air**
Oxygen / %	21	16
Carbon dioxide / %	0.04	4
Nitrogen / %	78	78
Moisture content	Very variable	High

9.3 Give explanations for each of the four differences or similarities between inspired and expired air shown in Table 9.1.

Keeping the lungs clean

The air around us contains dust particles and bacteria. The pathway to the lungs is designed to stop too many of these unwanted particles getting into the alveoli, where they could cause damage.

Figure 9.7 is a diagram of the lining of the trachea, magnified about 3000 times. The lining of all the passageways leading to the alveoli – inside the nose, the trachea and the bronchi – is like this.

Figure 9.7 ▶
The lining of the trachea.

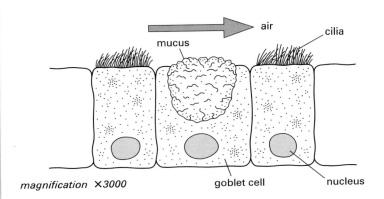

The lining contains two kinds of cells. Some cells are called **goblet cells**. These cells make sticky, slimy mucus. Many of the dust particles and bacteria in the air get trapped in the mucus.

The other cells have tiny, microscopic 'hairs' on them called **cilia**. (Cilia are not at all the same as real hairs – they are much, much smaller, and cannot be seen at all clearly with even the best school microscope.) The cilia beat in unison, like a field of grass rippling in the wind. They sweep the mucus upwards, towards the back of your throat. You swallow the mucus, together with all its trapped dust particles and bacteria. These are killed inside your stomach, by the hydrochloric acid and enzymes.

Despite this excellent filtering system, some dust and bacteria do get down into the lungs. Patrolling white blood cells constantly move around on the surface of

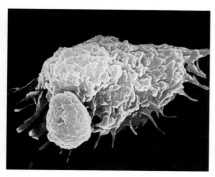

▲ Figure 9.8
A white blood cell about to engulf another cell. White blood cells like these patrol all over the body. In the lungs, they destroy bacteria and viruses that you might breathe in, often before they have a chance to make you ill.

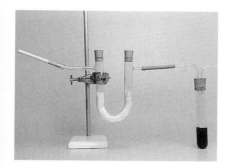

▲ Figure 9.9
This apparatus can be used to see some of the substances in cigarette smoke. The U-tube contains cotton wool, and the boiling tube contains Universal Indicator solution. You need to attach a pump to the right-hand end of the apparatus to suck the smoke through when the cigarette is lit.

the alveoli. They take in and digest any foreign material which they meet. Figure 9.8 shows one of these white cells in the lungs.

Cigarette smoke

Cigarette smoke contains many harmful substances. The most important ones are nicotine, tar and the gases carbon dioxide and carbon monoxide. All of these substances can cause damage and disease.

Nicotine is a drug that affects the brain. It makes people feel more relaxed. Nicotine is an **addictive** drug. This means that people who regularly smoke cannot easily give up smoking, because their bodies demand more nicotine.

Nicotine also affects the blood system. It increases the rate at which the heart beats, and increases blood pressure. This can put strain on the heart. People who smoke are more likely to suffer from **heart disease** than people who do not.

Tar in cigarette smoke can cause **cancer**. The most common cancer caused by smoking is lung cancer, but smoking can also increase the risk of suffering from many other kinds of cancer as well.

Cancer happens when cells divide uncontrollably. Usually, cells only divide when they need to. Sometimes, however, the DNA in a cell can be damaged in a way that makes the cell divide over and over again. A mass of cells called a **tumour** is formed. If the cells in this tumour go on and on dividing, and spread into other areas, then this is a cancer. Many cancers can be cured if caught early. The tumour can be removed by surgery, or the cancer cells can be killed with radiation or chemicals. Lung cancer, however, is very difficult to cure.

Tar in cigarette smoke can cause cancer by damaging the DNA in cells. This is most likely to happen in the lungs or in the tubes leading to the lungs. Some of the chemicals from the cigarette smoke also go into the blood and are carried around the body, where they can damage DNA in other cells and cause cancers there.

Tar also affects the lining of the tubes leading to the lungs. It destroys or paralyses the cilia, so that they can no longer sweep mucus up to the throat. The tar stimulates the goblet cells to make more mucus than

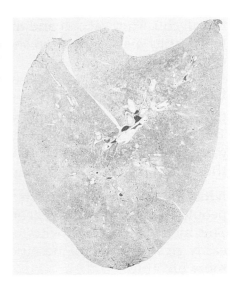
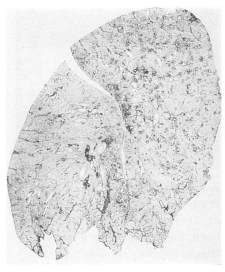

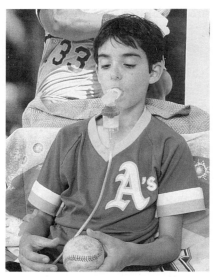

▲ Figure 9.11
In developed countries, asthma is becoming more and more common, especially in young people. This boy is using an inhaler. He breathes in a drug which helps to relax the muscles in his bronchioles, so that they get wider and make it easier for him to breathe.

usual. The mucus slides down into the lungs. Here, bacteria may breed in it, causing disease. The person tries to remove the mucus by coughing, which can damage the lungs and the lining of the tubes even more. This is **bronchitis**. Sometimes, the damage is so bad that the walls of the alveoli break down. This stops oxygen and carbon dioxide moving easily in and out of the blood, so the person finds it very difficult to get enough oxygen. They have **emphysema**.

Carbon monoxide in cigarette smoke diffuses into the blood from the alveoli. Like oxygen, it combines with haemoglobin. However, unlike oxygen, the carbon monoxide will not separate from the haemoglobin. It combines irreversibly. Up to 7% of a smoker's haemoglobin is combined with carbon monoxide. This haemoglobin cannot be used for carrying oxygen, so smokers are likely to run short of oxygen if they do anything very energetic.

Air pollution

Some air pollutants can make breathing problems worse. **Sulphur dioxide**, a gas produced when fossil fuels are burnt, can make bronchitis much worse than usual. Sulphur dioxide can make the bronchioles contract (get narrower) making it difficult for air to pass into the lungs. Concentrations of sulphur dioxide tend to be highest in cities where there is a lot of traffic, or industries that burn coal. **Dust** can also cause these problems, and may cause attacks of **hay fever** in people who have a tendency to suffer from this.

People who suffer from **asthma** are more likely to have an attack if they breathe polluted air. In an asthma attack, the muscles in the walls of the bronchioles contract so much that only a very narrow passageway is left for air to pass along. The person has difficulty in breathing. This happens because the body's defence system over-reacts to 'invasion' by something foreign in the air breathed in. Air pollutants such as nitrogen dioxide and sulphur dioxide can trigger an asthma attack, as can smoke and other irritant gases. People with asthma may be advised by their doctor not to do outdoor exercise on days when air pollution levels are high.

Supplement

Breathing

In order to maintain a good supply of oxygen to our blood, we need to move fresh air into the lungs and then push it out again. This is called **ventilation**. The movements we make to cause ventilation are called **breathing movements**. Figure 9.12 shows a section through the **thorax** or chest. The lungs are surrounded

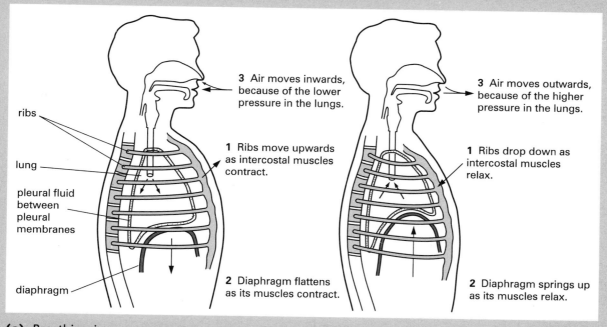

ribs

lung

pleural fluid between pleural membranes

diaphragm

3 Air moves inwards, because of the lower pressure in the lungs.

1 Ribs move upwards as intercostal muscles contract.

2 Diaphragm flattens as its muscles contract.

3 Air moves outwards, because of the higher pressure in the lungs.

1 Ribs drop down as intercostal muscles relax.

2 Diaphragm springs up as its muscles relax.

(a) Breathing in.
▲ **Figure 9.12**
Breathing movements.

(b) Breathing out.

by a pair of **pleural membranes**, which are completely airtight. Around these are the **ribs**. Between the ribs are **intercostal muscles**. Stretched right across between the lowest ribs, under the lungs, is the muscular **diaphragm**.

When you breathe in, the external intercostal muscles and the diaphragm muscles contract. The intercostal muscles pull the ribs upwards and outwards. The diaphragm muscles pull the diaphragm downwards. Both these movements make more space inside the thorax – they increase its volume. This decreases the pressure inside it. The pressure inside becomes lower than the air pressure outside. The air therefore rushes in from the high pressure area outside your body, to the lower pressure area inside your thorax. The only way into the thorax is through the trachea, along the bronchi and bronchioles and into the lungs. The air therefore goes into the lungs, and makes them inflate.

When you breathe out, the external intercostal muscles and the diaphragm muscles relax. This allows the ribs to drop back down again, and the diaphragm to spring back up. This increases the pressure in the thorax, squeezing air out of the lungs.

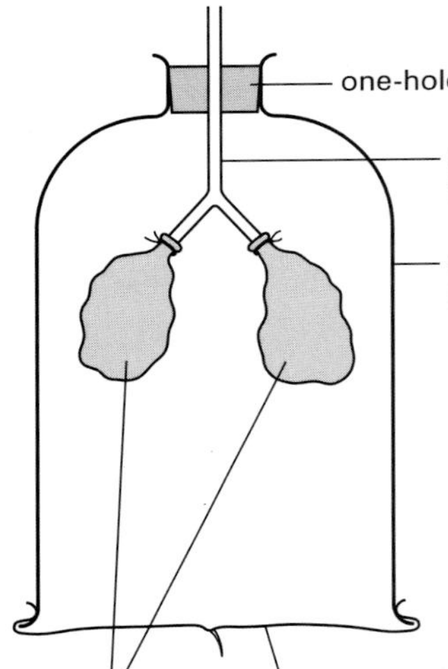

Investigation 9.3

How the diaphragm helps with breathing

The apparatus for this investigation is shown in Figure 9.13. It is a very simple model of a human thorax.

1 Compare the apparatus with Figure 9.12. Which part of the apparatus represents:

  • the lungs

  • the ribs and body wall

  • the diaphragm

  • the trachea and bronchi?

2 Pull down on the rubber sheet. What happens? Can you explain why?

3 Explain how the apparatus represents what happens when you breathe in and out.

4 What important structures are missing from this model?

one-hole bung

glass tubing

glass bell jar

balloons, tied tightly around the glass tubing – NOT inflated

plastic or rubber sheet tied around base, with something you can pull on in the middle

▲ **Figure 9.13**
Apparatus for investigating the action of the diaphragm in breathing.

Anaerobic respiration ▶

At the beginning of this chapter, we defined respiration as the breakdown of glucose to release energy, which cells can use. In humans, this is normally done by combining the glucose with oxygen. This is **aerobic respiration**, and can be defined as the release of energy from food by combining it with oxygen. However, some living things can release energy from glucose *without* using oxygen. This is called **anaerobic respiration**. Even humans can respire anaerobically for short periods.

Anaerobic respiration only releases a tiny amount of energy from glucose, compared with aerobic respiration. In aerobic respiration, about 19 times as much useful energy is released than in anaerobic respiration, from the same amount of glucose.

Anaerobic respiration in yeast

Figure 9.14 shows some yeast cells. Yeast is a single-celled fungus. Yeast is able to respire anaerobically. It releases energy from glucose by breaking it down into ethanol and carbon dioxide:

glucose → ethanol + carbon dioxide + energy

$$C_6H_{12}O_6 \rightarrow 2C_2H_5OH + 2CO_2 + energy$$

Anaerobic respiration by yeast is used in brewing. Yeast is added to a mixture of sugar and other substances, and it ferments the sugar to alcohol. In Brazil, sugar from sugar cane has been fermented in this way to produce alcohol, which is used as a fuel in car engines. In some countries, fermentation is used to make alcoholic drinks.

Respiration in yeast is also used in bread-making. The bubbles of carbon dioxide make the bread rise. You can read more about this on page 65.

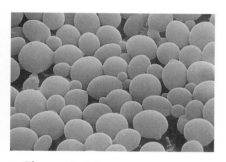

▲ **Figure 9.14**
Yeast cells. This picture was taken with a scanning electron microscope. The cells are magnified about 500 times.

Investigation 9.4

Anaerobic respiration in yeast
You will need:

- some yeast cells mixed up in water – the water should have been boiled and then cooled, so that it does not contain any dissolved air
- some sugar solution
- the test tubes, bungs and glass tubing shown in Figure 9.15
- a way of supporting your apparatus, such as a test tube rack or beaker

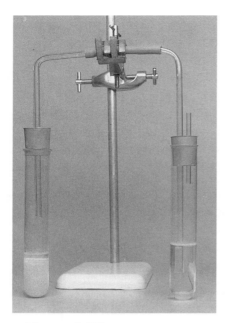

▲ **Figure 9.15**
Apparatus for showing anaerobic respiration in yeast. The yeast is in the left-hand tube. The right-hand tube contains limewater.

- some limewater
- some oil and a dropper pipette.

1 Put some of the yeast suspension into one of the test tubes, and add some sugar solution. The exact amounts are not important, but you should not fill your tube more than about half full.

2 Using a dropper pipette, gently trickle some oil into the tube, so that it makes a layer over the top of the yeast and sugar solution. This is to stop any oxygen diffusing in to the liquid.

3 Pour some limewater into the second tube, so that the bottom of the glass tubing is covered.

4 Push the bungs firmly into the tubes, as shown in Figure 9.15. You do not want any air leaks.

5 Stand your apparatus in a warm place. Have a look at it after half an hour, and again later if you can.

6 Write up your method, results and conclusions in the usual way.

Anaerobic respiration in humans

Unlike yeast, we cannot respire for long periods without oxygen. However, our muscle cells do quite often run out of oxygen when they are working hard. They can keep going for a while by respiring anaerobically. They do this in a different way from yeast, and produce **lactic acid** instead of ethanol and carbon dioxide:

glucose $\rightarrow$ lactic acid + energy

$C_6H_{12}O_6 \rightarrow 2C_3H_6O_3$ + energy

Lactic acid is toxic (poisonous). As it builds up in the muscles, it makes them feel tired and can cause painful cramps. Because of this, muscles can only respire anaerobically for quite a short period of time.

The lactic acid diffuses from the muscles into the blood, and is taken to the liver. The liver breaks it down by combining it with oxygen. Because of this, extra oxygen is needed. This is why you breathe faster when you have just finished exercising. You are paying off your **oxygen debt**, which you built up while your muscles were respiring anaerobically.

Question

9.4 When athletes train, many changes occur in their muscles and other parts of the body. These changes include:

- an increase in the blood supply to the muscles
- an increase in the amount of **myoglobin** (a substance very like haemoglobin, which stores oxygen) in the muscles
- an increase in the tolerance of the muscles to lactic acid.

How could each of these changes improve an athlete's performance?

Investigation 9.5

The effect of exercise on breathing rate

Design and carry out an investigation to test one of the following hypotheses:

- The longer you exercise, the longer it takes for your breathing rate to return to normal.
- The more vigorously you exercise, the longer it takes for your breathing rate to return to normal.
- If you do regular exercise for one week, the time taken for your breathing rate to return to normal becomes shorter.

Summary

- Respiration is a metabolic reaction in which glucose is broken down inside living cells, releasing energy from it that the cell can use.
- In aerobic respiration, the glucose is broken down by combining it with oxygen. Carbon dioxide is produced as a waste product. The word equation for aerobic respiration is:

  glucose + oxygen → carbon dioxide + water

- In humans, the oxygen needed for respiration diffuses into the blood from the alveoli. Carbon dioxide produced by respiration diffuses out of the blood into the alveoli. This is called gaseous exchange, and the surface of the alveoli is the gaseous exchange surface.

- Gaseous exchange surfaces usually have a very large surface area, to increase the rate at which gases can pass across them. They are kept moist, as otherwise the cells at the surface would dehydrate and die. A good blood supply helps to take away oxygen and bring more carbon dioxide, thus maintaining a diffusion gradient for each of these gases.

- Expired air contains less oxygen, more carbon dioxide and more water vapour than inspired air. Carbon dioxide can be detected by using limewater (which goes cloudy) or hydrogencarbonate indicator (which changes from red to yellow).

- Breathing takes place through rhythmic changes in the volume of the thorax, brought about by contraction and relaxation of the intercostal and diaphragm muscles. Breathing rate and depth increase during exercise.

- During inspiration, air flows through the nose and mouth, down the trachea, along the bronchi and into the bronchioles. Ciliated cells and mucus-secreting cells help to trap dirt and bacteria, keeping them out of the lungs.

- Carbon monoxide, nicotine and tar in cigarette smoke damage the lungs. Tobacco smoke stops cilia working, so that there is nothing to stop harmful particles reaching the lungs. Tar can cause lung cancer. Nicotine is addictive. Air pollution can cause similar damage.

- When breathing in, the external intercostal muscles and the diaphragm contract, increasing the volume of the thorax so that air flows in. When breathing out, these muscles relax, decreasing the volume of the thorax so that air is pushed out.

- When no oxygen is available, human muscle cells respire anaerobically. Glucose is broken down without oxygen, to form lactic acid. Yeast also respires anaerobically, producing ethanol and carbon dioxide.

Chapter 10

Excretion and homeostasis

Cells work best when they are surrounded by just the right conditions – the right amount of water, the right amount of glucose, and a temperature of about 37 °C. Keeping these conditions constant is called homeostasis. It is also important to remove from the body any unwanted waste materials produced by metabolism in the cells. This is excretion.

Excretion ▶

Metabolic waste products

Every moment of the day and night, thousands of chemical reactions are taking place in your cells. These reactions are called **metabolic reactions**, or metabolism. Respiration is one example of a metabolic reaction, but there are many, many more.

Many metabolic reactions produce substances that the body does not need. These substances are **waste products**. Some waste products are poisonous or **toxic**. Respiration, for example, produces the waste product carbon dioxide, which is toxic in large amounts.

Another source of waste products is substances we have more of in our bodies than we need. Many such substances can be stored, to be used later, but some cannot be stored and have to be removed from the body. Excess proteins, for example, cannot be stored.

Question

10.1 Suggest some substances that can be stored in the body until needed.

The body therefore has to get rid of these waste products or excess substances, in a process called **excretion**. One definition of excretion is: *the removal of waste products of metabolism (which may be toxic), and of substances in excess of requirements, from the body.*

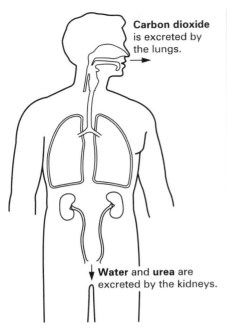

▲ Figure 10.1
The main excretory products of humans.

In Figure 10.1:
- Carbon dioxide is excreted by the lungs.
- **Water** and **urea** are excreted by the kidneys.

It is important to realise that the removal of undigested material as faeces from the alimentary canal is *not* excretion. This process is called **egestion**. This undigested material has never really been inside the body at all! The alimentary canal is just a tube running from mouth to anus. To get properly inside the body, food molecules have to pass through the walls of the alimentary canal and into the blood, in the process of absorption. So the waste substances in faeces have not been produced by metabolism, nor are they in excess of requirements – they have simply not been digested or absorbed.

Humans excrete three main substances, as shown in Figure 10.1. One is **carbon dioxide**, which is constantly being produced by all cells as they respire. The excretion of carbon dioxide by the lungs is described in Chapter 9. Another substance is **urea**, which is made by the liver from excess proteins, and then excreted by the kidneys. The third substance is **water**, which is sometimes in excess in the body, and which is removed by the kidneys. We also excrete substances produced in the body by the breakdown of our own hormones, and also by the breakdown of toxic substances like alcohol and other drugs.

Urea production and excretion

Urea is made in the **liver**. It is made from excess proteins and amino acids, as shown in Figure 10.2 opposite.

When protein is eaten, the protein molecules are digested to form amino acid molecules. The amino acids are absorbed into the blood, and pass into the hepatic portal vein. This takes them to the liver.

In the liver, several things may happen to the amino acids. They may simply pass through, and travel on around the body, here and there moving into cells that may need them for making proteins. Or the liver itself may use them, stringing them together to make proteins such as fibrinogen, the protein used in blood clotting.

Question

10.2 Make a list of five different proteins (other than fibrinogen) that are made in the body. Which types of cells will make each of these proteins?

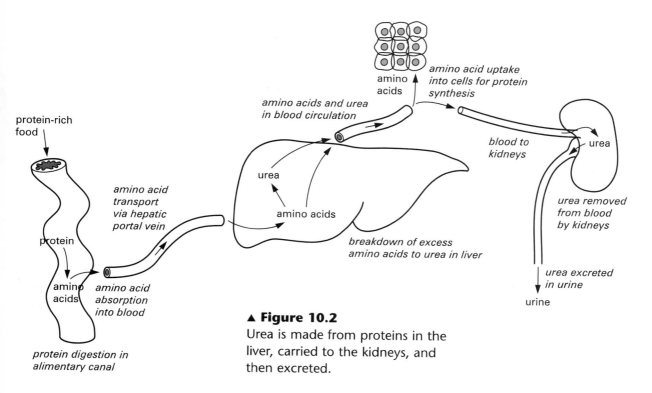

▲ Figure 10.2
Urea is made from proteins in the liver, carried to the kidneys, and then excreted.

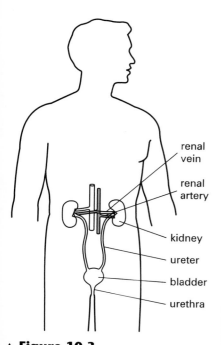

▲ Figure 10.3
The human urinary system.

However, the body may not need all the amino acids that arrive in the liver. If this is the case, then the liver breaks them down. It would be very wasteful just to excrete the amino acids as they are, so they are changed into carbohydrates or fats, which the body can store. This involves removing the nitrogen-containing part of the amino acid (you may remember that amino acids contain carbon, hydrogen, oxygen and nitrogen, while carbohydrates and fats contain only carbon, hydrogen and oxygen.) Removing the nitrogen-containing part is called **deamination**.

The nitrogen-containing part is made into a substance called **urea**. Because urea contains nitrogen, it is called a **nitrogenous excretory product**.

The urea is carried away from the liver in the blood. As the blood flows through the kidneys, the urea is taken out of the blood. The kidneys produce a solution of urea in water, called **urine**. The urine flows out of each kidney along a tube called the **ureter** (see Figure 10.3). The ureter carries the urine to the bladder, where it can be stored until it is released from the body along the **urethra**.

10.3 Put the events listed below in the right order, to explain how urine is produced and excreted.

- The liver deaminates excess amino acids.
- The kidneys remove urea from the blood.
- Amino acids travel along the hepatic portal vein.
- Urea passes into the blood.
- Some proteins are eaten.
- Urine flows into the urethra.
- Proteins are digested into amino acids.
- Urine is stored in the bladder.
- Amino acids are absorbed into the blood.
- Amino acids enter liver cells.
- Urea is produced.
- Urea is carried to the kidneys.
- Urine is produced.
- Urine flows along the ureter.

10.4 Explain the difference between each of the following pairs of words:

a excretion and egestion

b urine and urea

c ureter and urethra.

Removal of excess water

Water is a very important component of our bodies. The human body contains around 66% water. If you could totally dry a human body, you would be left with a dusty heap weighing only one-third of the weight of the living person.

It is important to keep the amount of water in the body roughly constant. If we had too little water, cells would begin to dry out, so that the metabolic reactions taking place inside them would slow down or even stop. If we had too much water, cells could take up so much by osmosis that they would burst.

The kidneys help to regulate the amount of water in the body. If there is too much, they excrete large amounts of watery urine. If there is not enough, much less urine is excreted, in a more concentrated form.

Other excretory substances

Many **hormones** are made in the human body. You will meet some of these later in this book, including insulin, adrenaline, oestrogen, progesterone and testosterone. These hormones are carried around the body in the blood. The liver breaks down many of these hormones. The breakdown products leave the liver in the blood, and are excreted by the kidneys, dissolved in urine.

The liver also breaks down many of the harmful substances that we may eat or drink, including drugs. One such drug is **alcohol**. Alcohol is very toxic to cells (you can find out more about this in Chapter 11). The liver cells break it down to harmless substances such as carbon dioxide and water. However, the liver cells may become damaged by the alcohol. A person who drinks a lot of alcohol over a long period of time may suffer permanent damage to the liver. The liver also breaks down many other drugs, such as nicotine and heroin.

Supplement

Kidney machines

Sometimes, a person's kidneys may stop working. This is often because of an infection, when damage may be done to the kidney cells. If this happens, then the kidneys can no longer remove urea or excess water from the blood. The person feels very ill, and will die if no treatment is available.

The best method of treatment is a **kidney transplant**, but this is not always possible. There may not be a suitable kidney available, or there may be no suitable hospital facilities nearby. Even if a transplant is done, the person's body may reject the transplanted kidney.

If a kidney transplant is not possible, then treatment can be given with a **dialysis** or **kidney machine**. Figure 10.4 shows a patient undergoing dialysis treatment and Figures 10.5 and 10.6 show how this works.

The patient's blood is passed through lots of tiny channels, made out of **dialysis tubing**. This is like the Visking tubing you may have used in biology experiments. It has very tiny, molecule-sized holes in it. Little molecules such as water, urea and glucose can fit through the holes, but big ones such as proteins cannot. The holes are far too small to let any cells through.

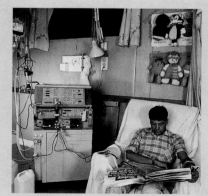

▲ **Figure 10.4**
A patient with kidney failure undergoing dialysis treatment.

Figure 10.5 ▶

A kidney dialysis machine.

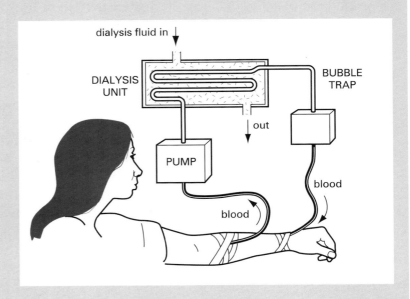

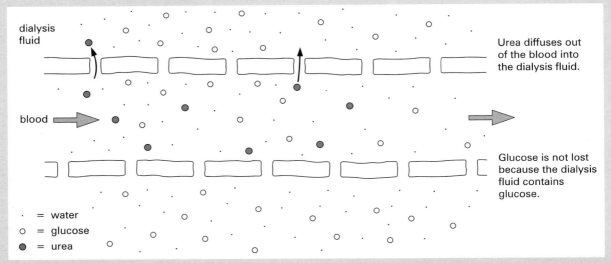

= water
o = glucose
● = urea

Urea diffuses out of the blood into the dialysis fluid.

Glucose is not lost because the dialysis fluid contains glucose.

▲ **Figure 10.6**

How kidney dialysis works.

Outside the dialysis tubing is a liquid called **dialysis fluid**. This is specially made up to have a similar composition to healthy human blood plasma. It is mostly water, with glucose and salts dissolved in it, but no urea. It must be absolutely sterile, with no bacteria or other living things in it. The dialysis fluid flows constantly through the machine in one direction, while the person's blood flows past it in the opposite direction.

All the molecules in the dialysis fluid and the blood are constantly bouncing around. Each will diffuse down its concentration gradient. As there is no urea in the dialysis fluid, urea will diffuse out of the patient's blood into the dialysis fluid. If there is more water in the blood than in the dialysis fluid, then water will diffuse *out* of the blood; if the concentration gradient is the other way round, then it will diffuse *in*. The same applies to glucose and salts. This process of diffusion of different molecules, each according to its own concentration gradient, through a partially permeable membrane, is called **dialysis**.

People with kidney failure have to have their blood 'cleaned' in a dialysis machine several times a week, for several hours at a time.

Most people would rather have a kidney transplant than have dialysis all their lives. They may feel sick during dialysis. They must be careful about what they eat. In many countries, there are not enough dialysis machines because the machines are expensive.

Although transplants cost more than dialysis to begin with, this is a 'one-off' cost. However, even a successful transplant has its disadvantages. The patient's immune system will reject the 'foreign' kidney unless immunosuppressant drugs are taken. Then the person is more susceptible to infections, because his or her immune system has been deliberately weakened.

Question

10.5 a Kidneys remove excess sodium chloride from the body. People with kidney failure must not eat too much salty food. However, they can eat as many salty things as they like while they are on a dialysis machine. Explain why this is so.

b Suggest one other type of food that a person suffering from kidney failure must not eat in excess.

Homeostasis ▶

Homeostasis can be defined as *the maintenance of a constant internal environment in the body.*

The regulation of the water content of the body by the kidneys is part of homeostasis. Two other features of the internal environment that are controlled are **temperature** and **glucose concentration**.

Temperature regulation

The normal human body temperature is about 37 °C. If the body temperature drops much below 37 °C, then metabolic reactions slow down, because molecules move more slowly at low temperatures. If the body temperature rises much above 37 °C, then metabolic reactions again slow down, because enzymes are denatured.

37 °C is quite a high temperature. In most parts of the world, the air temperature is normally quite a lot lower than this. For most people, for most of the time, the body is warmer than the environment around them. This means that heat is constantly being lost from the body to the environment. Heat is lost by conduction, convection and radiation. To keep the body temperature at 37 °C, we have to:

- produce heat inside the body, and

- prevent too much heat being lost from the body.

Inside the brain, there are cells that constantly monitor the temperature of the blood. These cells are in the **hypothalamus**. You can see where the hypothalamus is on Figure 11.8 on page 159. It is right in the middle of the head. Figures 10.7 and 10.8 (opposite) show how it regulates the blood temperature.

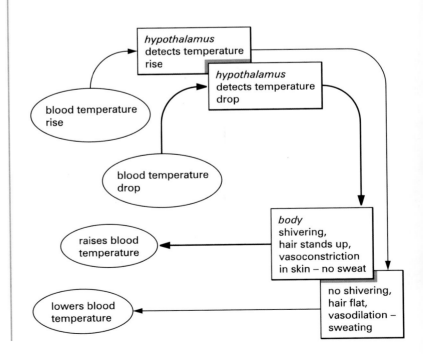

Figure 10.7 ▶
Flow diagram showing how body temperature is regulated.

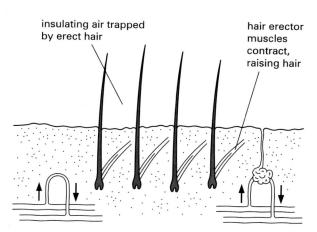

insulating air trapped by erect hair

hair erector muscles contract, raising hair

Constriction of arterioles supplies less blood to capillaries and sweat glands.

- more insulation by raised hairs
- less heat lost through evaporation of sweat
- less heat lost from skin capillaries by conduction and radiation
- heat generated by shivering of body muscles

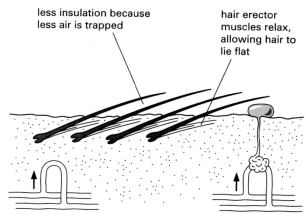

less insulation because less air is trapped

hair erector muscles relax, allowing hair to lie flat

Dilation of arterioles supplies more blood to skin capillaries. More heat is conducted to, and radiated from, skin surface.

More blood is supplied to sweat gland. More sweat is evaporated from the skin surface.

- less insulation by flattened hairs
- more sweating gives more heat loss through evaporation
- more heat lost from skin capillaries, by conduction and radiation

(a) How the skin responds when the body temperature changes.

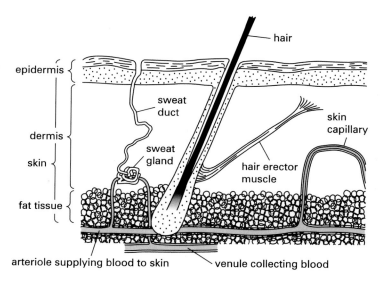

hair

epidermis

sweat duct

skin capillary

dermis

sweat gland

hair erector muscle

skin

fat tissue

arteriole supplying blood to skin

venule collecting blood

(b) The structure of the skin.

▲ **Figure 10.8**

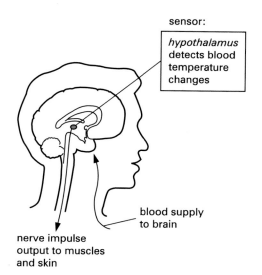

sensor:

hypothalamus detects blood temperature changes

blood supply to brain

nerve impulse output to muscles and skin

(c) The regulation of the blood temperature.

If the blood temperature *drops below 37 °C*, the hypothalamus sends messages along nerve fibres to the muscles and to the skin. These messages make the following events take place:

- Muscles in several parts of the body contract and relax very quickly. This is called **shivering**. The shivering muscles generate heat, which helps to raise the temperature of the blood.

- The muscles attached to the hair roots, called **erector muscles** (see Figure 10.8) contract. This pulls the hairs up on end. In humans, this does not help to keep us warm, but in animals with fur it does. The raised fur traps air next to the skin. Air is an excellent insulator, and reduces heat loss from the skin.

- Muscles around the arterioles leading to the upper layers of the skin contract. This closes off the blood vessels taking blood near to the surface of the body. This is called **vasoconstriction**. The blood takes a different route, flowing deep in the skin, below the fat layers. This means that there is a layer of insulation between the blood and the outside world, so reducing heat loss from the skin.

If the blood temperature *rises above 37 °C*, the hypothalamus again senses this, and sends different messages to the muscles and skin. This makes the following events take place.

- The erector muscles attached to the hair roots relax, so that the hair (or fur) lies close against the skin, no longer trapping so much air. Heat can more easily escape from the skin.

- The muscles around the arterioles leading to the skin surface relax, allowing the blood vessels to get wider. This is called **vasodilation**. The blood now flows close to the skin surface, where it can lose heat to the outside world.

- **Sweat glands** in the skin secrete sweat on to the surface of the skin. The water from the sweat evaporates, taking with it heat from the skin.

Question

10.6 Suggest explanations for each of the following.

   a You may sweat when you do a lot of vigorous exercise.

(a)

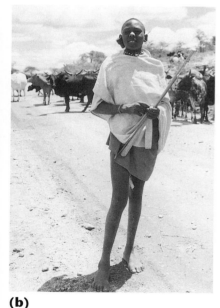

(b)

▲ **Figure 10.9**
(a) An Innuit from Northern Canada and **(b)** a Masai from Kenya have very different body shapes. How do these shapes adapt them for their environments?

b In very cold conditions, the blood supply to the fingers or toes may be cut off. (If this goes on for a long time, then cells in them die, and the person has frostbite.)

c In cold weather, you may need to eat more food than in warm weather.

d Several layers of thin clothes will keep you warmer than one thick layer.

e If someone falls into very cold water, you should remove their wet clothing as soon as they are back on land.

f In very hot conditions, it is easier to keep the body temperature cool if the air is dry than if it is very humid.

g You need to drink more when it is hot than when it is cold.

h Dogs have few sweat glands. They pant when they get too hot.

Investigation 10.1

Investigating factors that affect the rate of heat loss from the body

It is difficult to measure the rate of heat loss from a real body. In this investigation, you can use test tubes of hot water to represent a body. Although a human body would have a temperature of 37 °C, you will get better results if you start off with a temperature much higher than this, because this gives you a better chance of measuring the rate at which the temperature drops.

Design and carry out an investigation to test *one* of the following hypotheses:

- Short fat people lose heat more slowly than tall thin people of the same body weight.

- Several thin layers of clothing keep you warmer than one thick layer.

- Evaporation of water (for example in sweat) from the body surface speeds up the rate of cooling.

- Huddling together in groups can help animals to keep warm.

- A person in water loses heat more quickly than a person in air of the same temperature.

Glucose regulation

Glucose is one of the main fuels of the body. Cells need a constant supply of glucose so that they can respire. Glucose is transported around the body in solution in the blood plasma. A healthy person has a blood glucose concentration of about 100 mg of glucose in every 100 cm^3 of blood.

Cells in the **pancreas** constantly monitor the concentration of glucose in the blood. If you have eaten a meal containing a lot of starch or sugar, then there may be extra glucose in your blood. The cells in the pancreas detect this, and secrete a chemical called **insulin** into the blood. Insulin is a **hormone**; you will find out more about hormones in Chapter 11.

Insulin is carried in the blood all over the body. When it reaches the liver, it makes the liver cells take glucose from the blood. The liver cells use the glucose in several ways. They respire some of it. They change some of it into fat. They change some of it into **glycogen**.

Glycogen is a polysaccharide made of hundreds of glucose molecules linked together in a long chain. Glycogen is stored in the liver cells. A human liver can store about 50 g of glycogen for every kilogram of liver tissue.

Question

10.7 The liver makes up about 2.5% of an adult's body weight. Approximately how much glycogen could be stored in the liver of a man weighing 80 kg?

As the liver takes glucose out of the blood, the cells in the pancreas sense that the blood glucose concentration is falling. They stop secreting insulin and begin to secrete another hormone, **glucagon**. This makes cells take up less glucose from the blood. If the blood glucose level goes on dropping, then the liver cells will break down some of the glycogen they have stored. It is broken down into glucose again, and released into the blood, to keep the blood glucose concentration at the correct level. Figure 10.10 shows how the concentration of glucose is regulated.

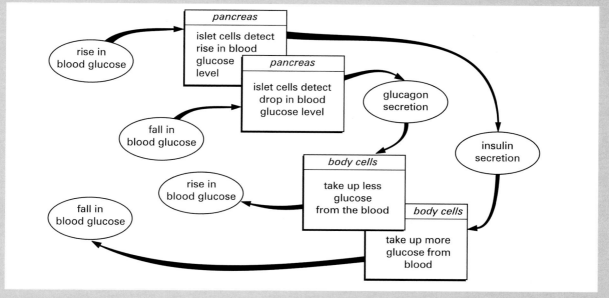

▲ **Figure 10.10**
Flow diagram showing how blood glucose concentration is regulated.

Negative feedback

If you look at Figures 10.7 and 10.10, you will see that the ways in which temperature and blood glucose are controlled are basically very similar. In both cases, there is a **sensor** which detects changes. This sensor then sends **messages** to a part of the body, called an **effector**, which does something about the change. The effector acts to bring back the temperature or glucose level towards normal. This is sensed by the sensor, which produces different messages to make the effector act to swing the changes back the other way.

Question

10.8 Copy and complete the following table, summarising the control mechanisms for temperature and blood glucose.

	Temperature	Blood glucose
Sensor		
Effector(s)		
How the effectors respond to a rise in the level		
How the effectors respond to a drop in the level		

This process is called **negative feedback**. The sensor detects a change, and gets an effector to do something to bring things back to normal. The results of this action are detected by the sensor. In other words, information about the effects of the sensor's actions are **fed back** to it. This makes the sensor stop doing what it was doing before, and do the opposite. The information has had a **negative** effect on the sensor.

▼ **Figure 10.11**
The effect of a meal containing carbohydrate on blood glucose and insulin concentrations. Can you explain the shapes of the curves?

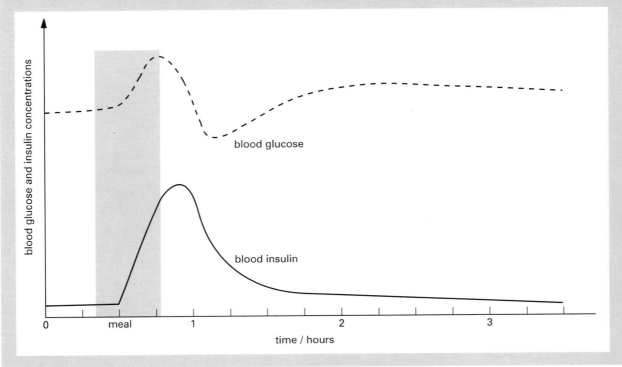

- Excretion is the removal of toxic materials, the waste products of metabolism and substances in excess of requirements.

- In the liver, excess amino acids are deaminated to form the nitrogenous excretory substance, urea.

- Urea is transported in the blood to the kidneys, where it is excreted in solution, as urine.

- Urine flows from the kidneys along the ureters to the bladder, where it is stored. It leaves the body via the urethra.

- The kidneys adjust the amount of water that they release in urine according to the amount of water in the blood. This helps to keep the amount of water in the body constant.

  - If kidneys become damaged and stop working, a person's blood can be cleaned using a dialysis machine. Alternatively, they can be given a kidney transplant.

- The liver breaks down hormones and drugs such as alcohol and heroin.

- Homeostasis is the maintenance of a constant environment within the body. It includes temperature regulation and regulation of the concentration of glucose in the blood.

- The hypothalamus coordinates temperature regulation. It receives information about body temperature, and responds by sending nerve impulses to skin and muscles. If too hot, then sweating increases and vasodilation occurs. If too cold, then hairs stand on end, vasoconstriction occurs and muscles shiver.

  - The pancreas and liver control glucose regulation. If blood glucose levels rise too high, the pancreas senses this and secretes insulin, which causes glucose to be taken up and used by liver and other cells. If blood glucose levels fall too low, it secretes glucagon, which causes the cells to decrease the rate at which they take up glucose. This is an example of negative feedback.

Coordination and response

All living things, including plants, are able to detect changes in their environment, and to respond to them. The parts of the body that detect the changes are called receptors, while those that respond are effectors. Information passes from receptors to effectors, and to other parts of the body, by means of nerves or hormones.

Nervous control ▶

Receptors

A **receptor** is a cell that can sense something about its environment. Humans have receptors that can sense five different types of information about the environment – light, sound, touch, temperature and chemicals. These types of information are called **stimuli**. The receptors change the energy in the stimuli into electrical energy in nerve cells, as shown in Figure 11.1. The receptor cells are often part of a **sense organ**.

Question

11.1 Copy and complete the following table.

Stimulus to which receptor cells are sensitive	Sense organ in which receptor cells are found
Light	
	Skin
	Ear
Touch	
	Mouth and nose

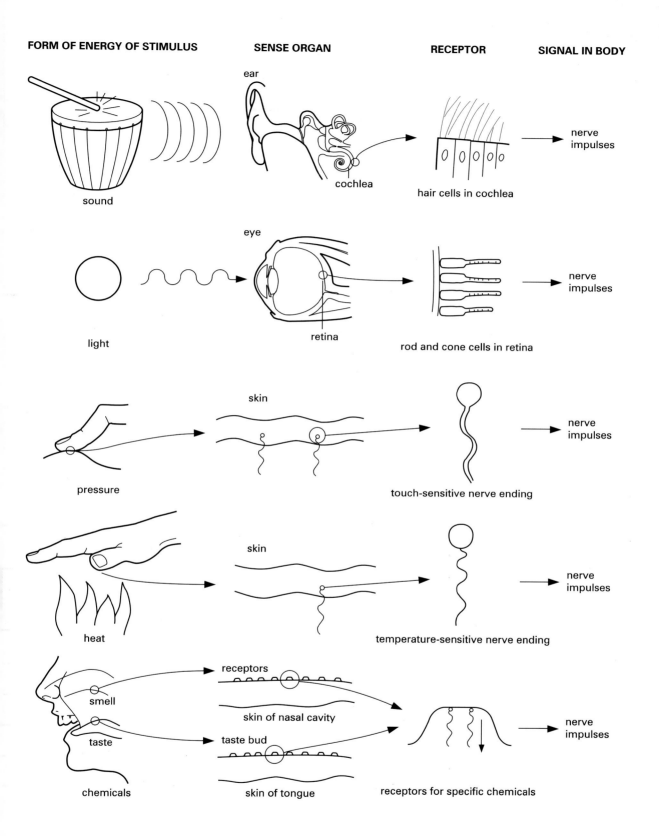

| FORM OF ENERGY OF STIMULUS | SENSE ORGAN | RECEPTOR | SIGNAL IN BODY |

sound

ear

cochlea

hair cells in cochlea

→ nerve impulses

light

eye

retina

rod and cone cells in retina

→ nerve impulses

pressure

skin

touch-sensitive nerve ending

→ nerve impulses

heat

skin

temperature-sensitive nerve ending

→ nerve impulses

chemicals

smell

taste

receptors

skin of nasal cavity

taste bud

skin of tongue

receptors for specific chemicals

→ nerve impulses

▲ Figure 11.1
Receptors in sense organs transfer different kinds of energy into nerve impulses.

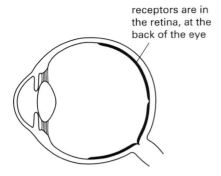

▲ Figure 11.2
The position of the receptors in the eye.

The human eye

Of all our receptors, we are probably most aware of those that are sensitive to light. These receptors are found in a thin layer at the back of the eye. They are called **rods** and **cones**. The thin layer in which they are found is the **retina**.

Figure 11.2 shows the position of the retina. When light falls onto the rods and cones in the retina, the light energy generates tiny electrical signals in them. These electrical signals rush to the brain, along the **optic nerve**, taking much less than a second to arrive there. The brain interprets the pattern of signals so that we 'see' an image.

The clarity of the image the brain 'sees' depends on the clarity of the image made by the light falling on the retina. The parts near the front of the eye **focus** the light coming into the eye, so that it forms a clear image on the retina.

Figure 11.3 ▶
Section through a human eye.

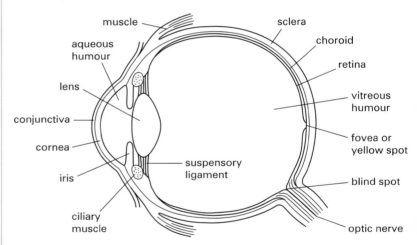

Focusing

Two of the parts of the eye that help to focus light onto the retina are the **cornea** and the **lens**. Most of the focusing is done by the cornea. The lens makes the fine adjustments. Figure 11.4 shows how they do this.

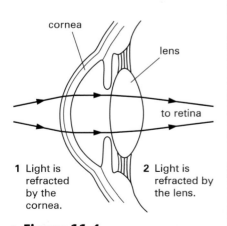

1 Light is refracted by the cornea.

2 Light is refracted by the lens.

▲ Figure 11.4
How light is refracted as it enters the eye.

When light hits the cornea at an angle, the light is bent or **refracted**. Your cornea acts as a **converging lens**. It bends the light rays inwards. The cornea is a fixed shape, and always bends similar light rays by the same amount.

The light rays then pass through the lens. Here, they are refracted a little more, just enough to bring them into perfect focus on the retina.

Accommodation

Unlike the cornea, the amount by which the lens refracts the light rays can be varied. The lens is stretchy and elastic, and can be pulled out into a thin shape, or allowed to fall back into its natural fat shape (Figure 11.5).

When you look at an object very close to your face, the light rays from it are spreading out, or **diverging**, when they reach your eye. They need to be bent sharply to bring them into focus on the retina. When you look at something close up, your brain automatically sends a message to the ring of muscles called **ciliary muscles** which help to hold the lens in position. The message tells the muscles to contract. The muscles do this, and so get shorter. This makes the ring smaller.

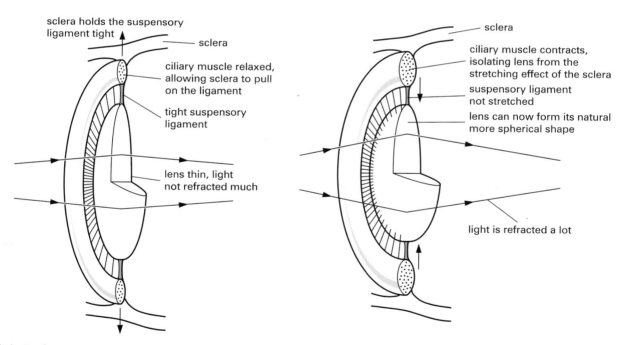

sclera holds the suspensory ligament tight

sclera

ciliary muscle relaxed, allowing sclera to pull on the ligament

tight suspensory ligament

lens thin, light not refracted much

sclera

ciliary muscle contracts, isolating lens from the stretching effect of the sclera

suspensory ligament not stretched

lens can now form its natural more spherical shape

light is refracted a lot

(a) To focus on a distant object, the lens is made thin.

(b) To focus on a nearby object, the lens is made fat.

▲ **Figure 11.5**
Accommodation.

The lens is held in the middle of the ring of muscles by strong fibres called **suspensory ligaments**. When the ciliary muscles contract and make the ring smaller, the suspensory ligaments go loose. Nothing is pulling outwards on the lens. The lens falls into its natural fat, rounded shape.

A fat, round lens refracts light rays much more than a thin, flat one. The diverging light rays are bent sharply inwards, bringing them into focus on the retina. The brain can sense how sharp the image is, and will quickly send more messages to the ciliary muscles to tell them to contract or relax a little bit more, until the focus is exactly right.

The changes that take place in your eye when you focus on objects at different distances away are called accommodation.

Questions

11.2 Write your own explanation of what happens, and why, when you look at an object in the far distance. You should mention the brain, the ciliary muscles, the suspensory ligaments, and the lens.

11.3 Make a copy of the eye shown in Figure 11.3.
Then make a second copy on transparent paper.

You are going to label your second copy with the functions of each of the parts, instead of their names. You will be making an 'overlay'. Then you can look at a diagram with just the names, a diagram with just the functions, or a diagram with both together.

The functions you should write are listed below. Use what you know about the eye, or what you can work out, to write each function by the appropriate part.

- contains receptor cells sensitive to light
- is full of a transparent fluid, which helps to hold the eye in shape
- refracts the light rays as they enter the eye; cannot change its shape
- responsible for fine adjustments to focusing; its shape can be changed
- strong fibres that hold the lens in position
- a ring of muscles that contract or relax to change the shape of the lens
- the coloured part of the eye
- a thin, transparent, protective covering over the front of the eye
- a tough, outer covering around the eye
- a dark layer behind the retina, which absorbs light so that it does not bounce around the eye.

Investigation *11.1*

The structure of the human eye

You will need:

- a partner or a mirror
- a ruler.

1 Use a mirror to look carefully at one of your own eyes, or look at a partner's eye. Make a drawing of it. Remember to put a scale on your diagram. Label as many parts of the diagram as you can, using your own knowledge and the names on Figure 11.3.

2 Suggest functions for each of the following: eyelids, eyelashes, tear ducts.

Investigation *11.2*

Looking at a sheep's eye

You may be able to do this investigation yourself, or your teacher may be able to demonstrate it to you. The eye will have come from a farm animal that has been killed for food, such as a sheep. If you are doing the investigation yourself, you will need:

- a sheep's eye
- a dish or board on which to work with the eye
- a pair of sharp dissection scissors, and perhaps a scalpel and forceps
- some thin disposable gloves
- some old newspaper.

Take care! Be very careful with scissors and scalpels.

1 Examine the eye carefully. If there is a lot of creamy-white fat around it, remove this using the scissors and scalpel. Be careful not to cut away the pale red **muscles**, or the white **optic nerve**. Look at Figure 11.6 to see what these look like, and where they are found.

2 Make a large, labelled diagram of the eye, from whatever angle you think will show the most information. Figures 11.3 and 11.6 will help you with your labels.

3 You are now going to cut the eye in half, along the line shown in Figure 11.6. Getting in is quite difficult, because the **sclera** is extremely tough. You don't need to worry about the insides of the eye squirting out at you – the part you are cutting into contains a jelly called the **vitreous humour**, rather than very

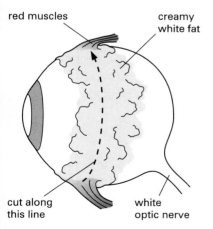

red muscles   **creamy white fat**

cut along this line   **white optic nerve**

▲ **Figure 11.6**
Dissecting an eye.

runny liquid. Use scissors rather than a scalpel. Notice that the eye collapses once the jelly drops out, showing that the jelly helps to hold the eye in shape.

4 Open out the two halves of the eye (you can leave them partly joined together if you like) and make a labelled diagram of what you can see. You may find that the contents have a lot of black pigment in them. This has come from the **choroid**, the black layer behind the retina.

5 Take the lens out of the eye, and put it over some newspaper print. You will see that it behaves like a magnifying glass.

6 Clear everything away, and wash your hands thoroughly, even though you were wearing gloves. Write a full description of what you have seen and done, to go with your two diagrams.

Supplement

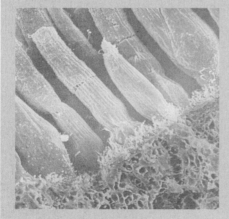

▲ **Figure 11.7**
Part of the retina of an eye, showing some of the thousands of rods and cones. The bases of the rods and cones are towards the bottom right of the picture, and they extend towards the top left. The cones are shorter than the rods.

Rods and cones

The two kinds of receptor cells in the retina are sensitive to different types of light. **Rods** are sensitive to quite dim light. It is your rod cells that send signals to the brain when you are looking at things at night. If your rod cells do not function, then you have **night blindness**. This can happen if you are very short of vitamin A, which is needed to help rod cells to work.

Cones are only sensitive to bright light. At night, they cannot sense the low light levels at all. However, they do have one great advantage over rods – they can sense the different colours of light, so that we see an image in colour. When only rods are working, we only see an image in black and white.

Most of the cones in the human eye are packed together in just one small part of the retina, called the **yellow spot**. You focus an image on this part of the eye when you look directly at an object. There are no rods in the yellow spot. The rods are spread out on the other parts of the retina.

Question

11.4 Suggest explanations for each of the following:

a Nocturnal mammals (which are active at night) often have no cones, only rods, in their eyes.

b In the dark, it is very difficult to tell what colour anything is.

c In the dark, it is difficult to see a clear image of an object if you look straight at it; you may be able to pick it out better if you look just to one side of it.

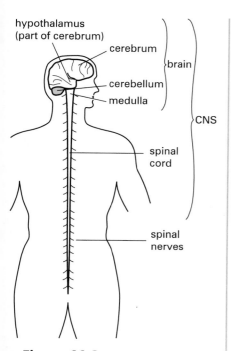

▲ **Figure 11.8**
The human central nervous system.

The nervous system

Receptors, such as the rods and cones in the eye, are a part of the **nervous system**. The nervous system is made up of all our receptors, nerves, and the brain and spinal cord.

The brain and spinal cord make up the **central nervous system**, often called the CNS for short. Figure 11.8 shows the main parts of the brain, and the spinal cord. The spinal cord runs all the way from the base of the brain to the end of your backbone. It runs inside a 'tunnel' through the vertebrae (bones in the backbone), which protect it from damage. All the rest of the nervous system apart from the CNS makes up the **peripheral nervous system**.

Information picked up by receptors is sent along nerves to the CNS. Inside the CNS, information coming in from different receptors and information generated within the brain itself, is processed and coordinated. As a result, messages are then sent out along nerves to muscles or glands, to tell them what to do. The muscles and glands are called **effectors** – they carry out actions in response to messages from the CNS.

Neurones

Both the peripheral nervous system and the CNS contain special cells called **nerve cells** or **neurones**. Figure 11.9(a) (overpage) shows a **motor neurone**, which means that it takes messages *from* the CNS *to* effectors such as muscles. ('Motor' means 'movement', and messages are carried by motor neurones to your muscles, to make them move.)

Like all animal cells, this neurone has a cell surface membrane, cytoplasm and a nucleus. It also has several features found only in neurones, not in other cells.

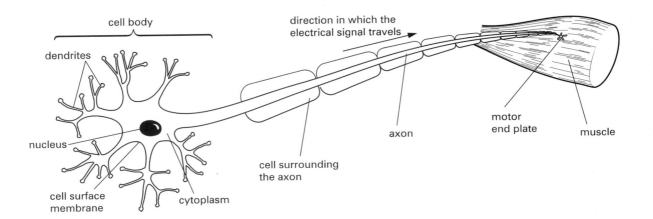

▲ Figure 11.9(a)
A motor neurone. The cells surrounding the axon of the neurone are called Schwann cells. They insulate the axon, which speeds up the rate at which nerve impulses travel along it.

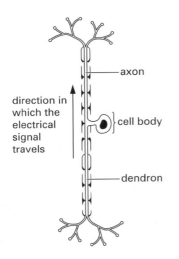

▲ Figure 11.9(b)
A sensory neurone. The structure is basically the same as in a motor neurone, but there is a long thread of cytoplasm called a dendron, as well as an axon.

The most striking thing about it is the long thread of cytoplasm called an **axon**, which stretches out from the cell body. Some human motor neurones have axons over a metre long. The axon has the job of allowing electrical signals to speed along it, from the nerve cell body to the motor end plate. This **motor end plate** is in a muscle, and it passes the electrical signals into the muscle fibres, to make them contract. You can also see several shorter threads of cytoplasm, called **dendrites**, coming out of the nerve cell body. Their function is to pick up electrical messages from other cells.

Figure 11.9(b) shows a **sensory neurone**. The function of a sensory neurone is to pass electrical messages *from* the receptor cell *to* the CNS.

In Figure 11.10, you can see where the different parts of a motor neurone are found in the body. Its cell body and dendrites are inside the spinal cord. The axon reaches all the way from the spinal cord into a muscle. Axons run in groups within the body, forming a bundle of axons called a **nerve**. A nerve is rather like an electricity cable containing many individual wires.

You can also see a sensory neurone in Figure 11.10. Sensory neurones have their nerve cell bodies very close to the spinal cord. Long threads of cytoplasm stretch out in two opposite directions – one into the spinal cord, and another even longer one out to a receptor cell.

The third type of neurone shown in Figure 11.10 is a **relay neurone**. The whole of this neurone is inside the spinal cord. It has many short dendrites, which pick up messages from many other neurones around it, and pass them on to other neighbouring neurones.

A reflex arc

Imagine that the receptor in Figure 11.10 is a pain receptor in your hand, and that you accidentally put your hand down onto a sharp pin. An electrical signal is generated in the pain receptor. This signal speeds along the nerve fibre of the sensory neurone, past its cell body, and on into the spinal cord. The signal is passed on to the relay neurone, and then to the motor neurone. It rushes down the motor neurone's nerve fibre, and into the muscle. The muscle contracts, and pulls your hand away from the pin.

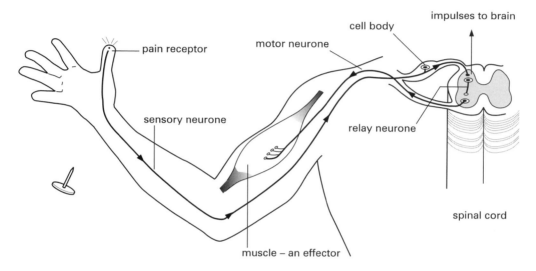

▲ **Figure 11.10**
A reflex arc. The spinal cord is drawn much larger in relation to the other structures shown than in real life.

This pathway, from the receptor in your hand to the muscle, is called a **reflex arc**. It takes only a fraction of a second for the signal to travel all the way from the receptor to the effector, so you respond very quickly to the pain. You respond without thinking about it. This kind of response is called a **reflex action**. A reflex action is a very quick, automatic response to a stimulus.

Supplement

Voluntary and involuntary actions

However, this is not quite all there is to your response to putting your hand on a pin.

When the electrical signal from the pain receptor arrives in the spinal cord, it not only is passed to the relay neurone and the motor neurone, but also to other neurones which will pass the message up to your brain. By the time it gets there, the signal going the other way may already have reached your muscle, in which case you will not have time to stop your hand pulling away, even if you wanted to. The signal to your brain makes you aware of what is going on, but probably too late to do anything about it.

If, however, you *knew* that you were going to put your hand onto the pin, you could prevent yourself from pulling it away, even if your pain receptor was stimulated. Before you touched the pin, your brain could send electrical signals down the spinal cord to the relay or motor neurones in the reflex arc, telling them *not* to send a message to your arm muscle. So, when the message arrives from the pain receptor, it is not passed on to the motor neurone, and your arm muscle does not contract.

The reflex action of automatically pulling your hand away from the pin is an example of an **involuntary action**. You do not think about it, and are not conscious of it until after it has happened. Stopping your hand from pulling away from the pin is an example of a **voluntary action**. You consciously think about it, and make a decision about what to do or what not to do.

Question

11.5 Copy and complete the following table. The first line has been done for you. There are many possible correct answers you could suggest. Try to put in some voluntary and some involuntary responses. If you like, you could add some more examples of stimuli to the table.

Stimulus	Receptor	Effector	Response	Voluntary or involuntary?
Sight of object moving quickly towards your eye	Rods or cones in retina	Muscle in eyelid	Eyelid closes	Involuntary
Loud bang just behind you				
Smell of good food cooking				
Sight of someone you know across the road from you				

The pupil reflex

You may have noticed that the size of a person's **pupil** (the dark part in the middle of the eye) changes in bright or dim light. In bright light the pupil is small, but it widens in dim light. This change is a reflex action.

Figure 11.11 shows the pupil, looking from the front of the eye. The pupil is just a gap in the middle of the coloured part of the eye, the **iris**. The function of the iris is to stop too much light getting into the eye. A lot of very bright light falling onto the retina could damage the rods and cones. So, in bright light, the iris closes inwards, narrowing the hole through which light can pass.

The iris contains two sets of muscles. One set runs around the iris, and these are called **circular muscles**. The other set runs from the centre to the outside, and these are called **radial muscles**.

Imagine what will happen when the *circular* muscles contract. As the muscles get shorter, they will make the circle smaller. The iris will close in, making the pupil smaller. When the *radial* muscles contract, the opposite happens. They pull the iris into a narrower shape, which makes the pupil larger.

When you walk from a dim room into bright sunlight, the bright light falling on the rods and cones in your retina sets up electrical signals which go to your brain.

▼ **Figure 11.11**
How the iris changes the size of the pupil.

In bright light, the circular muscles contract. This makes them shorter, and squeezes the iris inwards over the pupil, making it narrower. This allows less light through the pupil.

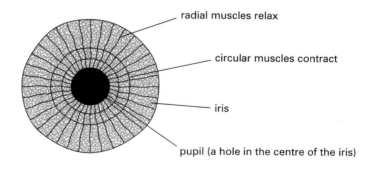

radial muscles relax

circular muscles contract

iris

pupil (a hole in the centre of the iris)

In dim light, the radial muscles contract. This makes them shorter, and pulls the iris away from the centre, making the pupil wider. This allows more light through the pupil.

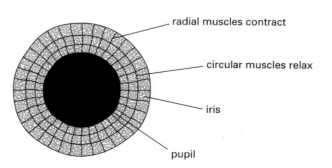

radial muscles contract

circular muscles relax

iris

pupil

From here, they are sent back along motor neurones to the muscles in your iris. The signals make the circular muscles contract, making the pupil smaller, cutting down the amount of light getting into the eye. This reaction is a reflex action, just like pulling your hand away from the pin. It is an automatic reaction, it happens very quickly, and you do not think about it. Although the message goes into your brain, it does not go directly into a part where you do your conscious thinking.

Drugs and the nervous system

A drug can be defined as a substance that changes how the body works. Most people take drugs at some time or another. Many of these are medicinal drugs, such as aspirin which relieves pain, or antiobiotics that kill bacteria that are making us ill. Often, though, they are drugs that we do not really need, but that we take because it makes us feel better, or because other people take them and we want to feel included in the group.

For example, many people drink coffee and tea. These contain a drug called **caffeine**, which makes our brains feel more alert. Drugs which do this are called **stimulants**. There is little evidence that caffeine does any real harm to people, although it is probably not a good idea to take too much of it.

Alcohol

Another drug that many people use is **alcohol**. Alcohol slows down the activity of the brain. Drugs which do this are called **depressants**. In many parts of the world, drinking alcohol is a very common activity, and people may feel left out if they choose not to drink alcoholic drinks. In other countries and societies, alcohol is completely forbidden.

Alcohol slows down reflex actions, by reducing the rate at which neurones can conduct nerve impulses. This can be extremely dangerous if the person is in a situation where they need to be able to think clearly and quickly, such as when driving a car. A very high proportion of injuries and deaths from car accidents occur when either a driver or a pedestrian has been drinking alcohol. Most countries have strict laws preventing people from driving when they have alcohol in their blood.

A concentration of around 500 mg of alcohol in every 100 cm^3 of alcohol will make a person unconscious.

Many people have died in these circumstances, by choking on their own vomit while unconscious. In larger doses, alcohol can kill because of its effects on the brain, such as stopping the signals that usually keep you breathing regularly. Young people are particularly likely to run these risks as they may not be aware of the real dangers of drinking large quantities of alcoholic drinks.

Alcohol also reduces the ability of different parts of the brain to communicate with one another. This can result in a loss of inhibition, so that people do things that normally common sense would stop them doing. For example, some people become more agressive and violent than usual. Antisocial behaviour resulting from the drinking of alcohol can cause problems both for the person who has been drinking, and also for others who get caught up in it.

Many people are able to drink small amounts of alcohol without coming to any harm. However, for some people, the need to drink alcohol becomes greater and greater, so that eventually they cannot manage without it. They have become **addicted** to it. Eventually, they may spend most of their time under the influence of alcohol, and no longer be able to keep a job or live with their family. They may end up living rough on the streets.

People who drink large amounts of alcohol over a long time period often suffer from liver damage. We have seen that one of the functions of the liver is to break down drugs, such as alcohol. This can damage the liver cells, and a disease called cirrhosis of the liver can result.

Heroin

Heroin belongs to a group of drugs called **narcotics**. These are drugs that can relieve pain and produce sleep. Some narcotics, such as codeine and morphine, are used in medicine to relieve severe pain.

Heroin, like codeine and morphine, is made from the juice of the opium poppy. However, heroin is not normally used in medicine, because for some people it is extremely addictive. In most countries it is illegal to take heroin. Despite this, some people take heroin because it gives them a feeling of euphoria – that is, everything seems absolutely wonderful and all worries and problems disappear. Although not everyone will become addicted, many people do. For these people, the need to go on taking heroin gets stronger and stronger. Higher doses are needed to get the same effect, and when heroin is not available the addict suffers from very unpleasant withdrawal symptoms. Heroin addicts will often go to any lengths to get money so that they can buy more heroin, and are prepared to commit crimes or leave their families in order to get their drug. Everything in their lives, except obtaining heroin, stops having any importance at all.

Some heroin users inject the drug directly into their veins. If this is done using an unsterilised needle, then there is a risk of introducing bacteria or viruses into the blood that can cause disease. For example, many people have become infected with the HIV virus that causes Aids, by sharing needles for injecting drugs.

Behaviour

Reflex actions play only a small part in human behaviour. Many of the things we do are voluntary actions. We may think about a variety of possible actions, and then do whatever seems best at the time. On a different day, we might make a quite different decision. Human behaviour is very variable, and often quite unpredictable.

Many other animals, however, have simpler behaviour patterns. Many invertebrates have quite small, simple central nervous systems. Much of the behaviour of these animals is made up of reflex actions. The same stimulus will often produce the same response.

Many moths, for example, will fly towards a bright light. Cockroaches, on the other hand, will always move away from a bright light. Neither the moths nor the cockroaches think about what they are doing. This kind of behaviour is called a **taxis**. A taxis can be defined as *a movement in response to a stimulus, in which the direction of the movement is determined by the direction of the stimulus.*

The examples of the moth and the cockroach are both responses to light, and can be called **phototaxis**. In the case of the moths, the direction of movement is towards the stimulus, so this is **positive phototaxis**. The cockroaches show **negative phototaxis**. Other taxes which animals may show include **geotaxis** (response to gravity) or **chemotaxis** (response to chemicals).

Investigation *11.3*

Investigating phototaxis in maggots

Maggots are the larvae of houseflies. You must only use maggots which have been specially bred and kept in a clean environment, as maggots collected from the wild are very likely to carry harmful bacteria.

You will need:

- several active maggots
- a stopclock, or a watch or clock with a second hand
- a large sheet of squared paper
- a lamp or other source of bright light
- a way of shading your squared paper from other people's lights.

1 Number the squares on your paper along two sides, as though they were the axes of a graph.

2 Set up the squared paper and lamp as shown in Figure 11.12. Make sure the paper is lying absolutely flat, with no slope or bumps. Arrange shading around your paper so that most of the light falling onto it comes from your lamp and not from anywhere else.

Figure 11.12 ▶
Method for Investigation 11.3.

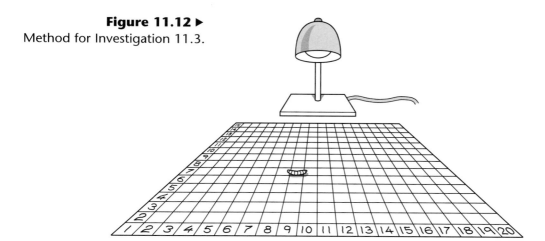

3 Place one maggot in the centre of your squared paper, and start a stopclock. Every 10 seconds, record the coordinates of the square the maggot is in. (If it is moving very quickly or very slowly, you may like to change the time interval.) Keep doing this until the maggot moves off the paper. As well as these records, take note of the way in which the maggot appears to sense the light, and any other points about its behaviour.

4 Repeat with at least five more maggots, until you think you can see a pattern in your results.

5 Write up your experiment in the usual way.

How muscles work to produce movement

You have already met some muscles in this chapter. You know something about two sets of muscles in the eye – the ciliary muscles, which control the shape of the lens, and the iris muscles, which control the shape of the iris.

Figure 11.13 shows another set of muscles. These are two of the largest muscles in your arm, the **biceps** and the **triceps**.

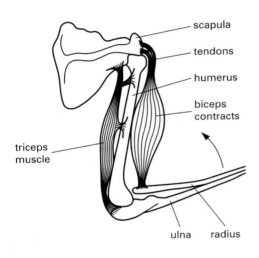

(a) Bending or flexing the arm.

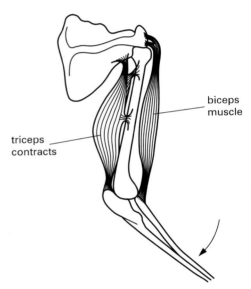

(b) Straightening or extending the arm.

▲ **Figure 11.13**
Action of antagonistic muscles in the arm.

The upper arm contains a single bone, called the **humerus**. This bone fits into a spherical socket in the shoulder bone, or **scapula**. At the elbow, the humerus forms a joint with one of the two bones of the lower arm, called the **ulna**. The second bone in the lower arm is called the **radius**.

The biceps muscle is joined to the scapula and humerus at one end, and to the ulna at the other. The triceps muscle is joined to the scapula at one end, and to the ulna at the other. The 'bi' and 'tri' in their names refer to the number of places at which they are joined at the upper end – the biceps is joined in two places, and the triceps is joined in three. Each muscle is joined to the bones by a bundle of strong, non-stretchy fibres called a **tendon**.

When you want to bend your arm at the elbow, your brain sends an electrical signal along a motor nerve fibre to your biceps muscle, and another to your triceps muscle. The signals tell the biceps muscle to contract, and the triceps muscle to relax. As the biceps contracts, it gets shorter, pulling the bones to which it is attached closer together. The arm bends, or **flexes**. The relaxed triceps muscle gets pulled longer and thinner as this happens.

When you want to straighten your arm again, signals are sent to the biceps to relax, and to the triceps to contract. As the triceps shortens, it pulls the arm straight. This pulls the relaxed biceps into a longer, thinner shape again. The arm has been **extended**.

You need to have two muscles because each of them is only able to pull one way. Muscles cannot push – they can only pull. You need one muscle, the biceps, to pull on the bones to bend the arm. The other, the triceps, pulls on the bones to straighten the arm. The biceps is called a **flexor muscle**, and the triceps an **extensor muscle**. The two muscles form an **antagonistic pair** of muscles. The radial and circular muscles in the iris are also an antagonistic pair.

Hormonal control ▶

Hormones and endocrine glands

Electrical signals travelling along nerve cells are not the only way information is passed around the body. We also use chemicals called **hormones**.

Hormones are made in organs called **endocrine glands**. An endocrine gland is made up of many secretory cells. A network of **blood capillaries** runs through the gland. The secretory cells make the hormone, and release it into the blood. The hormone is carried all around the body, in solution in the blood plasma.

Figure 11.14 (overpage) shows some of the endocrine glands in the human body. Table 11.1 (overpage) summarises the functions of these glands.

Hormones are carried to every part of the body in the bloodstream. However, they only affect certain organs, known as their **target organs**. One of the target organs of insulin, for example, is the liver.

Endocrine gland	Hormone	Function of hormone
Adrenal gland	Adrenaline	Prepares body for 'fight or flight'
Pancreas	Insulin Glucagon	Reduces blood glucose level Increases blood glucose level
Testis	Testosterone	Produces male secondary sexual characteristics
Ovary	Oestrogen	Produces female secondary sexual characteristics, and is involved in the control of the menstrual cycle
Ovary	Progesterone	Involved in the control of the menstrual cycle, and in pregnancy

▲ **Table 11.1**
Hormones and their functions.

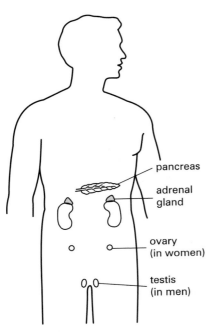

▲ **Figure 11.14**
The positions of some human endocrine glands.

Most hormones do not last for very long in the bloodstream. They are broken down by enzymes, and the products of this breakdown are excreted by the kidneys.

The role of the hormones **insulin** and **glucagon** have already been described on pages 148–149. Testosterone, oestrogen and progesterone are described on page 84. Here, we shall look at the hormone adrenaline.

Adrenaline

Adrenaline is a hormone secreted by the **adrenal glands**, which lie just above the kidneys. Adrenaline is secreted whenever you are nervous or excited. Your brain sends messages along nerves to your adrenal glands, stimulating them to secrete adrenaline into the blood.

The function of adrenaline is to increase the rate of metabolic activity, in order to prepare you to deal with whatever is making you nervous. It is sometimes called the 'fright, fight or flight' hormone, because it helps to give you extra energy and muscle power to fight, or run away from, danger. Unfortunately, many of the 'dangers' people face cannot be dealt with by fighting or running away. Examinations, for example, may make you secrete adrenaline, as may a visit to the dentist.

You are probably aware of the some of the effects of adrenaline. One of the most obvious is that it makes the heart beat faster. Adrenaline also causes the liver to break down some of its glycogen stores, releasing extra glucose into the blood. Both these actions result in an increase in your metabolic rate. Adrenaline also causes the arterioles leading to your digestive system to constrict, while those leading to your muscles dilate; this may make you feel you have 'butterflies in the stomach'. It can cause the bronchioles to get wider, so allowing more air to move in and out of the lungs with each breath.

11.6 a For each of the effects of adrenaline described above, explain how it might help you to fight off, or flee from, a danger.

   b The adrenaline secreted into your bloodstream only lasts for a very short time before it is broken down by enzymes. If you need to go on reacting to the danger, then your adrenal glands keep secreting more adrenaline. Suggest why the system works like this, rather than leaving the adrenaline for a long time before breaking it down.

Supplement

The use of BST in milk production

In some countries, a hormone called bovine somatotropin, or BST for short, is used to increase milk production in cattle.

BST is a hormone that all cattle produce naturally. However, if extra BST is given to a cow, she will produce larger amounts of milk. If the cost of the BST is less than the increased returns that the farmer gets from selling the milk, then this is economically worth doing.

However, there are some arguments against using BST in this way. For example, many people see no need for using this hormone; they think that if we want more milk, we should just keep more cows. Moreover, in many countries there is already more than enough milk being produced, so we do not need to produce more. And it is probably not very good for a cow to make very large amounts of milk. There is some evidence that cows given extra BST are more likely to get infections of their udders than untreated cows.

Comparing nervous and hormonal control

Both the nervous system and the hormonal system are very important in controlling and coordinating actions in the human body. Each has its own particular characteristics, with its own advantages in particular situations.

The nervous system transmits information much more swiftly than the hormonal system. Information passes around the nervous system in the form of electrical signals, which travel along neurones at speeds of several metres per second. Information in the form of hormones travels in the blood; the average flow rate of blood through the different kinds of blood vessels is much slower than the average speed of the transmission of electrical signals along nerves.

The nervous system delivers its messages directly to or from a particular part of the body. Hormones are taken everywhere in the blood, rather than directly to the organ which is to respond to them. Some hormones, such as adrenaline, have many target organs, and so there is a widespread response to their secretion. The nervous system tends to produce a more localised response, such as the contraction of a particular muscle to pull your hand away from a sharp pin.

Despite the fact that hormones such as adrenaline are rapidly broken down in the blood, they still last longer than an electrical signal travelling along a nerve. Hormones tend to produce longer lasting responses than nerve signals.

Question

11.7 Draw up a comparison table to show the similarities and differences between nervous and hormonal control systems.

Responses in plants ▶

Plants, like animals, respond to stimuli. Most of these responses are much slower than those of animals. But some responses are very fast. One plant that can respond very quickly to touch is the Venus flytrap. The leaves of this plant are especially designed for catching insects. There is a 'hinge' down the centre, with a broad pad on either side. On each pad there are three small spines. If an insect touches one of these spines, the leaves instantly fold over at the hinge, closing together and trapping the insect inside. The leaf cells then secrete enzymes on to the insect, digesting it. The soluble substances produced by this digestion are then absorbed into the leaf.

This response of the Venus flytrap is brought about by electrical signals, rather like the signals that run along nerves in animals. Many other plant responses, however, do not use electrical signals to transmit information, but use chemicals, rather like the hormonal system of animals. These chemicals are sometimes called **plant hormones**, or sometimes **plant growth substances**.

Investigation *11.4*

The response of cress seedlings to light

You will need:

- three small dishes with lids, for example plastic Petri dishes
- a little cotton wool or filter paper
- some cress seeds (or other seeds as supplied by your teacher)
- three cardboard boxes.

Figure 11.15 ▶
Method for Investigation 11.4.

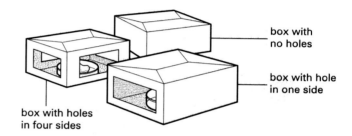

box with no holes

box with hole in one side

box with holes in four sides

1 Cover the bottom of each dish with cotton wool or filter paper. Add enough water to moisten the cotton wool or paper, but not so much that there are puddles of water in the dish. Sprinkle a few seeds in each dish. Put on the lid.

2 Cut a hole in one side of one of the cardboard boxes, and in all four sides of another, as shown in Figure 11.15. Put all three boxes upside down on a flat surface, in a light place. Put one of your dishes of seeds under each box.

3 Look at your seeds each day. Make sure you always keep the dish in exactly the same position in the box – you must not turn it round. Once the seeds have germinated, you can take off the lid of the dish, but you will then have to make sure that the seedlings do not dry out.

4 After a few days, when the seedlings in each dish have grown, take the dishes out of the cardboard boxes. Make a labelled drawing of one seedling from each dish. Make careful notes of any differences between them.

Tropisms

Plants often respond to a stimulus by growing towards it or away from it. This is called a **tropism**. A tropism is a growth response by a plant, in which the direction of the growth is determined by the direction of the stimulus. 'Photo' means light, so phototropism is a growth response to light. As the plant shoot grows *towards* the light, this can be described as **positive phototropism**.

As well as light, plants also respond to gravity. Shoots tend to grow away from the pull of gravity, while roots tend to grow with the pull. Shoots are **negatively geotropic**, while roots are **positively geotropic**.

Supplement

Auxins

Auxin is a plant hormone, or growth substance. Unlike animal hormones, auxin is not made in an endocrine gland. It is made by cells near the tips of plant shoots and roots. This is where the plant cells are dividing, as the plant grows.

All the time, new cells are being produced by the dividing region at the tip, and these new cells eventually find themselves further back from the tip as even newer cells are constantly made at the end. These slightly older cells do not divide, but they *do* grow. They grow by getting longer.

It is auxin that makes the cells get longer. The auxin made by the dividing cells diffuses backwards, away from the tip. Auxin stimulates cells to lengthen. Like animal hormones, auxin is eventually broken down by enzymes in the plant.

If light shines from one direction onto a plant, the auxin tends to accumulate on the shady side. The cells on this side therefore lengthen faster than those on the sunny side. This makes the shoot bend towards the light as it grows.

Using plant hormones

Auxin is only one of several plant hormones. There are many others, most of which can now be chemically synthesised. People who grow plants sometimes use plant hormones to increase the quantity or quality of their crops.

Some plant hormones are used as **selective weedkillers**. Auxin can be used in this way. When sprayed onto cereal crops, it is taken up by plants that have broad leaves, but not by the crop, which has narrow leaves. The weeds therefore take up the auxin in such large quantities that they 'outgrow themselves' and are killed, whereas the cereal crop is unharmed.

Another use of auxin is in **rooting cuttings**. Growers who want to produce many plants with identical characteristics to the parent plant can cut off a piece of the parent, dip the base into a 'hormone rooting powder', and place it in damp compost. The rooting powder contains auxin, which stimulates new roots to grow from the cut stem.

A hormone called **gibberellin** also has many uses. For example, it is sprayed onto bananas after they have been harvested, to stop them ripening too quickly. It is also used by growers of sugar cane, as it can help to increase its growth in low temperatures.

Summary

- Receptors are cells that detect stimuli. They are often part of a sense organ.
- The receptors in the eye respond to light, and they are situated in the retina. Light is focused onto the retina by the cornea and lens. The shape of the lens can be changed in order to focus light from objects at different distances; this is called accommodation.

  - The receptors in the retina are rods and cones. Rods are sensitive to dim light, and see in black and white. Cones are only sensitive to brighter light, and see in colour. Most cones are near the fovea, while most rods are in other parts of the retina.

- The nervous system is made up of the central nervous system (brain and spinal cord) and the peripheral nervous system (nerves and sense organs).
- Neurones carrying impulses from the CNS to effectors (muscles and glands) are called motor neurones. Those carrying impulses from sense organs to the CNS are called sensory neurones. The path along which an impulse passes from a receptor to the CNS and then to an effector is called a reflex arc.
- A reflex action is a fast, automatic response to a stimulus.

continued ...

- Voluntary actions are ones which we consciously decide to do. Involuntary actions are those which happen without us thinking about it.

- Invertebrates often show very simple and predictable behaviour patterns. One example is a taxis, in which the animal moves towards or away from a stimulus.

- Muscles are examples of effectors. In the upper arm, the biceps and triceps work antagonistically to raise and lower the arm at the elbow joint.

- Adrenaline is a hormone that is secreted in response to fear. It prepares the body for fight or flight.

- The misuse of drugs such as alcohol and heroin can have harmful effects both on the user and on society.

- Hormones secreted by plants include auxin, which is involved in the growth responses to light and gravity. These growth responses are called tropisms.

- Both animal and plant hormones can be used in food production. BST is used to increase milk production in cows. Gibberellin is used to increase growth of sugar cane.

Chapter 12

Reproduction

Living things may reproduce asexually, or sexually. Both plants and mammals use sexual reproduction, which involves gametes and fertilisation. Many plants and other organisms use asexual reproduction, or both sexual and asexual reproduction.

Asexual reproduction ▶

'Asexual' means 'not sexual'. In **asexual reproduction**, an organism simply grows a new organism from itself. Only one parent is involved. The new organism is genetically identical to its parent.

Figure 12.1 ▶
Asexual reproduction in a bacterium.

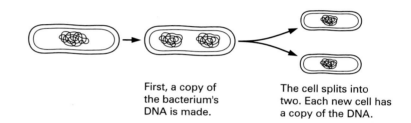

First, a copy of the bacterium's DNA is made.

The cell splits into two. Each new cell has a copy of the DNA.

Figure 12.2 ▶
Asexual reproduction in a fungus. This fungus is *Mucor*, a mould which sometimes grows on bread.

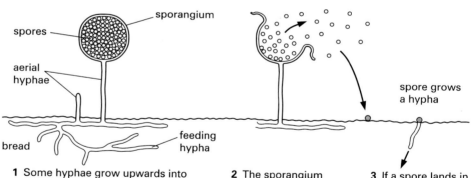

1 Some hyphae grow upwards into the air. A sporangium forms on top of an aerial hypha. Spores are formed inside the sporangium.

2 The sporangium bursts open, releasing the spores.

3 If a spore lands in a suitable place, it will grow into a new fungus.

Figure 12.3 ▶
Asexual reproduction in an Irish potato plant.

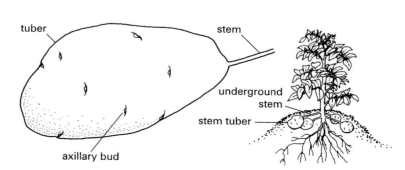

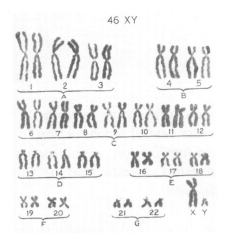

46 XY

▲ Figure 12.4
Chromosomes from a human male. The chromosomes have been arranged in their pairs, beginning with the largest. The sex chromosomes are at the bottom right.

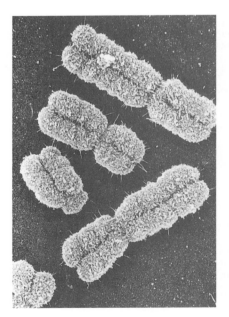

▲ Figure 12.5
A scanning electron micrograph (which shows things in three dimensions) of human chromosomes. You can see that each one is made of two chromatids lying side by side. The place where the chromatids are joined is the centromere.

Figures 12.1, 12.2 and 12.3 on the previous page show three different organisms reproducing asexually. **Bacteria** are made up of single cells. They reproduce by division, each cell splitting into two (Figure 12.1). At warm temperatures, around 35 °C, they may divide every 20 minutes.

Fungi can also reproduce asexually. The fungus shown in Figure 12.2 is a mould which grows on food, such as bread. Some of the hyphae (see page 10) grow upwards. At the tops of these hyphae, cells divide to produce **spores**, which are kept inside a **sporangium**. The sporangium bursts open, and the spores are scattered in the air, or carried on the feet of houseflies. If the spores land on a suitable food material, they will grow into a new fungus.

Irish potato plants reproduce asexually by producing **stem tubers** (Figure 12.3). As the plant grows, some stems grow down into the ground, instead of upwards. Food made in the leaves of the plant is transported to these stems. The stems grow swellings, called tubers, in which this food is stored in the form of sugar and starch. Eventually, the parent plant dies, leaving the tubers in the ground. In warm weather, the tubers will begin to sprout stems and roots, using the stored food materials. Each tuber grows into a complete new plant.

Mitosis

The kind of cell division that happens in asexual reproduction is called **mitosis**.

Inside the nucleus of every cell, there are threads of DNA called **chromosomes**, shown in Figures 12.4 and 12.5. Each chromosome is made up of many **genes**. The genes are a code or recipe for making the cell, and for the activities it will carry out.

In mitosis, each new cell gets a complete set of chromosomes, identical to the ones its parent cell had. This is why the organisms produced by asexual reproduction are identical to their parents. They have identical chromosomes and genes, so the instructions for making the new organism are just the same as the instructions for making the parent.

Before mitosis can happen, each thread of DNA, or chromosome, makes an exact copy of itself. This is called DNA replication. Mitosis can then begin. First, the chromosomes become shorter and fatter by coiling into a spiral. This is probably so that they do not get tangled up during mitosis. They become so short and fat that you can see them with a good light microscope.

When the chromosomes are visible, you can see that each one is made up of two threads. Each chromosome moves to the middle of the cell. Then the two threads separate, one going to each end of the cell. The cell then divides down the middle, making two new cells, each with one copy of each chromosome. Figure 12.6 shows a cell dividing by mitosis.

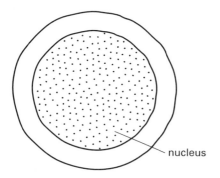

1 Resting cell. DNA replication takes place during this stage.

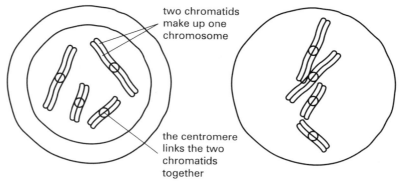

2 The chromosomes shorten. Each is in the form of two identical chromatids joined by a centromere.

3 The four chromosomes line up at the equator of the cell.

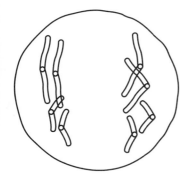

4 The centromeres split, allowing the chromatids to separate. The chromatids move to opposite ends of the cell.

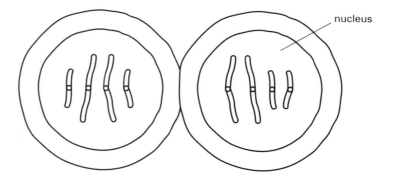

5 The nucleus divides and the cell splits into two. The chromosomes lengthen and eventually become invisible again.

▲ **Figure 12.6**
Mitosis.

Question

12.1 What will have to happen before the newly formed cells can divide again?

Sexual reproduction ▶

Sexual reproduction is more complicated than asexual reproduction. In sexual reproduction, an organism produces sex cells or **gametes**. In humans, for example, the gametes are eggs (produced by the female) and sperm (produced by the male). Two different gametes fuse together in a process called **fertilisation**, to form a new cell called a **zygote**. The zygote then divides repeatedly to form a new organism.

Often sexual reproduction involves two organisms, a male and a female. However, many organisms can reproduce sexually all by themselves. Many flowers, for example, produce male and female gametes in the same flower, and can fertilise themselves. This is still sexual reproduction, because it involves gametes and fertilisation.

The young organisms produced by sexual reproduction are not identical with each other, nor with their parents. There are two reasons for this. First, the gametes are made by a process called **meiosis**, which shuffles the chromosomes so that each gamete gets a slightly different collection of genes from all the other gametes. Second, fertilisation brings together chromosomes from two different parents, which means even more mixing of chromosomes. Figure 12.7 outlines the process of sexual reproduction.

▼ **Figure 12.7**
Sexual reproduction.

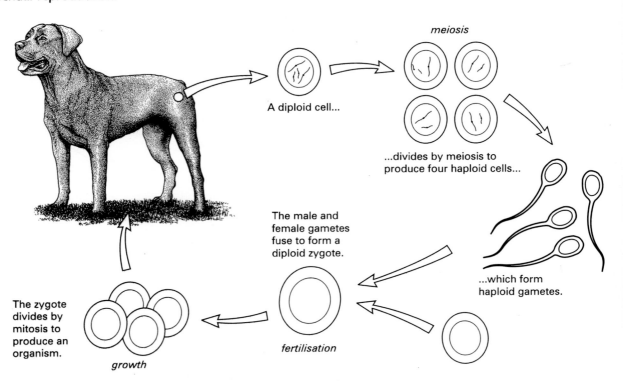

meiosis

A diploid cell...

...divides by meiosis to produce four haploid cells...

...which form haploid gametes.

The male and female gametes fuse to form a diploid zygote.

The zygote divides by mitosis to produce an organism.

fertilisation

growth

Question

12.2 In the form of a table, make a comparison between asexual and sexual reproduction.

Meiosis

Figure 12.8 shows how meiosis happens.

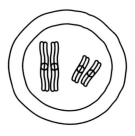

1 Each chromosome pairs up with one like itself.

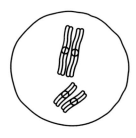

2 The pairs line up at the equator of the cell.

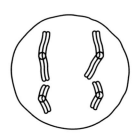

3 The individual chromosomes separate from their partners and move to opposite ends. The cell divides into two.

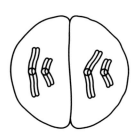

4 The chromosomes line up at the equators of the new cells, just as in mitosis.

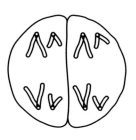

5 The chromatids separate and move to opposite ends of the cells.

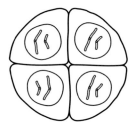

6 Each cell divides, forming four cells in total.

7 The cells differentiate to form gametes.

▲ **Figure 12.8**
Meiosis.

The purpose of cell division by meiosis is to produce new cells – the gametes – with *half* the normal number of chromosomes. This is necessary so that when two gametes fuse together, they will produce a cell with the correct number of chromosomes. In humans, for example, most cells have 46 chromosomes. Eggs and sperm have 23 each, so that when they fuse together they form a zygote with 46 chromosomes.

The 46 chromosomes in a human cell can be arranged into 23 pairs, as shown in Figure 12.4 on page 178. Each cell has *two of each kind* of chromosome. A cell like this is said to be **diploid**.

Before meiosis begins, each chromosome makes a copy of itself, just as in mitosis. Then, just as in mitosis, each chromosome coils and so becomes visible with a light microscope. But from then on the behaviour of the chromosomes in meiosis and mitosis is different.

Instead of each chromosome moving around on its own, as in mitosis, the chromosomes undergoing meiosis **pair up**. Each chromosome finds its matching partner, and lies very closely alongside it. In their pairs, the chromosomes move to the middle of the cell. They then separate from their partners, and move to opposite ends of the cell. The cell then divides into two. Each of the new cells now has only *one of each kind* of chromosome. It is said to be **haploid**.

Each of the haploid cells now divides again, in the same way as in mitosis. So, at the end of meiosis, there are four new cells for every one parent cell.

These new cells also carry different combinations of genes from each other. When the chromosomes pair up, bits of them often get mixed up with each other, so that each chromosome may end up with some of its partner's genes. Also, when the pairs of chromosomes line up, each pair can be either way up. This means that there are many possible groupings of chromosomes in the new cells that are made. Each gamete will have a different combination of genes from every other gamete. Therefore each offspring will be different from every other offspring.

The female reproductive organs

Sexual reproduction in humans ▶

Figure 12.9 opposite shows the reproductive organs of a woman. The eggs, which are the female gametes, are made in the two **ovaries**. The eggs are made by meiosis, from diploid cells in the ovaries.

Once a month, one egg leaves one of the ovaries. This is called **ovulation**. The egg is swept into the funnel-shaped opening of the **oviduct**, or **Fallopian tube**, by the movement of cilia which line the tube. The tiny egg, only about the size of a full stop on this page, is swept very slowly along the oviduct. It takes several days for it to move all the way to the **uterus** or **womb**.

The uterus is the place where a baby will develop if the egg is fertilised. The wall of the uterus has two layers. The inner lining is a soft, spongy layer containing many

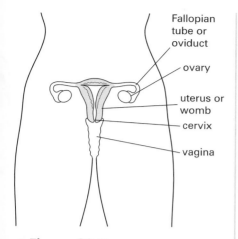

▲ Figure 12.9
The reproductive organs of a human female.

blood vessels. These blood vessels can supply a developing embryo with food and oxygen. The outer layer is mostly muscle. This can contract to push the baby out when it is ready to be born.

At the base of the uterus is a ring of muscle called the **cervix**. The cervix separates the uterus from the **vagina**, which opens to the outside of the body.

The menstrual cycle

Normally, one egg leaves one of the ovaries once a month. When this happens, the inner lining of the uterus becomes ready to receive the fertilised egg. It becomes full of tiny blood vessels and is soft and spongy. However, if the egg is not fertilised, then this thick lining is not needed. It gradually breaks down, and is lost through the vagina over a period of about four to seven days. This is called **menstruation**. It happens roughly once a month, in women between the ages of about 12 and 50.

Figure 12.10 shows the timing of these events. This is called the **menstrual cycle**. The exact timing, and the length of the cycle, varies between different women. It may also vary in any one woman, especially if she is ill or has changes in her life such as a long journey.

Figure 12.10 ▶
The human menstrual cycle. The numbers in the circle represent days.

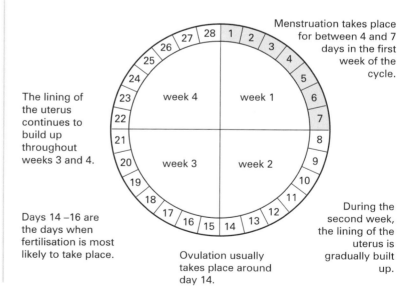

Hormones and the menstrual cycle

The menstrual cycle is controlled by hormones. Two of these hormones are produced by the ovaries. They are called **oestrogen** and **progesterone**. Their levels in the blood at different stages of the menstrual cycle are shown in Figure 12.11.

Figure 12.11 ▶
Oestrogen and progesterone levels through the menstrual cycle.

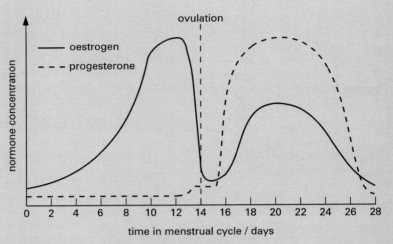

Progesterone levels are low for the first 14 days of the cycle. After ovulation, the ovary begins to secrete progesterone. Progesterone is secreted at this time because it causes the lining of the uterus to thicken, ready to receive the fertilised egg. If the egg is not fertilised, the ovary stops secreting progesterone. The fall in progesterone levels causes the lining of the uterus to break away, so that menstruation occurs.

Oestrogen levels, like progesterone levels, are low during menstruation. Then the ovaries begin to secrete oestrogen. Oestrogen levels gradually build up, until they reach their maximum at around 12–13 days after menstruation began. The high level of oestrogen affects the pituitary gland, and this in turn produces hormones which cause ovulation to occur. Ovulation occurs around the 14th day.

The levels of oestrogen start to fall just before ovulation, as the ovary slows down its secretion of this hormone. It begins secreting it again after ovulation, but the levels do not rise as high as earlier in the cycle. The function of oestrogen in this second half of the cycle is to work together with progesterone, to build up the lining of the uterus.

The male reproductive system

Figure 12.12 shows the reproductive system of a man. The spermatozoa, or **sperm**, which are the male gametes, are made in the two **testes**. The sperm are made by meiosis, from diploid cells in the testes. The testes also have the function of producing the hormone **testosterone**.

Figure 12.12 ▶
The reproductive organs of a
human male.

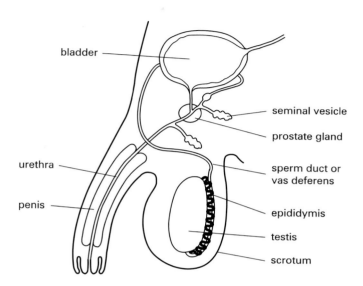

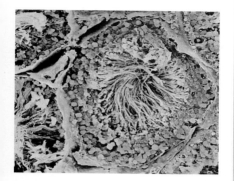

▲ Figure 12.13
A section across a seminiferous tubule in a testis. The sperm can be seen in the centre of the tubule, their heads towards the outside and their tails towards the middle.

The testes are enclosed within a sac of skin, called the **scrotum**. Each testis is made up of a tangle of coiled tubes. Figure 12.13 shows a cross-section of one of these tubes. You can see the sperm collecting in the centre of the tube.

The tubes in the testis all lead to the **epididymis**, where the sperm can be stored. A tube called the **sperm duct** or **vas deferens** leads from the epididymis. The sperm ducts from the two testes join with each other just below the bladder. They both lead into the **urethra**, which is also the tube that carries urine from the bladder to the outside. When sperm are passing through the urethra, a valve closes to stop urine from passing through at the same time.

Close to where the sperm ducts meet the urethra, there are two glands. One is called the **prostate gland**, and the other the **seminal vesicle**. Both these glands make fluids in which the sperm can swim. The fluids contain sugars, to provide energy for the sperm. The sperm and the fluids together form **semen**.

The urethra passes to the outside of the body through the **penis**.

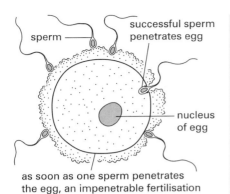

as soon as one sperm penetrates
the egg, an impenetrable fertilisation
membrane stops other sperm
getting in

▲ **Figure 12.14**
Fertilisation.

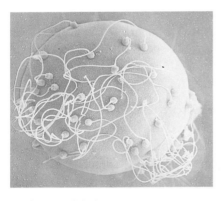

▲ **Figure 12.15**
Fertilisation. This takes place in
the oviduct (Fallopian tube). The
actual moment of fertilisation is
when the nucleus of the sperm
reaches the nucleus of the egg.

Fertilisation

During sexual intercourse, the blood pressure is increased
in the penis. This causes the penis to become stiff and
erect. It can then be inserted into the woman's vagina.

Stimulation of the end of the penis causes the muscles
along the sperm ducts to contract in a wave-like motion.
These contractions squeeze sperm past the seminal vesicle
and prostate gland, where fluid is added to them. The
muscular contractions force the semen out of the urethra.
This is called **ejaculation**. Millions of sperm leave the
urethra in a single ejaculation.

The semen is deposited at the top of the vagina, just
below the cervix. The sperm now set out on a hazardous
journey towards the egg. They have to swim, using their
tails, through the cervix, and then through the film of
moisture lining the wall of the uterus.

If there is an egg in one of the oviducts, some of the
sperm may eventually reach it. They are attracted towards
it by the chemicals it produces – it is as though they
'smell' their way to the egg. An egg only lives for a few
days after its release from the ovary, so if it has already
reached the uterus by the time the sperm find it, they
will be too late to fertilise it. Fertilisation will only
occur if the egg is still 'fresh', which means it will be
in the oviduct.

Figures 12.14 and 12.15 show how a sperm fertilises an
egg. Many sperm cluster around the egg, each trying to
force its way through the outer covering. Each sperm
has a sac of enzymes at the tip of its head, which can
digest a way into the egg. Once one sperm has succeeded
in penetrating the membrane of the egg, a lightning-
quick change takes place around the egg, producing
a **fertilisation membrane**. This stops any more sperm
getting in.

The successful sperm enters the egg. The nucleus of
the sperm and the nucleus of the egg fuse together.
This is **fertilisation**.

Question

12.3 Name the part(s) of the reproductive system in which each of the following occurs:
  a meiosis
  b production of sperm
  c production of eggs
  d addition of fluid to sperm to form semen
  e fertilisation
  f development of the embryo

Implantation and development

The fertilised egg is called a **zygote**. As both the egg and the sperm were haploid cells with 23 chromosomes each, the zygote is a diploid cell, with 46 chromosomes.

The zygote begins to divide very soon after fertilisation. It divides by mitosis. It does this over and over again, until a ball of cells is formed. The whole ball is no bigger than the original egg cell. It is called an **embryo**.

While it is dividing, the ball of cells moves slowly down the oviduct until it reaches the uterus. Here, about seven days after fertilisation, the tiny embryo sinks into the soft lining of the uterus. This is called **implantation**.

You have seen how, if the egg is *not* fertilised, the lining of the uterus breaks down and is lost during menstruation. This does not happen if the egg is fertilised. This is because the ovary keeps on secreting the hormone progesterone. The progesterone maintains the lining of the uterus.

The placenta

Some of the cells of the embryo grow into projections, or **villi**, which fix into the wall of the uterus. Other cells form a bag, called the **amnion**. But most of the cells divide and divide, eventually producing a **fetus**. Figure 12.16 (overpage) shows a fetus in the uterus.

The villi that grow from the embryo become firmly attached to the wall of the uterus. The uterus also grows projections. The two sets of projections, one from the embryo and the other from the mother's uterus, grow closely together, and form the **placenta**. The placenta gets bigger and bigger as the fetus grows, eventually reaching a diameter of about 30 cm when the baby is born.

Inside the villi on the fetus's side of the placenta, there are millions of tiny blood capillaries. The blood in these comes from the fetus, inside two blood vessels called the **umbilical arteries**, which run inside the **umbilical cord**. The blood is taken back to the fetus inside the **umbilical vein**. The placenta is shown in Figure 12.17.

Figure 12.16 ▶
A human fetus just before birth.

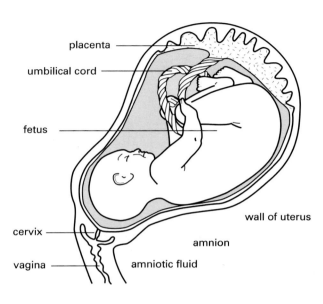

placenta

umbilical cord

fetus

cervix

vagina

wall of uterus

amnion

amniotic fluid

▼ Figure 12.17
The placenta.

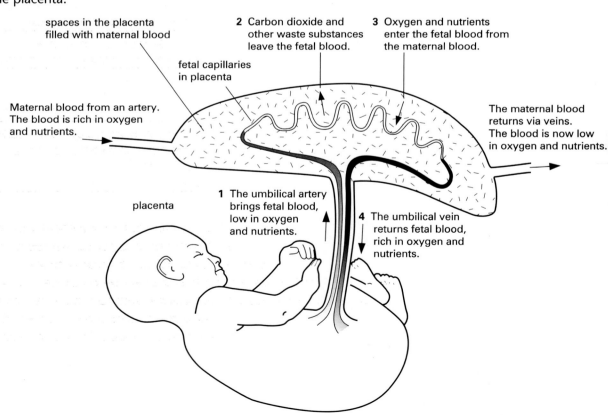

spaces in the placenta filled with maternal blood

2 Carbon dioxide and other waste substances leave the fetal blood.

3 Oxygen and nutrients enter the fetal blood from the maternal blood.

fetal capillaries in placenta

Maternal blood from an artery. The blood is rich in oxygen and nutrients.

The maternal blood returns via veins. The blood is now low in oxygen and nutrients.

placenta

1 The umbilical artery brings fetal blood, low in oxygen and nutrients.

4 The umbilical vein returns fetal blood, rich in oxygen and nutrients.

On the mother's side of the placenta, the projections contain large blood spaces filled with the mother's blood. The mother's and fetus's blood do not come into direct contact with one another. If this did happen, it could make the mother and the fetus very ill. This is because the mother and her baby might have different blood groups and their blood cells might clump together if mixed.

However, the mother's and fetus's blood are brought as close together as possible in the placenta. This allows many substances to pass between them. This happens by diffusion. Table 12.1 lists some of the substances that diffuse across the placenta.

Table 12.1 ▶
Substances that diffuse across the placenta

Type of substance	To fetus from mother	To mother from fetus
Respiratory gases	Oxygen	Carbon dioxide
Soluble nutrients	Amino acids Glucose Fatty acids Glycerol Vitamins Minerals Water	
Disease-preventing substances	Antibodies Antibiotics	
Nitrogenous excretory substances		Urea
Potentially harmful substances	Alcohol, nicotine and other drugs Viruses Bacteria	

As well as allowing the transfer of substances between the mother and her fetus, the placenta has another very important function. It secretes the hormones **progesterone** and **oestrogen**. These hormones keep the uterus lining in good order. They also stimulate growth of milk-producing tissue in the woman's breasts. In addition, they prevent any more eggs being released from the ovaries.

12.4 Discuss the ways in which the structure and function of the small intestine and the placenta are similar to each other.

Supplement

The amnion

A thin, but very strong, sac surrounds the fetus while it is growing inside the uterus. This is the **amnion**, or **amniotic sac**. The sac secretes a fluid called **amniotic fluid**. The developing fetus is completely surrounded by this fluid.

The fluid supports the fetus. It also protects the fetus from mechanical shock. It does not matter that the fetus is totally submerged in fluid, because it gets all its oxygen from the placenta, via the umbilical cord.

Ante-natal care

'Ante-natal' means 'before birth'. A pregnant woman can do several things to take care of herself and her developing fetus. This can help the fetus to develop into a healthy baby, and can make the birth easier for both the mother and her baby.

Diet is especially important during pregnancy. Table 12.2 shows the dietary requirements of a non-pregnant and a pregnant woman.

Table 12.2 ▶

Nutrients needed for pregnant and non-pregnant women.

Nutrient	Requirements for non-pregnant woman	Requirements for pregnant woman
Protein/ g	55	60
Calcium/ mg	500	1200
Iron/ mg	12	14
Vitamin C/ mg	30	60
Total energy/ kJ	9000	10000

The growing fetus needs plenty of **protein**, for building new cells, and the mother will need to eat more protein than usual, to provide for both herself and her baby. To a lesser extent, her intake of **carbohydrate** and **fat** will also need to increase. This is because she will need extra energy to move herself and her growing fetus around, and because the fetus itself needs an energy supply.

A good intake of **minerals** is especially important during pregnancy. In particular, **calcium** is needed to build the fetus's bones. If the mother does not eat enough calcium, then calcium may move from her own bones and teeth into the baby. A pregnant woman should have extra dental check-ups to make sure that her teeth remain healthy. **Iron** is also important, to make extra haemoglobin. This is partly for the fetus's blood, and partly to make extra blood for the mother. During pregnancy, a woman's total volume of blood increases by about 20%.

The increased need for calcium can normally be met by taking care with diet, such as drinking plenty of milk or eating milk products such as cheese. The increased need for iron is harder to achieve by diet alone, and many pregnant women are prescribed iron tablets by their doctor.

Drugs should, wherever possible, be avoided during pregnancy. Almost every drug a pregnant woman takes can cross the placenta and enter the fetus's bloodstream. A drug that may not harm the mother may cause considerable harm to a developing fetus. This is especially likely to happen during the first 11 weeks of pregnancy, when the different organs of the fetus are being formed.

For example, **smoking** during pregnancy can result in a smaller, less healthy baby. This is because the nicotine and carbon monoxide from cigarette smoke can cross the placenta. The carbon monoxide reduces the amount of oxygen supplied to the fetus (see page 130). Nicotine makes the fetus's heart beat too quickly, which may put extra strain on its circulatory system.

Alcohol can also be harmful to the fetus. A woman who drinks regularly and heavily throughout her pregnancy runs a greater than normal risk of giving birth prematurely, or of giving birth to a baby with some form of abnormality.

Other drugs that may normally be prescribed for illnesses by a doctor may also be unsuitable for use during pregnancy. A pregnant woman's doctor will be able to advise her on this.

Diseases that the mother suffers during pregnancy may have very damaging effects on a fetus. One such disease is **German measles** or **rubella**. This disease is caused by a virus. If a pregnant woman catches rubella, the virus crosses the placenta and infects the fetus. It can do great harm, frequently causing deafness and other disabilities. In many countries, teenage girls are vaccinated against rubella, to make sure that they do not get the disease if and when they become pregnant, later in life.

Exercise is especially important during pregnancy. Exercise helps the mother to keep fit, which may help her with the birth of her baby. It also helps to keep her circulatory system working efficiently, and may help her to feel cheerful and in control of her pregnancy. Good exercises include walking and swimming.

Birth

The baby is normally ready to be born about 9 months after fertilisation. A few weeks before this, it usually turns over in the uterus, so that it is head downwards.

Birth begins with the muscles of the uterus wall contracting slowly and rhythmically. Sometimes, this results in the amnion breaking, releasing the amniotic fluid. This may be the first sign that birth is about to begin. Sometimes, however, the amnion does not break until the contractions have been going on for some time.

To begin with, the contractions are quite gentle, and there is quite a long time between each one. Gradually, the contractions become stronger and closer together. They feel like strong cramp pains. The mother can help to make them less painful by relaxing, and breathing in a special way, which she may have been taught by her doctor or midwife. She will be able to keep moving around and being active for much of the first part of the birth.

The muscular contractions slowly cause the opening of the cervix to become wider. After several hours, when the cervix is wide enough to allow the baby's head to pass through, the contractions change. Now they begin to push the baby down through the cervix. The mother may be able to help actively with this, helping to push the baby out. This usually takes around 45 minutes.

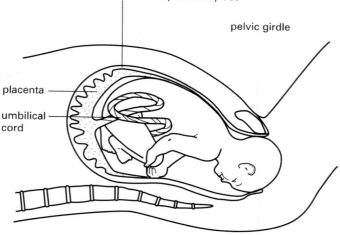

Figure 12.18 ▶ Birth.

muscular uterus wall contracts to push baby out

pelvic girdle

placenta

umbilical cord

cervix and vagina widen to allow baby through

Once the head of the baby has been pushed out through the cervix and vagina, as in Figure 12.18, the rest of its body slides out quite quickly. Suddenly, the baby's environment has completely changed. From being inside a warm, protective body, floating in the amniotic fluid, it finds itself in the outside world, surrounded by air. It takes its first breath, and its lungs inflate for the first time.

The baby is still attached to the placenta by the umbilical cord. The midwife now cuts the cord, and ties or clamps it to prevent infection entering the baby through it. Cutting the cord does not hurt either the mother or the baby, as there are no nerves in it. After a short while, the placenta falls away from the mother's uterus, and passes out of her vagina as the afterbirth.

Supplement

Feeding a young baby

During pregnancy, progesterone and oestrogen cause the milk-producing tissue in the mother's breasts to grow. After the birth of the baby, this tissue begins to produce **milk**.

Human breast milk is the perfect food for a growing baby. It contains easily digestible proteins, fat, the sugar lactose, vitamins, and minerals such as calcium.

If the mother cannot breast feed her baby, she can bottle feed. Baby milk powder is manufactured to be as similar to human breast milk as possible. It is mixed with boiled, cooled water and warmed to body temperature before being given to the baby.

However, bottle feeding is very much second best compared with breast feeding. Human breast milk contains not only the nutrients mentioned above, but also antibodies which can help the baby to fight off infections. Very young babies do not have well-developed immune systems, and are quite susceptible to infectious disease. Moreover, there is always the chance that milk given in a bottle may contain harmful bacteria, and great care has to be taken in its preparation to make sure that everything is spotlessly clean. Breast feeding can also help to build a close bond between mother and baby. Another important consideration is cost. A breast-feeding mother does have to eat more than she would if she were not feeding her baby, but the cost of the extra food she needs is likely to be far less than the cost of milk powder.

Family planning

Many couples wish to choose the time when they have their children, or to limit the number of children they have. A couple can use **family planning** to make sure that they only have the number of children they want, and that they do not have children at a time when they will not be able to care for them properly.

There are many methods of family planning. There are **natural**, **chemical**, **mechanical** and **surgical** methods. Every couple should be able to choose one of these methods which is suitable for them to use.

Natural methods Natural methods of family planning are the most widely used methods of family planning in the world today. They can be very successful if used carefully.

The most successful method of family planning is not to have sexual intercourse at all. This method is 100% successful in preventing pregnancy! However, it is not suitable for most couples, who may prefer to use the **rhythm method**.

The rhythm method depends on a woman understanding her menstrual cycle, and making sure that she does not have sexual intercourse during the time of the month when an egg is in her oviduct. She can be taught how to recognise the signs that ovulation is about to occur. These signs include a change in the natural secretions in her vagina, and a small but distinct rise in her body temperature.

If the woman is well taught, and if the couple always avoid sexual intercourse in the days around the time of ovulation, then this is a very reliable method of family planning. It also has the great advantage that it is an entirely natural method, and so is acceptable to people of all religions and cultures. However, not all women are able to tell exactly when ovulation occurs, perhaps because they have not been properly taught, or because their signs are not very clear, or because their menstrual cycle is rather irregular and unpredictable. Pregnancy can also result if the couple do not rigorously avoid sexual intercourse during the 'danger' time of the cycle.

Chemical methods These methods involve the use of chemicals, or drugs, which prevent ovulation, or which prevent the fertilised egg from implanting in the uterus.

The **contraceptive pill** is a very widely used, and very effective, method of family planning. It contains the hormones oestrogen and progesterone, which prevent an egg from being released from the ovary. If there is no egg, then there can be no fertilisation.

A woman on 'the pill' has to remember to take it every day for three weeks. She then stops taking it for one week, during which she will menstruate. If she forgets her pill, there is a chance that she may ovulate and become pregnant. However, so long as she takes it regularly, this is a very effective method of preventing pregnancy.

Some women do not like taking the pill, because they suffer from unpleasant side effects such as weight gain. Also, some women run a slightly greater risk of suffering dangerous circulatory diseases, such as strokes, if they are on the pill. For this reason, the pill can normally only be obtained on prescription from a doctor, and the woman is given regular check-ups to make sure that she stays healthy.

Another form of chemical family planning is the so-called **'morning-after' pill**. This pill also contains hormones. It is taken by a woman *after* she has had intercourse, and it works by preventing the fertilised egg from implanting in the uterus. It is not a pill to be taken regularly. It is most useful if a woman has had

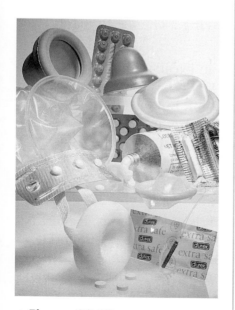

▲ **Figure 12.19**
A range of contraceptives.

intercourse without using any other kind of family planning, and fears that she might become pregnant. It will work up to several days after intercourse has taken place. However, no woman should rely on this pill as a normal method of family planning – it is really just an 'emergency' measure.

A third type of chemical family planning is the use of **spermicidal cream**. This is a soft, creamy substance that kills sperm. It can be put inside the woman's vagina before she has sexual intercourse. It is not entirely effective on its own, but can be used together with a mechanical form of family planning such as a condom or sheath (see below). It is important to realise that it is quite useless to use spermicidal cream *after* sexual intercourse has taken place, because by then many sperm will already be well on their way towards the oviducts.

Mechanical methods These methods of family planning use some kind of barrier to prevent fertilisation or implantation.

Perhaps the best known mechanical method is the **condom** or sheath. A condom is a piece of stretchy, impermeable material which is pulled over the erect penis. The condom has a space at the tip to collect semen. The condom provides a complete barrier between the man's penis and the woman's vagina, so that sexual intercourse and ejaculation can take place without any sperm having a chance to enter the woman's body.

Properly used, a condom is an excellent and very reliable method of family planning. It also has the great advantage that it not only prevents sperm, but also viruses and bacteria, from passing between the man and the woman. It is therefore a good safeguard against the transfer of HIV, and other viruses and bacteria which may cause sexually transmitted diseases. These diseases are described on pages 199–202.

It is important that a condom is used properly. It must be put on before any semen leaves the man's penis, and it must not be taken off until there is no chance of any further contact between the man's penis and the woman's vagina. Care must be taken that the condom does not slide off as the penis is withdrawn from the vagina.

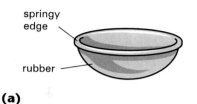

springy
edge

rubber

(a)

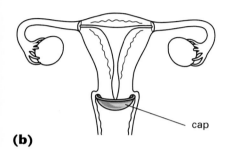

cap

(b)

▲ **Figure 12.20**
(a) A cap **(b)** A cap in position.

A condom may also become leaky if it is kept too long before use and it must *never* be used more than once.

Women can use a **femidom**, which is similar to a condom but is placed inside the vagina rather than over the penis.

Another mechanical method is the **cap**. This is a circular piece of rubber with a spring around its edge, which fits over the woman's cervix, as shown in Figure 12.20. Spermicidal cream can be put around the edge, to make doubly sure that no sperm can get past it. This is quite a reliable method of family planning if used carefully. A woman needs to have a cap of the right size, to fit her cervix, so she will need to go to her doctor when she first decides to use one. After that, however, she can easily insert and take out her cap by herself.

A third mechanical method is the **intra-uterine device** or **IUD**. This is a coil, made of copper or plastic, which fits inside the uterus, as shown in Figure 12.21. It is inserted by a doctor, and can be left inside the uterus for many months. It is an effective method of family planning, but some women find that it has unpleasant side effects, such as making their periods heavier than usual. It can also occasionally make it more difficult for a woman to conceive after it has been removed, so it is normally only recommended for women who already have as many children as they want.

Figure 12.21 ▶
An IUD in position. The IUD is put into the uterus, through the vagina, inside a small tube which holds it straight. When the tube is removed, the IUD springs into the shape shown in the diagram.

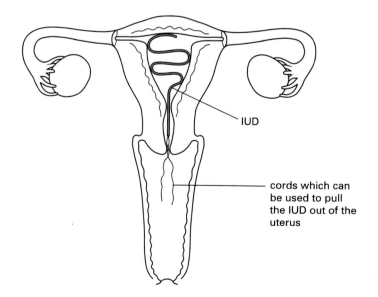

IUD

cords which can be used to pull the IUD out of the uterus

Surgical methods When a couple have as many children as they want, they may decide that one of them should have surgery to ensure that they will not have any more. This type of surgery is called **sterilisation**.

A woman can have her **oviducts** cut and sealed, so that no eggs can pass down them to the uterus, and no sperm can pass up them to fertilise an egg. A man can have his **sperm ducts** cut and sealed, so that no sperm can pass down them. The operation is slightly easier on a man than a woman. Both these methods are very reliable in preventing pregnancy, and mean that the couple can forget about family planning for the rest of their lives. However, once done it is not usually possible to reverse the operation, and anyone choosing these surgical methods of sterilisation should be certain that they are never going to want to have more children.

Question

12.5 Draw up a table summarising the different methods of family planning. Include brief descriptions of the advantages and disadvantages of each method, as well as an explanation of how it works.

Supplement

Increasing fertility

While many people wish to avoid having children, there are others who want to have children but cannot. There are many reasons for this. Perhaps the woman does not release eggs, or has blocked oviducts. Perhaps the man does not produce enough healthy sperm.

If the problem is the lack of egg production, the woman may be prescribed **hormones**, or 'fertility drugs', to make her ovulate. A hormone often used is called follicle-stimulating hormone (FSH). Just the right amount of drugs must be given, or she may produce several eggs at once, becoming pregnant with twins, triplets or even more babies at once.

If the problem is with her oviducts, or with the activity of the man's sperm, then *in vitro* **fertilisation** may be used. '*In vitro*' means 'in glass', and this refers to the fact that the fertilisation is made to take place in glassware such as

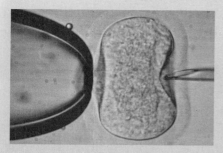

Figure 12.22

In vitro fertilisation. Usually, sperm are added to eggs in a Petri dish, and left to fertilise the egg themselves. The technique shown here, however is a relatively new one, only tried out for the first time in 1993. The sperm are actually injected into the egg. You can see the egg in the middle of the picture, being held in place by a pipette on the left. The sperm are in the needle on the right.

Petri dishes. People sometimes call this 'test tube fertilisation', although test tubes are not really used.

First, the woman is given hormones, such as FSH, so that she produces a lot of eggs. These are removed from her ovaries, and placed in a sterile dish with some of her partner's sperm. Fertilisation happens in the dish, and two or three of the resulting zygotes are then placed into her uterus. If all goes well, at least one of these will implant into her uterus in the normal way, and she will give birth normally in nine months' time.

In some cases, the man's sperm may not be active at all, so that it is impossible for him to fertilise his partner's eggs. The couple may then choose to use sperm from a donor. Normally, the identity of the donor is kept secret. The donor sperm may be inserted into the woman's vagina, so that fertilisation can occur in the normal way. This is called **artificial insemination**. Alternatively, *in vitro* fertilisation may be used.

There is much argument about whether these methods of allowing couples to have children are right. Some people think that, with the human population growing almost out of control, couples should not be helped to have children. Moreover, some of these methods involve great expense, and it can be argued that money spent on this would be better spent in curing people of diseases. However, others think that a couple who desperately want children should be helped if at all possible.

Sexually transmitted diseases

Sexually transmitted diseases are caused by bacteria or viruses which pass from one person to another during sexual intercourse. Two such diseases are **gonorrhoea** and **AIDS**.

Gonorrhoea is caused by a bacterium. The bacterium lives and breeds in the linings of the male or female reproductive organs. It needs moisture and a temperature of around 37 °C to survive, and so can normally only be passed on during sexual intercourse; it cannot live on lavatory seats, for example.

Gonorrhoea is a serious disease, because if left untreated it can cause great damage to the urinary and reproductive organs, and may cause sterility. It can also cause eye infection in a baby born to a mother with the disease, because the bacteria can get into the baby's eyes as it is born.

The symptoms of gonorrhoea are easier to spot in a man than in a woman. A man will probably develop a sore on his penis, and will have a discharge from his urethra and pain when passing urine. A woman, however, may show little or no signs in the early stages, except perhaps a discharge from her vagina; however, this discharge may not be noticeably different from her normal vaginal discharge. It is therefore very important that, if a man is diagnosed as having gonorrhoea, his sexual partner or partners are tested as soon as possible.

Gonorrhoea is easy to treat. The patient takes a course of antibiotics, which are drugs that kill bacteria inside the body. However, the number of people with gonorrheoa is still increasing in many countries, including developed ones such as the United States of America. The spread of gonorrhoea could be reduced if:

- people reduced the number of sexual partners they have, ideally remaining faithful to just one person

- people used condoms, which stop the bacterium from passing from one person to another

- people were treated promptly with antibiotics as soon as infection was suspected.

AIDS is caused by HIV, the **human immunodeficiency virus**. The virus lives in body fluids, such as blood and fluids in the reproductive tract. It is unable to survive for any length of time outside the body, and so can only be passed from one person to another by direct contact between their blood, or fluids in the reproductive tract.

The virus lives and breeds inside lymphocytes, the white blood cells of the immune system. It may live inside the body for many years before it begins to produce the symptoms of the disease **acquired immune deficiency syndrome**, or **AIDS**.

HIV prevents the lymphocytes from defending the body against disease, and a person with AIDS is very vulnerable to infection from other viruses or bacteria. Eventually, one or more of these infections causes death.

There is no cure for AIDS. All over the world, scientists are trying to find a vaccine to protect people against infection, or drugs to kill the virus inside the body. Much progress has been made, and a cure may one day be found. However, at the moment the only way to avoid AIDS is to make sure that you never become infected with the virus. Understanding how the virus is passed from one person to another can help you to do this.

The methods of transfer are:

- sexual intercourse with someone infected with the virus
- blood transfusions using blood containing the virus
- injections with needles previously used by someone with the virus.

Sexual intercourse is the most common method of infection with HIV. The more partners a person has, the greater risk they run of coming into contact with HIV. If each person had only one sexual partner, HIV would not spread at all.

The use of a condom can greatly decrease the risk of the virus passing from one person to another, although it is not 100% foolproof.

In the past, before people knew about HIV, infected blood was given to people in blood transfusions, and many people got AIDS as a result of this. However, in most countries people who offer to donate blood are now tested to make sure that they do not have HIV before their blood is accepted. In addition, all blood used in transfusions in most countries is now screened to make sure that it does not carry HIV, so that blood transfusions are now safe.

A needle used to give an injection to a person whose blood contains HIV may pick up some of the person's blood. If the same needle is then used by someone else, the HIV can pass into their blood. No one should ever be given an injection with an unsterilised needle. Just *cleaning* a needle is not enough – it needs to be *sterilised*. Better still, any used needle should be disposed of, and only brand new needles should be used for giving injections. People who inject drugs often share needles with one another, and this has been an important way in which AIDS has spread.

AIDS is still spreading fast. In some developing countries, 50% of the population are thought to be infected with HIV. It is very important that everyone learns about how the disease is spread, and takes steps to make sure that they do not do anything which runs a risk of infection with the virus.

Growth and development

Every person begins life as a fertilised egg, or zygote. Soon after fertilisation, the zygote starts dividing by mitosis. You may remember that mitosis produces two new cells from one cell, each cell containing identical genetical information. Mitosis continues throughout the nine months while the fetus is in the uterus, and after birth until it is an adult. From the one cell of the zygote, around one million million cells are eventually produced.

In the first few mitotic divisions of the zygote, the ball of cells does not get any bigger. It does not grow. The cell divisions simply make lots of small cells out of one larger one. Soon, however, the cells in the ball begin to grow, as they take in nutrients such as amino acids. A pattern of growth begins in which an individual cell grows to a certain size, and then divides to form two smaller cells. Each of these cells grows, and then divides again. **Growth** is therefore a result of *cell growth* and *cell division*. Growth can be defined as *an increase in size*.

As the ball of cells gets bigger, or grows, it also **develops**. To begin with, all the cells in the tiny ball are very similar. As time goes on, and more and more cells are produced, they begin to take on different shapes and functions. Organs, such as the brain, spinal cord, heart and bones, are formed. This all happens during the first 11 weeks after fertilisation. Development can be defined as an increase in complexity of an organism as it grows to adulthood.

Growth patterns

Both growth and development continue after the baby is born. Figure 12.23 opposite shows the pattern of growth in a boy. You can see that growth is fastest in the first year or two after birth, then slows down, then

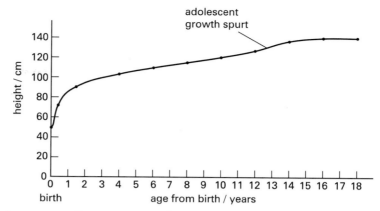

Figure 12.23 ▶
Growth curve for a boy.

shows another spurt as the person reaches their early teens. This time is called **adolescence**.

As well as rapid growth, rapid development takes place during adolescence. Adolescence is the time when a person changes from being a child to being a sexually mature person. The time at which the sex organs become mature is called **puberty**. The exact age at which puberty occurs varies quite a lot between different people, but is usually somewhere between the ages of 11 and 17. It generally happens earlier in girls than in boys.

During this time, the ovaries and testes begin secreting larger amounts of the sex hormones **oestrogen** (in girls) and **testosterone** (in boys). These two hormones cause many changes in the person's body. In a girl, the ovaries become fully mature and begin to release eggs, so that her periods begin. Her breasts develop, and her hips widen. In a boy, the testes become fully mature and begin to produce sperm. His shoulders become broader, his voice deepens, and he may begin to grow hair on his face. In both boys and girls, hair grows around the openings of the sexual organs, and under the arms, and sweat glands become more active. All of these features are called **secondary sexual characteristics**.

Sexual reproduction in flowering plants ▶

Flowering plants, like humans, reproduce sexually. They produce male and female gametes, which fuse to form a zygote. The zygote then grows into a new plant.

Flowers

The reproductive organs of a plant are in its **flowers**. Figure 12.24 (overpage) shows a typical flower.

The male gametes are produced inside the **anthers**. The female gametes are produced inside the **ovules**. As in a human, the gametes are made by meiosis.

However, unlike humans, most flowers produce both male and female gametes. They are said to be **hermaphrodite**. (There are some hermaphrodite animals. Earthworms and snails, for example, are hermaphrodite.)

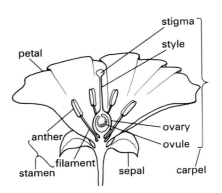

▲ **Figure 12.24**
An insect-pollinated flower.

Investigation 12.1

Investigating a flower

You are going to look carefully at the structure of a flower, and work out the function of each part. You can use Figure 12.24 to help you. However, each kind of flower is slightly different, so your flower will probably not be quite the same as the one in the diagram.

You will need:

- one or more flowers and flower buds from an insect-pollinated plant
- a hand lens or, if available, a microscope and some glass slides
- a sharp knife or a scalpel
- a tile or other surface on which to work.

Take care! Be careful with knives and scalpels.

As you work through the steps of this investigation, keep a record of what you see. You could make drawings, and annotate them with your answers to the questions. You might like to stick the parts of the flower into your notebook. You could write annotations next to the different parts of the flower.

1 Write down the name of the flower.

2 Look first at a flower bud. Find the **sepals** round the outside of it. Now find the sepals of an open flower. What do they look like? How many are there? What is their function?

3 Carefully remove all the sepals from a fully opened flower. The next layer is made up of a ring of **petals**. What do they look like? How many are there? What is their function?

4 Carefully remove all the petals. As you do so, look at the base of each one. You may be able to see a small gland called a **nectary**, which makes a sugary fluid called **nectar**. (You could also look for nectaries at the base of the stamens or around the ovary when you get to steps **5** and **6**.) In some flowers, there is enough nectar for you to be able to taste it – but do not try this unless your teacher tells you that it is safe to do so! What do you think is the function of the nectaries? Can you suggest why they are right at the base of the flower?

5 Once the petals have all been removed, you can clearly see the ring of **stamens**. The stamens are the male sexual organs

of the flower. Each stamen is made up of a stalk or **filament**, and an **anther**. **Pollen grains**, which contain the male gametes, are made in the anthers. Can you see any pollen grains on the anthers? If you can, then look at them with a hand lens or under a microscope. How big are they? What do they look like? Are there any pollen grains on the anthers inside a flower bud?

6 Carefully remove all the stamens. You are left with the female sexual organs of the flower, the carpel. Look for one or more **stigmas**, which are on top of the **ovaries**, to which they are attached by the **style**. (In some flowers, the style is very short, while others have long styles.) Look at a stigma using a hand lens, or a microscope. What does it look like? Are there any pollen grains on it? If so, can you suggest how they might have got there?

7 Using a sharp knife or a scalpel, carefully cut open the ovary. Look for tiny round **ovules** inside it. The female gametes are made inside the ovules. How many ovules are there? What do they look like?

Pollination

Sexual reproduction depends on a male gamete fusing with a female gamete. In humans, the male gametes can swim to the female gametes. But in flowers, the male gametes are in the pollen grains in the anthers, while the female gametes are in the ovules in the ovary. The male gametes cannot swim to the female gametes, because there is air, not liquid, between them. The male gametes would dry out long before they reached a female gamete.

The journey of a male gamete to a female gamete in a flower takes place in two stages. First, the male gametes are carried, inside the pollen grains, to a stigma. Second, the pollen grain grows a tube from the stigma to the ovule, through which the male gamete can safely travel to the female gamete.

The first stage of this journey, in which pollen grains are transferred from anther to stigma, is called **pollination**.

Insect and wind pollination

In the flower you looked at in the investigation, pollination is done by **insects**. The insects come to the flower to collect nectar or pollen for food. The coloured petals, and perhaps a scent, advertise the presence of

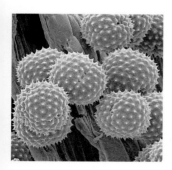

▲ **Figure 12.25**
Pollen grains from ragweed. The spikes help them to stick to the bodies of insects.

the food, attracting insects to the flower. As they push down to the nectaries, they brush past the anthers. Pollen grains stick to their bodies. When the insects feed at a second flower, some of the pollen grains may be brushed on to the stigma.

Some flowers do not use insects for pollination. They rely on the **wind**. These flowers do not need to produce nectar, nor do they need brightly coloured petals. Wind-pollinated flowers are usually dull green or brown. Their anthers and stigmas hang outside the flower, to catch the wind. Figure 12.26 shows wind-pollinated flowers. They often produce larger amounts of pollen than insect-pollinated flowers, to allow for the wastage that occurs; the wind, unlike an insect, will not carry the pollen directly to another flower.

▲ **Figure 12.26(a)**
Sorghum flowers. They are wind pollinated. They have fluffy stigmas – mostly visible on the left here, but a few on the right as well – and dangling anthers.

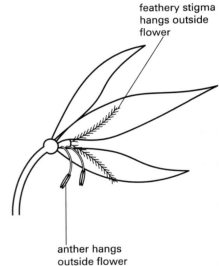

feathery stigma hangs outside flower

anther hangs outside flower

▲ **Figure 12.26(b)**
A wind-pollinated flower.

Question

12.6 Draw up a table to compare the structure of insect-pollinated and wind-pollinated flowers. You could include a column giving a brief explanation of the reason for each difference you describe.

Pollen may be carried from an anther to a stigma on the *same* plant. This is called **self-pollination**. Alternatively, it may be carried to a stigma on a *different* plant, of the same species. This is called **cross-pollination** (Figure 12.27).

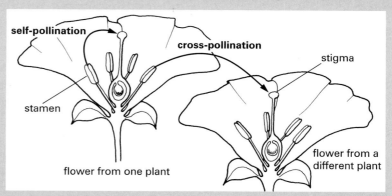

Figure 12.27 ▶
Self- and cross-pollination.

Fertilisation

Having arrived on a stigma, a pollen grain will begin to grow a **tube** (Figure 12.28). It is stimulated to do this by chemicals, which usually include sugars, secreted by the stigma. Different species of flowers secrete slightly different combinations of chemicals, so pollen grains will normally only grow tubes if they land on a stigma of their own species.

The tube grows right down through the style, towards an ovule inside the ovary. Enzymes are secreted from the tip of the pollen tube and these enzymes digest the tissues of the style. Inside the tube, the male gamete travels to the ovule. The male gamete is not a complete cell like a sperm cell; it is simply a haploid nucleus.

When the tube, and the male gamete inside it, arrive at an ovule, the male gamete enters the ovule through a small hole in its outer covering, and fuses with the female gamete. Fertilisation has occurred. A diploid zygote has been formed. Just as in humans, this diploid zygote will now divide repeatedly by mitosis, producing an embryo plant.

Seeds and fruits

Once fertilisation has taken place, many changes take place in the flower. All the parts that are no longer needed, such as sepals, petals and stamens, often wither and fall off.

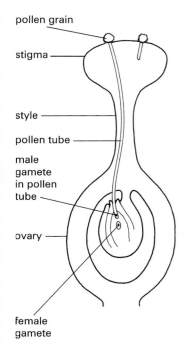

▲ **Figure 12.28**
Fertilisation in a flower. The moment of fertilisation is when the male nucleus fuses with the female nucleus in the ovule.

Each ovule that has been fertilised begins to develop into a **seed**. Inside the seed, the zygote forms an **embryo plant**. Food is brought to the developing seed from the rest of the plant, and is stored inside it, in structures called **cotyledons**. The outside wall of the ovule grows thicker and harder, becoming the **testa** of the seed. The tiny hole in this outside wall, through which the pollen tube entered, is still there; it is called the **micropyle**.

Once the seed has grown to its full size, it begins to lose water. The water moves out of the seed, back into the parent plant. The seed becomes dehydrated. Metabolic reactions in the seed stop; it is said to be **dormant**. In this state, the seed can last a long time before it germinates. Dormancy allows the seed to survive in difficult conditions, such as a very cold or dry season, which would kill an actively growing plant.

At the same time as all this is happening, the ovary is changing as well. The ovary, which will contain one or more ovules turning into seeds, begins to change into a **fruit**. This happens in different ways in different plants. You will see some examples if you carry out investigation 12.3. Fruits have the function of containing and protecting the seeds inside them, and of helping these seeds to be spread away, or **dispersed**, from the parent plant.

Question

12.7 Suggest why it is useful for seeds to be dispersed away from the parent plant.

Investigation 12.2

The structure of a seed

You will need:

- a pea or bean pod
- a tile or other hard surface on which to work
- a soaked bean.

1 Look first at the pea or bean pod. This pod was once the **ovary** of a flower. What would you expect to have been growing from the top of an ovary? Can you see any remains of these structures?

2 Carefully open the pod along one long side. Inside, you will see several developing **seeds**. They were once **ovules**. How many are there? How big are they? Are they all the same size? Do they all seem to be developing into seeds? If not, can you suggest why?

3 Notice that each developing seed is attached to the pod by a small **stalk**. What substances do you think might be transported through this stalk, and in which direction?

4 Make an annotated diagram of the opened pod.

5 Now look at the fully mature bean seed. It has been soaked in water to make it easier to dissect. Look for the scar where the seed has been broken away from the pod; this is called the **hilum**. If you look very carefully, you may be able to see the tiny **micropyle** near one end of the hilum. The outer covering of the seed is the **testa**: how has it changed since the seed was an ovule in a pod? What functions do you think the testa has?

6 Make an annotated diagram of the bean seed.

7 Carefully remove the testa from the seed. Beneath it, there are two creamy coloured **cotyledons**. These contain food stores for the developing embryo. What kind of food do you think might be stored in the cotyledons? How could you check your ideas? How did the food get there?

8 Very gently, pull the two cotyledons apart. Between them lies the **embryo**. Look for the **plumule**, which will develop into the shoot of the new plant, and the **radicle**, which will develop into the root.

9 Make an annotated diagram of one half of the seed, to show the embryo plant and a cotyledon.

Investigation *12.3*

Fruits

A fruit is a structure that has developed from an ovary after fertilisation. A fruit contains seeds. Although many fruits, such as oranges, are edible, there are many that are not.

You will be given several different fruits. For *each* fruit:

1 Look carefully at its **structure**. Can you imagine what it looked like when it was part of a flower? If possible, look at a flower in which the fruit has not yet fully developed. Which parts of the flower have become the different parts of the fruit? If you are told to do so, cut open the fruit, and look for the seeds inside.

2 Think about how the fruit helps to **disperse** the seeds. Some different dispersal mechanisms include:

- Animal dispersal – the fruit may be designed to stick to an animal's fur, or to be eaten by an animal; in this case, the seeds may pass right through the animal's alimentary canal, and be deposited on the ground in its faeces.
- Wind dispersal – the fruit may have wings, hairs or a 'parachute' to help it to be carried some distance by the wind.
- Self-dispersal – the fruit may be designed to dry out and explode, shooting the seeds out.

These are not the only mechanisms of seed dispersal, so be prepared for anything when you look at your fruits!

3 Make an annotated diagram of each fruit you look at. Your annotations should include notes on the structure of the fruit, and also on its dispersal mechanism.

Seed germination

You have seen how a seed, formed within a fruit, dries out and becomes dormant. The seed will not become active and begin to grow until its environment is suitable. If you carry out investigations 12.4 and 12.5, you can find out what conditions are needed for a seed to germinate, and how it grows into a new plant.

Investigation *12.4*

What conditions are needed for seed germination?

You will need:

- some small seeds, such as mustard, which will germinate quite quickly when given the right conditions
- several test tubes
- cotton wool
- black paper, scissors and sticky tape
- some boiled, cooled water
- soil.

Design and carry out an investigation to find out which of the following conditions are needed by these seeds for germination:

- light
- air
- moisture
- soil
- warmth.

Investigation 12.5

How a bean seed germinates

You will need:

- two or three bean seeds
- some blotting paper
- a glass jar.

1 Cut a piece of blotting paper to the same length as the height of your jar. Roll it up, and stand it in the jar, as shown in Figure 12.29.

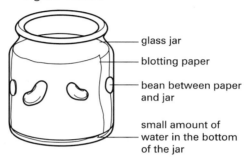

glass jar

blotting paper

bean between paper and jar

small amount of water in the bottom of the jar

Figure 12.29 ▶
Method for Investigation 12.5.

2 Drop the bean seeds between the blotting paper and the wall of the jar, as shown in Figure 12.29. It does not matter which way up they are.

3 Pour about 0.5 cm depth of water into the jar. It will soak up into the blotting paper. Pour in a little more water if it does not quite spread to the top of the paper. Do not leave too much water in the bottom of the jar – you want just enough to keep the beans moist, but not to drown them!

4 Put the jar into a warm place. Each day, make a record of what happens to the beans. You could use a combination of writing and labelled diagrams. As well as your descriptions, answer these two questions when the beans get to the appropriate stages:

a Which emerges first from the bean – the root or the shoot? Can you suggest why it is useful that they should emerge in this order?

b Do the root, the shoot or both show any tropic responses (see pages 173–174)? If so, what are they, and why is this useful to the plant?

The advantages and disadvantages of sexual and asexual reproduction

Humans can only reproduce sexually. Bacteria, fungi and many flowering plants can reproduce both sexually and asexually. Are there any advantages in being able to reproduce in these different ways?

On page 177, you saw how a potato plant can reproduce asexually, by forming stem tubers. Potato plants are flowering plants, and can also reproduce sexually, forming seeds. They use both of these methods because both have their own advantages and disadvantages.

Asexual reproduction has the advantage that only one parent is needed. If a plant is growing on its own, then it can reproduce even if there are no others of its own species growing near by. However, sexual reproduction may also be possible in these circumstances if the plant can self-pollinate.

Asexual reproduction uses mitosis, so the new plants produced are genetically identical to the parent plant. If the parent is well adapted to the conditions in which it is living, this is a very good way of producing many other well-adapted plants living in the same area. Sexual reproduction produces gametes by meiosis, and so the offspring vary from each other and from their parents. This can be useful if the plant is colonising a new environment, or if the environment is changing. Some of the offspring may turn out to be better adapted, and more successful, than the parent plant.

You will remember that flowers may be either self-pollinated or cross-pollinated. In self-pollination, pollen is carried from the anther to the stigma of the same plant. In cross-pollination, the pollen comes from a different plant. After pollination, the male gametes inside the pollen grains fertilise the female gametes in the ovules. So both types of pollination result in sexual reproduction. They can both produce variation in the offspring. However, cross-pollination is likely to produce greater variation, because it is likely that the plant that produced the pollen, and the plant that produced the ovules, have different genes. Reproduction resulting from self-pollination tends to produce little or no variation amongst the offspring.

Summary

- Asexual reproduction involves a single parent which produces offspring by simple division. Sexual reproduction involves male and female gametes, which fuse together in a process called fertilisation, to form a zygote. There may be either one or two parents in sexual reproduction.

- In asexual reproduction or growth, cells divide by mitosis, which produces new cells exactly like the parent cell. Gametes, however, are formed as cells divide by meiosis, which produces new cells with half the normal number of chromosomes.

- In humans, the female gametes are eggs and they are made in the ovaries. One egg is normally released each month. The lining of the uterus becomes richly supplied with blood, in order to receive the fertilised egg. If the egg is not fertilised, the uterus lining is lost during menstruation.

- The menstrual cycle is controlled by the hormones oestrogen and progesterone, produced by the ovaries.

- The male gametes are sperm and they are made in the testes.

- Sperm fertilise eggs in the woman's oviducts. The zygote implants into the uterus wall, and develops into an embryo. A placenta forms, through which materials can be exchanged between the blood of the embryo and the blood of the mother.

- Breast feeding is normally considered to be preferable to bottle feeding.

- Birth control can prevent unwanted pregnancies. Methods may be natural, chemical, mechanical or surgical.

- Hormones can be used to increase a woman's fertility.

- Gonorrhoea and AIDS can be transmitted by sexual intercourse.

- Growth can be defined as a permanent increase in size, resulting from the enlargement of cells and their division by mitosis.

- Flowers are the organs of a plant that are responsible for sexual reproduction. Female gametes are made in the ovules, and male gametes in the pollen grains. Pollen is carried to the stigma by insects or the wind; this is called pollination. The male gametes then travel down a tube to the female gametes, and fuse with them to form a zygote. This develops into an embryo plant, inside a seed.

- Seeds develop inside fruits. Fruits help to disperse seeds. This is important as it provides an opportunity for the plant to colonise new areas, and reduces competition.

- Asexual reproduction produces new individuals just like the parent, which is good if the organism is well adapted to its environment. Sexual reproduction produces variation amongst offspring, which can form the basis for evolution.

Genetics and evolution

Many characteristics of living organisms are caused by their genes, which are passed on from parents to offspring. Differences in genes, and differences in environments, cause variation between individuals. Through natural or artificial selection, only those organisms with the set of inherited characteristics that best suit them to their environment survive and reproduce. This can result in evolution.

Genetics ▶

Genes and chromosomes

You may remember that the nucleus of every cell contains threads of DNA, called **chromosomes**. Humans have 46 chromosomes in each cell; other kinds of organisms may have many more or less than this.

Each chromosome carries a collection of recipes for making proteins. A recipe for one protein is called a **gene**. A gene could be defined as *a length of DNA, making up part of a chromosome, which carries instructions for making a protein molecule.* Each of your cells contains hundreds of thousands of these recipes – hundreds of thousands of genes.

Protein molecules are made of many amino acid molecules strung together. There are 20 different amino acids. The order in which they are arranged determines what kind of protein is formed. The protein haemoglobin will have a completely different set of amino acids, in a completely different order, from the protein keratin. The genes in your cells carry a code that tells your cells the order in which to string together amino acids to make proteins.

Amazingly, by doing this, your genes determine a tremendous number of things about you. This is partly because all **enzymes** are proteins. Your genes tell your cells how to make your enzymes. Although you have probably only learnt about a few enzymes, especially those involved in digestion, it is important to realise that you have thousands of different enzymes in your body. Each enzyme catalyses a different metabolic reaction. If you have slightly different genes from someone else, then you and they will have slightly different metabolic reactions. This could produce quite noticeable differences between you. Your noses might grow into different shapes for example, or one of you might grow taller than the other.

In most cases, we do not yet know just how the different protein recipes that genes carry result in a different characteristic. No-one has the slightest idea why having a gene to make a particular sort of protein should result in a different shaped nose! So, when we are talking about the effects of genes, we often don't bother to talk about proteins at all. We just say that a particular gene produces a particular characteristic.

There is still a tremendous amount that we do not know about all the different human genes, and just what effects they have on us. However, we *do* know about how genes are inherited, and that is what this chapter is mostly about.

Alleles, genotypes and phenotypes

If you look back at Figure 12.4 on page 178, you can see that the 46 chromosomes in a human cell can be arranged in 23 pairs. You have two of each kind of chromosome. The two chromosomes in a pair have genes for the same characteristics in the same position. They are called **homologous chromosomes** ('homo' means 'the same', and 'logous' means 'place'). So you have *two* genes in each of your cells for each characteristic. This is true for all animals and plants – they always have two genes for each characteristic.

Imagine an animal that can have either black or white hair (Figure 13.1). The colour of its hair is determined by its genes. The hair colour gene comes in two different forms – it can either be a recipe for black hair, or a recipe for white hair. These different forms of a gene are called **alleles**. We can use letters to represent them. The allele for black hair could be **B**, and the allele for white hair **b**.

Because the animal has two alleles for each gene, there are three possible combinations of alleles it might have. They are **BB**, **Bb** or **bb**. These are the three possible **genotypes** of the animal as shown in Figure 13.2.

▲ Figure 13.1
The hair of this animal can be either black or white. This is because the gene which determines its hair colour has two forms, or alleles.

Figure 13.2 ▶
Homologous chromosomes carry the same genes in the same position. If there are two alleles of a gene, **B** and **b**, then there are three possible combinations of these alleles.

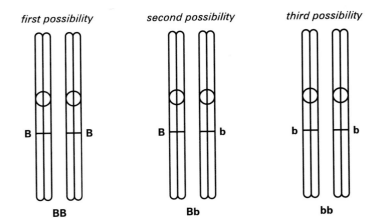

first possibility *second possibility* *third possibility*

B   B   B   b   b   b

BB   Bb   bb

The **phenotype** of the animal is the characteristic that you can see. In this example, the phenotype is the colour of the animal's hair. What colour hair will animals with these three genotypes have? **BB** is no problem – this animal will have black hair. Similarly, an animal with the genotype **bb** will have white hair. But what about **Bb**? Will it have grey hair? Or be black with white patches?

If one of the alleles is **dominant** over the other, then neither of these possibilities is correct. Let us say that the allele for black hair is dominant over the allele for white hair. In this case, an animal with the genotype **Bb** will have black hair – just as black as an animal with the genotype **BB**. The allele **b** is said to be **recessive**.

We can summarise this in a table:

Genotype	Phenotype
BB	black
Bb	black
bb	white

You may have noticed that we have represented the dominant allele with a capital letter, and the recessive allele with a small letter. This is always a good idea – it helps you to remember which is which. There are two other things to think about when you are choosing letters to represent alleles. First, keep to the same letter – do not use **B** for black and **W** for white, for example. Second, choose a letter that looks really different when you write it as a capital and a small letter. If you choose something like **W** and **w**, you will find that neither you nor an examiner can tell which is which when you write quickly!

Homozygous and heterozygous

You have already met several new words in this chapter – and here are two more.

An organism whose alleles for a characteristic are the *same* is said to be **homozygous**. In the example above, an organism with the genotype **BB** is homozygous, and so is one with the genotype **bb**. An organism whose alleles for a characteristic are *different* is said to be **heterozygous**. In the example above, an organism with the genotype **Bb** is heterozygous.

Questions

13.1 Explain the difference between each of the following pairs of terms:
   a gene and allele
   b genotype and phenotype
   c homozygous and heterozygous.

13.2 In a breed of dog, the allele for long legs is dominant to the allele for short legs.
   a Choose suitable letters to represent these two alleles.
   b Draw a table, like the one on page 216, listing the three different genotypes and the two different phenotypes a dog may have.

13.3 In maize, plants with the genotype **Tt** are tall, while those with the genotype **tt** are short.
   a What is the phenotype of a plant with the genotype **TT**?
   b Which is the recessive allele?

13.4 Cows may have horns or no horns. Heterozygous cows always have horns.
   a Which is the dominant allele – the one for horns or the one for no horns?
   b Choose suitable letters to represent the two alleles.
   c What is the genotype of a cow with no horns?
   d What is the phenotype of a cow that is homozygous for the dominant allele?

Inheriting genes

Genes are passed on from parents to offspring inside **gametes**.

You may remember that, in humans, gametes only have 23 chromosomes, compared with the usual 46. (If you have forgotten about this, look back at page 181.)

Ordinary human cells, with 46 chromosomes, have *two* of each kind of chromosome, and are said to be **diploid** cells. Gametes, however, have only *one* of each kind of chromosome, and are said to be **haploid** cells.

If gametes only have *one* of each kind of chromosome, then they can only have *one* of each kind of gene. It is extremely important that you remember this. *Gametes have only one copy of a gene for each characteristic.*

Imagine a male animal with the genotype **Bb**. When sperm are made inside his testes, each sperm will only get one of the two alleles. Each sperm will have either the genotype **B**, or the genotype **b**. There will be roughly equal numbers of each kind (see Figure 13.3).

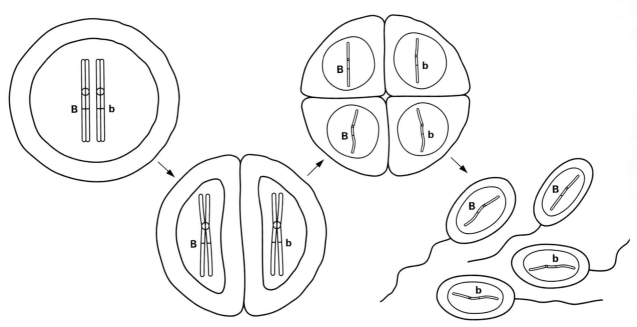

▲ **Figure 13.3**
A cell with genotype **Bb** can divide by meiosis to form sperms with genotype **B** or **b**.

Imagine a female animal with genotype **bb**. When eggs are made inside her ovaries, each egg will only get one of the **b** alleles. Each egg will have the genotype **b**.

What will happen if these two animals mate? As there are equal numbers of **B** and **b** sperm, there are equal chances that either kind of sperm will fertilise the female's eggs. When the sperm and egg fuse together, they will form a zygote. If a **B** sperm fertilises an egg, the genotype of the zygote will be **Bb**. If a **b** sperm fertilises an egg, the genotype of the zygote will be **bb**. We can show this in a genetic diagram.

▲ Figure 13.4
If an animal with genotype **Bb** and one with genotype **bb** have offspring, we would expect half to be black and half to be white.

Parents' phenotypes	Black male White female
Parents' genotypes	**Bb** **bb**
Gametes	Ⓑ and ⓑ ⓑ
Offspring genotypes	

Gametes	ⓑ
Ⓑ	Bb
ⓑ	bb

Offspring phenotypes	**Bb** = black, **bb** = white
Ratios	Equal numbers of black and white offspring would be expected.

The 1:1 ratio

Do not fall into the trap of thinking that the genetic diagram shows that the animals will have two offspring, one black and one white! We have no idea how many offspring they will have – they might have one, or five, or twelve … What the diagram tells us is that there are *equal chances* of producing black or white offspring. We can say that the ratio of black to white offspring is expected to be 1:1.

This 1:1 ratio of phenotypes in the offspring is always what is expected when a heterozygous animal mates with a homozygous recessive animal. If you see a 1:1 ratio in a genetics question, this is almost certainly what is going on.

However, you probably realise that things don't always work out as you expect them to. Try tossing a coin four times – you would expect it to come down heads twice and tails twice, but you would not be particularly surprised if it did not. It is the same with genetics. If the animals had four offspring, we would expect two to be black and two to be white, but we should not be particularly surprised if they were in some other ratio. Genetics diagrams only tell you the *probability* of the offspring genotypes and phenotypes, not what will *actually* happen.

The 3:1 ratio

Now follow through this cross between two heterozygous animals.

Parents' phenotypes	Black	Black
Parents' genotypes	**Bb**	**Bb**
Gametes	Ⓑ and ⓑ	Ⓑ and ⓑ

Offspring genotypes

Gametes	Ⓑ	ⓑ
Ⓑ	**BB**	**Bb**
ⓑ	**Bb**	**bb**

Offspring phenotypes

BB = black, **Bb** = black, **bb** = white

Ratios

A ratio of 3 black : 1 white offspring would be expected.

This 3:1 ratio of phenotypes in the offspring is what is expected when two heterozygous organisms cross.

Questions

13.5 In a species of cactus, the allele for red spines, **R**, is dominant to the allele for brown spines, **r**.

Draw a genetic diagram to show the phenotypic ratios you would expect from a cross between two cacti with the genotypes **Rr** and **rr**.

13.6 Two plants with yellow flowers were crossed. Roughly three-quarters of the offspring had yellow flowers, while one quarter had white flowers. Choose suitable symbols for the alleles for flower colour, and then draw a genetic diagram to explain these results.

13.7 A goat with long hair and one with short hair were mated on several occasions. Over the years, they produced a total of 7 offspring, 4 of which had long hair and 3 of which had short hair.

    a There are two possible explanations for these results. What are they?

    b Suggest a breeding experiment you could carry out to find which of your explanations is correct.

Test crosses

In answering the questions above, you may have realised that, while you can sometimes tell the genotype of an organism from its phenotype, this is not always so. If the phenotype shows the recessive characteristic, you know that it must be homozygous for the recessive allele, like the white animal in the earlier example. But

▲ Figure 13.5
You cannot tell the genotype of an animal showing the phenotype given by the dominant allele. To find this out, you need to do a test cross.

if the phenotype shows the dominant characteristic, there are two possibilities for its genotype – it could be heterozygous, or it could be homozygous for the dominant allele. How could you find out which genotype it has?

The way to do this is to cross your 'unknown' organism with one showing the recessive phenotype. This is called a **test cross**. By looking at the offspring, you can work out the genotype of the 'unknown' parent.

Question

13.8 In rabbits, the allele for brown eyes, **E** is dominant to the allele for blue eyes, **e**.

   a What are the two possible genotypes for a brown-eyed rabbit?

   b What is the only possible genotype for a blue-eyed rabbit?

   c Draw a genetic diagram to show the expected phenotypes in the offspring from a cross between a homozygous brown-eyed rabbit and a blue-eyed rabbit.

   d Draw a genetic diagram to show the expected phenotypes in the offspring from a cross between a heterozygous brown-eyed rabbit and a blue-eyed rabbit.

   e A brown-eyed rabbit was crossed with a blue-eyed rabbit. They had nine baby rabbits, of which four had brown eyes and five had blue eyes. What was the genotype of the brown-eyed rabbit?

   f A rabbit breeder crossed a brown-eyed rabbit with a blue-eyed rabbit. The rabbits had three babies, all with brown eyes. The breeder said that this proved that the brown-eyed rabbit must have the genotype **EE**, but her daughter said that she could not be certain, and should do the cross again to make sure. Who was right – the breeder or her daughter?

Supplement

Codominance

So far in this chapter, we have assumed that one of a pair of alleles is always dominant over the other. But this is not always true. Sometimes, both alleles have an effect in a heterozygous organism. When this happens, the alleles are said to be **codominant**.

Supplement

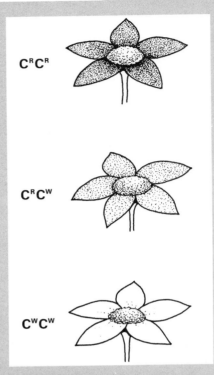

C^RC^R

C^RC^W

C^WC^W

▲ **Figure 13.6**
Two codominant alleles can give three different phenotypes.

For example, imagine a plant in which there are two alleles for flower colour. Allele C^R gives red flowers, and allele C^W gives white flowers. In a heterozygous plant, the flowers are pink. Figure 13.6 shows these phenotypes and genotypes.

Genotype	Phenotype
C^RC^R	Red flowers
C^RC^W	Pink flowers
C^WC^W	White flowers

Notice that, instead of using a capital letter and a small letter for the two alleles, we use the same letter for each – in this case C – with a different capital letter written just above and to the right of it. This is what you should always do when choosing symbols for codominant alleles. If you used a capital and a small letter, it would suggest that one was dominant and the other recessive, which would be wrong.

Questions

13.9 In a certain breed of cattle, coat colour may be red, white or roan. Roan is a mixture of red and white hairs.

   a Choose suitable symbols for the alleles for red hair and white hair.

   b Draw a table listing the three genotypes and the three phenotypes.

   c Draw a genetic diagram to show the results of a cross between two roan cattle.

13.10 In a variety of tomato plant, the leaves may be pure green, pure white, or variegated (a mixture of green and white).

   a Choose suitable symbols for the alleles involved.

   b When two variegated plants were crossed, 87 offspring were produced. Of these, 20 were green, 46 were variegated, and the remaining 21 died soon after germination. Draw a genetic diagram to explain these results. Why did 21 of the young plants die?

Blood groups

Human blood groups are determined by genes. The blood group gene has three alleles, I^A, I^B and I^O. Allele I^A gives blood group A. Allele I^B gives blood group B. Allele I^O gives blood group O.

Alleles I^A and I^B are codominant. Both of these are dominant to allele I^O, which is recessive. This gives the following pattern of possible genotypes and phenotypes:

Genotype	Phenotype
$I^A I^A$	Group A
$I^A I^B$	Group AB
$I^A I^O$	Group A
$I^B I^B$	Group B
$I^B I^O$	Group B
$I^O I^O$	Group O

Questions

13.11 Draw a genetic diagram to show the possible blood groups of the children born to a man with blood group O and a woman with blood group AB.

13.12 A man with blood group A and a woman with blood group B had three children. One child had blood group O, one had blood group A and one had blood group B. Draw a genetic diagram to explain this.

13.13 In a hospital, two mothers had babies at the same time. A nurse took both babies away to wash them, and forgot which was which. To make sure that the right baby was given to the right mother, the two babies, the two mothers and the two fathers all had their blood groups checked. The results were:

Mrs X	group A	Mr X	group A
Mrs Y	group B	Mr Y	group AB
Baby P	group O	Baby Q	group A

Which baby belonged to which parents?

Sex inheritance

Of the 46 chromosomes in a human cell, two are sex chromosomes. There are two sorts, called X and Y chromosomes because of their shapes. You can see them in Figure 12.4 (on page 178).

Females have two X chromosomes, so they have the genotype **XX**. Males have one X and one Y chromosome, so they have the genotype **XY**.

You can draw a genetic diagram to show how sex is inherited in the same way as any genetic diagram. The only difference is that we use the symbols **X** and **Y** to represent whole chromosomes, rather than genes.

	Male	Female
Parents' phenotypes	Male	Female
Parents' genotypes	XY	XX
Gametes	Ⓧ and Ⓨ	Ⓧ

Offspring genotypes

Gametes	Ⓧ
Ⓧ	XX
Ⓨ	XY

Offspring phenotypes XX = female, XY = male

Ratios Male and female offspring in equal numbers would be expected.

Question

13.14 Which gamete determines the sex of a baby – the egg or the sperm?

Variation and selection ▶

Discontinuous and continuous variation

In most of the genetics problems you have worked through in this chapter, you will have seen that the offspring have a variety of different phenotypes. This variation is caused by their **genes**. An example of variation caused entirely by a person's genes is **blood groups**.

There are four blood groups – groups A, B, AB and O. Each person has one or other of these blood groups. This kind of variation is called **discontinuous variation**. If you counted up the numbers of people out of 100 with each blood group, you could draw a bar chart like the one in Figure 13.7. Each category is quite distinct – no-one has a blood group part way between one and another.

Figure 13.7 ▶
The frequency of the four blood groups in West Africa. This is an example of discontinuous variation.

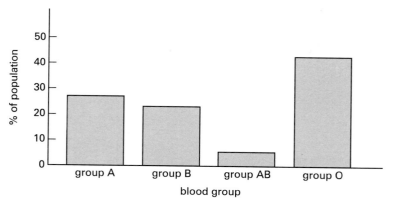

However, what result would you find if you measured the **heights** of these same people? Here, there would be no neat categories. A person can be any height at all, between the smallest and tallest extremes. If you wanted to draw a graph showing the variation in height, you would have to invent categories.

For example, for just 10 of your sample of people you might get the results shown in Table 13.2.

To draw your graph, you need to arrange these results into categories. The smallest height is 1.29 m, and the tallest 1.51 m. We could split these up into six categories: 1.25–1.29 m, 1.30–1.34 m, and so on. (It makes it much easier to draw your graph if you make each category cover the same range of heights.) You can then draw up a second table, like the one in Table 13.3.

Finally, you can use these results to draw a histogram, like the one in Figure 13.8 (overpage). Notice how, this time, the bars are drawn right next to each other, not separate as they were for the blood groups. This is because the blood groups were quite separate categories, with no 'link' or continuation between them. The heights, though, are not really separate – we have artificially created the categories. So we can draw the bars touching, because there is a continuation between one height category and the next. Human height is an example of **continuous variation**.

The variation in human height is caused partly by a person's genes, but also by their **environment**. You might inherit genes for tallness from your parents, but,

Person	Height / m
A	1.51
B	1.37
C	1.29
D	1.42
E	1.39
F	1.46
G	1.32
H	1.40
I	1.43
J	1.48

▲ **Table 13.2**

Height / m	Number of people
1.25–1.29	1
1.30–1.34	1
1.35–1.39	2
1.40–1.44	3
1.45–1.49	2
1.50–1.54	1

▲ **Table 13.3**

unless you have a good diet while you are growing, you may not grow as tall as your genetic potential would allow you to.

Figure 13.8 ▶
The frequency of heights in a class of 16-year-olds. This is an example of continuous variation.

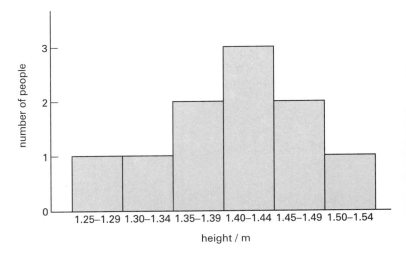

Question

13.15 **a** List *two* characteristics, other than blood groups, which are caused *only* by a person's genes.

b List *five* characteristics, other than height, which are caused partly by a person's genes, and partly by their environment.

c Which of the seven characteristics you have listed show continuous variation, and which show discontinuous variation?

Investigation *13.1*

Human variation

You will need:

- a ruler or a tape measure, depending on what you decide to measure.

1 Choose a characteristic that shows continuous variation in the people in your class – one you can measure. Possible characteristics include wrist circumference, length of big toe, arm length from elbow to tip of little finger, and so on. Decide exactly how you are going to measure it, so that you can do it in exactly the same way on each of your subjects.

2 Measure the characteristic on as many people as possible. Record your results in a table.

3 Divide your measurements into categories. Ideally, you should have something between 6 and 12 categories, each covering

the same range of measurements. Make a second results table showing how many people fit into each category.

4 Draw a histogram to display your results.

Mutations

Genetic variation, such as the variation in human blood groups, is handed on from parents to children. You inherited your blood group genes from your mother and father. If two parents know their blood groups, then they can work out the possible blood groups of their children.

But sometimes, a new genetic variation suddenly appears in a family. An unpredictable change can occur in the genes, so that a baby may be born with a characteristic that has never been seen in the family before. This unpredictable change in a person's genes is called a **mutation**.

An example of a characteristic produced by a mutation is **albinism**. In most people, there is a gene that causes the production of the brown pigment melanin. Although people from different parts of the world have different alleles of this gene, which produce different amounts of melanin, most people have at least some melanin in their skin. However, this gene may mutate to produce an allele that does not code for the production of melanin at all. A person with two copies of this allele will have no melanin, and will have very pale skin and hair.

Another example of a characteristic caused by mutation is **Down's syndrome**. This is caused when the cell division that produces an egg in the mother's ovaries goes wrong. Instead of sharing out the chromosomes evenly, the two number 21 chromosomes may both go into the same cell. The cell that does not get any number 21 chromosomes dies, but the egg cell that gets two of them may survive. If this egg is then fertilised, the baby will have three number 21 chromosomes (one from its father and two from its mother) instead of two, and it is this which produces the features of Down's syndrome. Children with Down's syndrome may have a shorter life expectancy than normal, because they are prone to heart defects and infectious diseases, although this can often be treated with surgery and antibiotics. They are often exceptionally affectionate and happy, but have some degree of mental retardation.

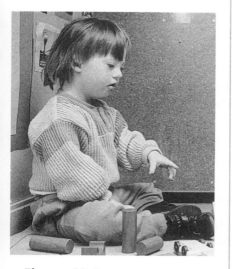
▲ **Figure 13.9**
Child with Down's syndrome.

What causes mutation? Many mutations simply occur by chance, with no apparent reason for them. In the case of Down's syndrome, there is a close relationship between the age of the mother and the frequency of occurrence of the mutation – older mothers are much more likely to have a child with the syndrome than young mothers. Another factor that can increase the risk of mutation is **ionising radiation**, and so can some **chemicals**. Both radiation and chemicals can damage the structure of the DNA that makes up genes.

Artificial selection

Humans make use of variation to breed animals and plants that are useful to them. For example, a farmer may have a herd of cattle, which he uses to produce milk. The cows in his herd will vary in the quantity and quality of milk they produce. To improve the herd, the farmer will pick out the one or two cows that produce the largest quantities of the best milk, and breed from them. He will use a bull that has a mother or sisters who are good milk producers, or that is known to produce offspring who are good milk producers.

The farmer can continue his selective breeding programme for many generations, each time picking only the best milk producers to be the mothers of the next generation. The milk production of his herd will gradually increase.

This process is called **artificial selection**. Another way of carrying out artifical selection is to choose two individuals which have two different, desirable characteristics and breed them together. For example, a variety of rice with high resistance to a disease could be crossed with a different rice variety which gives very high yields. The breeder then grows large numbers of the offspring, and chooses the ones with the best combination of resistance to disease and high yield to breed in the next generation.

(a) Cattle in the USA.

(b) Cattle in India.

▲ **Figure 13.10**
What differences can you see between these two types of cattle? Why do you think these features have been selected by cattle breeders in these two countries?

Question

13.16 This question will involve you in doing some research, probably outside school.

a Choose one crop, or one breed of animal, which is of importance in your area. Find out what characteristics of this crop or animal are important in providing good economic returns to the people who grow or farm it. Don't forget that characteristics such as resistance to disease, or ability to grow on poor soils, may be just as important as the ability to provide a very high yield.

b Try to find out if anyone is carrying out artificial selection on your chosen crop or animal. (With crop plants, farmers often buy their seed from a supplier, so the farmers will probably not be carrying out artificial selection. However, the suppliers of the seeds may be doing this.) Are people just carrying on keeping, and breeding from, all the individuals in a population, or are they breeding selectively?

Supplement

Natural selection

In nature, a similar process to artificial selection is going on all the time. Only the 'best' individuals within a varied population are 'chosen' to breed. This is called **natural selection**.

For example, zebras must be able to run fast in order to escape from predators such as lions. In a population of zebras, there will be variation in the ability to run. Those zebras that are not good runners are more likely to be killed by lions than those that are above-average runners.

This means that zebras that are especially good runners are more likely to survive long enough to breed than those that are not. If the ability to run fast was caused by the zebra's genes, then it can pass on this ability to its offspring. The next generation of zebras will inherit the ability to run fast. The slow zebras will probably not live long enough to reproduce, so their genes will not get passed on to the next generation.

This process has been going on for thousands of years. We can imagine that, over this time, natural selection has been producing generations of zebras each able to run just a little faster than the previous generation. If we could compare a present-day population of zebras with those which lived ten thousand years ago, we might be able to see a measurable difference in their average speeds. We might see that the zebras have **evolved** from a relatively slow-running species into one that can run faster.

Bacteria and antibiotics

Another example of natural selection is happening in bacteria. In the 1940s, **antibiotics** were discovered. These are substances that can kill bacteria without harming humans. Antibiotics revolutionised medicine; for the first time, people with bacterial infections could be treated with pills or injections of antibiotics. Diseases that used to be fatal could now be cured. One such disease was **tuberculosis**, or TB.

However, through natural selection, the bacteria that cause TB have now developed resistance to many of the antibiotics that have been used to treat the disease. Imagine a population of TB bacteria reproducing inside a person's lungs. The person is diagnosed as having TB, and her doctor prescribes an antibiotic to kill the bacteria and cure the disease. The antibiotic kills almost all the bacteria in the person's lungs – but just one or two of the bacteria are different from the others, and are resistant to the antibiotic. They are not killed.

These resistant bacteria now find themselves in an ideal situation. All their rivals, with whom they were previously competing for food in the victim's lungs, are now dead. The resistant bacteria multiply rapidly. Before long, there are large numbers of these resistant bacteria. A strain of resistant bacteria has evolved.

What can be done about this? First, we can reduce the chances of this sort of resistance developing by being careful how we use antibiotics. In the past, antibiotics were prescribed very frequently and carelessly, so that people were given antibiotics when they did not really need them. The more the antibiotics were prescribed, the more likely it was that resistant strains of bacteria would develop. Now, more care is taken about this, as people realise that antibiotics should be used sparingly.

Second, new antibiotics can be developed. It is a sort of 'race' between the bacteria that develop resistance to the antibiotics, and the biochemists who develop new antibiotics to which bacteria are not yet resistant.

Supplement

Figure 13.11
The distribution of malaria in Africa, the Middle East and India.

Figure 13.12
The distribution of sickle cell anaemia in Africa, the Middle East and India.

Sickle cell anaemia

In some parts of the world, especially those shown on the map in Figure 13.11, the disease **malaria** is an important and potentially dangerous disease. Thousands of people die from malaria each year. It is caused by a parasite, which lives and breeds inside a person's red blood cells. The parasite is carried from one person to another by mosquitoes. If a mosquito sucks blood from someone who is infected with the parasite, the parasite is sucked up into the mosquito's body. When the mosquito bites another person, the parasite is injected into the person's blood. The distribution of malaria in the world closely matches the distribution of the particular kinds of mosquitoes which can carry this parasite.

The distribution of malaria also matches something else – the distribution of a disease called **sickle cell anaemia**. This is shown in Figure 13.12. There is a very interesting explanation for this relationship.

Sickle cell anaemia is caused by a codominant allele, H^S, of the gene that codes the production of haemoglobin. People with two copies of the normal allele, H^A, have normal haemoglobin. People with the genotype $H^S H^S$ have abnormal haemoglobin. People who are heterozygous, $H^A H^S$, have some normal and some abnormal haemoglobin.

The abnormal haemoglobin produced by the allele H^S does not carry oxygen very well. People with the genotype $H^S H^S$, who have only abnormal haemoglobin in their cells, have the disease sickle cell anaemia. If they become short of oxygen – perhaps because they are doing exercise – the abnormal haemoglobin causes their red blood cells to go out of shape. The cells stop carrying oxygen, and can get stuck inside small blood vessels, causing great pain. Without medical treatment, a person with sickle cell anaemia is likely to die of the disease while they are quite young.

From what we know about natural selection, we would expect that people with the genotype $H^S H^S$ would be less likely to reproduce than those people with the genotype $H^A H^A$. This should mean that, over many generations, the allele H^S would be lost from the population. But this has not happened. Why has natural selection not 'selected' people with normal haemoglobin? Why do we still have people with sickle cell anaemia in human populations in some parts of the world?

The answer is – malaria. People with the genotype $H^A H^A$, with only normal haemoglobin, are more likely to suffer and die from malaria than people with abnormal haemoglobin. Thus, the three different genotypes have different advantages and disadvantages in the struggle for survival. People with $H^A H^A$ do not suffer from sickle cell anaemia, but in some parts of the world they are susceptible to malaria. People with $H^S H^S$ suffer from sickle cell anaemia, but they do not suffer from malaria. People with the genotype $H^A H^S$ have the best of both worlds – they do not have sickle cell anaemia, and they are much less susceptible to malaria than those with the genotype $H^A H^A$. Thus, these heterozygous people have a great selective advantage over the others, and are more likely to survive, reproduce, and pass their genes on to the next generation than are people with either of the other two genotypes.

Question

13.17 What effect do you think each of the following may have on the incidence of sickle cell anaemia in different parts of the world?

a Modern medicine has increased the chances of a person with sickle cell anaemia being able to survive and have children.

b It is now possible for couples to be tested to find out if they are carriers of (heterozygous for) the sickle cell allele.

c Many people from the parts of Africa where malaria is common have emigrated to other countries, such as the United States of America.

d The parasite that causes malaria, and the mosquitoes that carry it, are becoming resistant to the drugs and chemicals used to kill them.

- Cell nuclei contain long threads of DNA called chromosomes. Each chromosome is made up of many genes.

- A gene is a part of a chromosome that provides instructions for making a particular protein, and therefore helps to determine a particular characteristic of an organism. Different varieties of a gene are called alleles.

- Most cells are diploid cells. They have two sets of chromosomes and therefore two copies of each gene. Gametes are haploid cells. They have one set of chromosomes and one copy of each gene.

- If a cell has two identical alleles of a particular gene, it is said to be homozygous. If it has two different alleles, it is heterozygous. The alleles that an organism has make up its genotype. Its appearance is its phenotype.

- A dominant allele always shows in the phenotype. A recessive allele only shows in the phenotype if no dominant allele is present.

- If both alleles affect the phenotype in a heterozygous organism, they are said to be codominant. Blood groups are determined by three alleles of the blood group gene. Two of these alleles are codominant, while the third is recessive.

- If a homozygous recessive organism is crossed with a heterozygous one, the offspring are likely to be in the ratio of 1 showing the dominant feature : 1 showing the recessive feature.

- If two heterozygous organisms are crossed, the offspring are likely to be in the ratio of 3 showing the dominant feature : 1 showing the recessive feature.

- In continuous variation, a complete range of phenotypes is shown, for example hair colour. In discontinuous variation, only a few different phenotypes are shown, for example blood groups.

- A mutation is a sudden and unpredictable change in a gene or chromosome.

- Animal and plant breeders make use of natural variation to breed together animals and plants with the best characteristics. This is called artificial selection.

- In a wild population, organisms with the most advantageous characteristics are more likely to survive and reproduce, passing on their genes to their offspring. This is called natural selection and can lead to evolution.

14 Organisms in their environment

Living organisms and their environments make up ecosystems. Energy flows through ecosystems, while nutrients circulate within them. Population sizes are controlled by interaction between organisms and their environments.

Energy flow in ecosystems ▶

Ecosystems

An **ecosystem** is a group of living organisms and their environment. A pond and all the things that live in it is an ecosystem. A tree and all the things that live in it is an ecosystem.

Consider a pond. There will probably be many different species of living organisms in the pond. There may be fish, frogs, water beetles, snails and plants. All the different kinds of organisms make up the pond **community**. All of one kind of organism, for example all the individuals of one particular species of fish, make up a **population**. The pond community is made up of many different populations.

The pond is the **habitat** of all the organisms that live in it. A habitat is a place where an organism lives. Within the pond, each species of organism will have its own particular habitat. Some species of fish, for example, may live on the bottom of the pond, while others will swim high in the water.

The pond community and the pond itself make up an **ecosystem**. An ecosystem is made up of a particular area, and all the living organisms in it. The pond ecosystem consists of all the animals and plants living in the pond, plus the pond water, the mud on the bottom, the stones in it, and the gases such as oxygen and carbon dioxide dissolved in the water.

Investigating an ecosystem

In this investigation, you will look closely at an ecosystem, and try to find out what lives in it.

The apparatus you need will depend on the kind of ecosystem you investigate. Your teacher will give you guidance on this.

1 Find a comfortable place where you can sit and look at the ecosystem you are going to investigate. Describe it in as much detail as you can. You could do this in writing, or as an annotated diagram, or both. In your description, include:

- the approximate size of the ecosystem
- the non-living parts of it (for example, soil, water, air, stones), including the amount of sunlight it gets, whether it is windy or sheltered and so on
- any living parts of it that you can see (these are likely to be mostly plants, but you may see some animals as well).

2 Try to identify some of the living components of the ecosystem. For the **plants**, you may be able to look them up in an identification book. Some of the **animals** may be as easy to find as the plants – for example, slugs and snails. Others may be well hidden, for example mice. Your teacher may be able to suggest some ways of finding some of these hidden animals. Make a list of all the plants and animals which you find. This is the **community**.

3 Choose one plant and one animal, and look closely at the particular area in which they live. This is their **habitat**. Describe the habitat of your chosen plant and animal.

Question

14.1 Distinguish between:
- a a community and a population
- b a habitat and an ecosystem.

Food chains

The animals in an ecosystem get food by eating each other or eating plants. The plants get food by using the energy from sunlight in photosynthesis. All the food in the ecosystem is made by the plants. The plants are the **producers** of food for the whole community.

The plants convert energy from sunlight into chemical energy in food. They will store some of this food, often in the form of starch. When the plants need energy, for example to build new cells, they can release some of the energy in their food stores, by the process of respiration.

Animals get their energy by eating food containing chemical energy. They eat food that has been made by plants. Animals are **consumers**. An animal that eats plants is a **herbivore** or **primary consumer**. An animal that eats primary consumers is a **carnivore** or **secondary consumer**. An animal that eats secondary consumers is a **tertiary consumer**.

We can show how the Sun's energy is passed from plant to animal to animal by drawing a **food chain** (Figure 14.1). A food chain shows how energy is passed along from one organism to another. Food chains always begin with a plant, because plants are the producers. The arrows in a food chain show the direction of energy flow from one organism to the next.

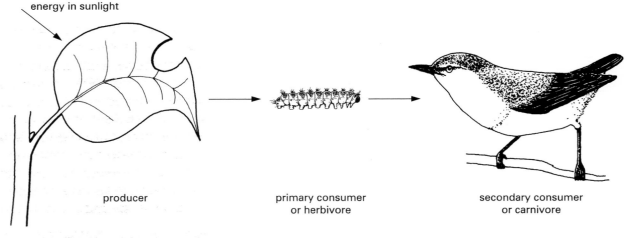

energy in sunlight

producer

primary consumer
or herbivore

secondary consumer
or carnivore

▲ **Figure 14.1**
A food chain. The arrows show the direction of energy flow.

Question

14.2 a Draw two different food chains for the ecosystem you investigated. You may already have a good idea of what eats what. You could also use books to find out what different sorts of animals feed on, or your teacher may be able to help you.
  b Draw a food chain with five organisms in it.
  c Draw a food chain that ends with a human.

Energy loss in food chains

Every time energy is transferred from one form to another, some of it gets lost as **heat** (Figure 14.2). The heat energy simply disappears into the environment.

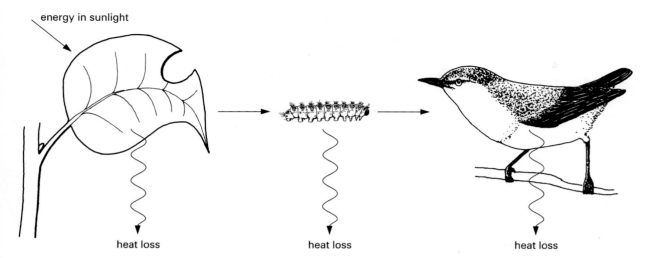

energy in sunlight

heat loss   heat loss   heat loss

▲ **Figure 14.2**
Energy is lost as heat as it passes along a food chain.

When a plant respires, converting some of the chemical energy in starch into another form of energy, quite a lot of the energy is lost from the plant as heat. This energy is lost from the ecosystem. It simply goes into the atmosphere.

When an animal eats the plant, there is not as much energy for the animal as the plant had, because the plant has already lost some as heat. Nor can the animal use all of the energy left in the plant. For example, it may only be able to eat the leaves of the plant, so that the energy in the roots is unavailable to it. It may not be able to absorb all of the plant molecules into its blood from its digestive system, so that quite a lot of these energy-containing molecules are lost from the animal's body as faeces. So a lot of energy is lost in being transferred from the plant to the animal.

The animal will then release some of the energy in the molecules it has eaten, in respiration. As in the plant, a lot of this energy will be lost as heat. By the time a carnivore comes to eat the herbivore, only a tiny fraction of the energy originally captured by the plant in photosynthesis is left. The rest has all been lost to the environment.

Question

14.3 You may have found it difficult to answer question **14.2b**. You will probably find it extremely difficult, if not impossible, to think of a food chain that has six links in it. From what you know about energy and food chains, can you suggest why food chains do not go on for ever?

Food webs

A food chain is a very simplified picture of how energy passes from one organism to another. In practice, many different kinds of herbivores feed on a particular kind of plant, and many kinds of carnivores feed on these herbivores. All of these interacting food chains make up a **food web**. Figure 14.3 shows one example.

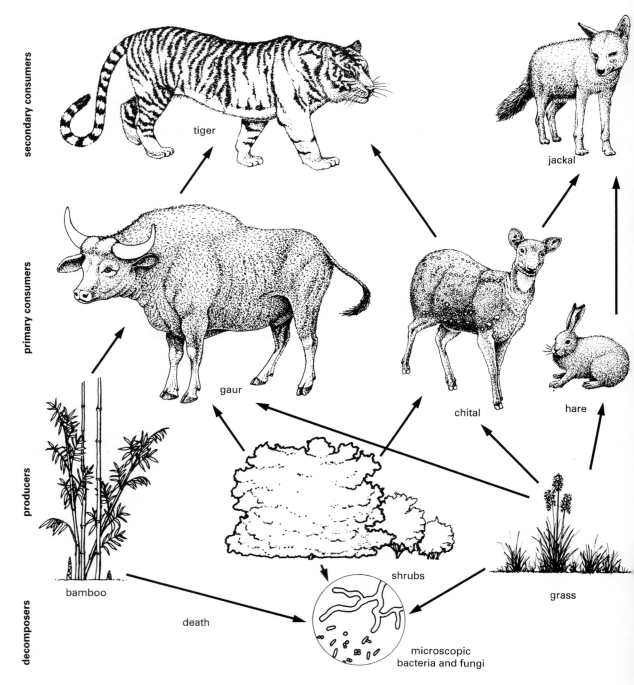

secondary consumers

tiger

jackal

primary consumers

gaur

chital

hare

producers

bamboo

shrubs

grass

decomposers

death

microscopic bacteria and fungi

Notice that the food web includes a group of organisms we have not mentioned before. Many organisms do not feed on living plants and animals, but on their remains. For example, they may feed on dead leaves, or dead animals, or their faeces. These organisms are called **decomposers**. They are some of the most important organisms in an ecosystem, because they help in the recycling of the nutrients inside these remains. You will find out more about this on pages 245–246.

You may have found some decomposers, such as earthworms, in your ecosystem, but millions of them will have escaped your notice. This is because many of them live in the soil, and are very, very small. They include **bacteria** and **fungi**. There are usually more decomposers in an ecosystem than any other group of organisms.

Question

14.4 Draw a food web to represent the energy flow through the ecosystem which you studied in Investigation 14.1. You will not be able to include every kind of animal and plant, so do not worry if your web is not complete.

Pyramids of numbers

Consider the food chain:

$$\text{grass} \longrightarrow \text{antelope} \longrightarrow \text{leopard}$$

If we looked at one square kilometre of African grassland, we might find that within that area there were millions of grass plants, a few hundred antelope and just one leopard. We could show this information in a diagram called a **pyramid of numbers**, as in Figure 14.4. The area within each box represents the number of organisms. Each box represents a different stage within the food chain. The lowest box represents the

Figure 14.4 ▶
A pyramid of numbers for the food chain: grass → antelope → leopard.

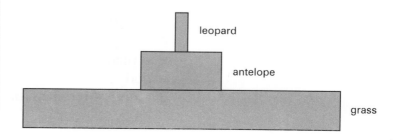

producers, the one above it the primary consumers, and the one above that the secondary consumers. We call each of these levels in the pyramid a **trophic level**. 'Trophic' simply means 'feeding'.

Pyramids of biomass

Would you always get a pyramid shaped like this, for any food chain? You might expect to, because you know that energy is lost as you go along a food chain. So you would expect the number of organisms in the chain to get smaller and smaller as you go along it, because there is less and less energy available. But consider this food chain:

tree → leaf-eating → insect-eating → birds of
          insects   birds   prey

If we drew a pyramid of numbers for this food chain, it would look like Figure 14.5(a). This is rather an odd pyramid! It suggests that a very small amount of tree can support a much larger amount of insects. From what we know about energy losses along food chains, this does not make sense.

(a)

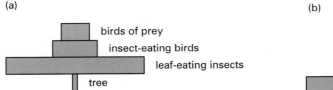

(b)

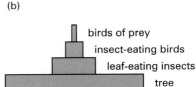

▲ **Figure 14.5**
Pyramids of **(a)** numbers and **(b)** biomass for the food chain: tree → insects → birds → birds of prey

You can probably see what is wrong. A tree is enormous compared with an insect. If we could find the *mass* of the tree, we would find that it was much larger than the mass of the insects that were eating its leaves. The mass of a living organism is called its **biomass**. If we knew the biomass of the populations of all of the organisms in this food chain, we could draw a **pyramid of biomass**. It would look like Figure 14.5(b).

Pyramids of energy

Even a pyramid of biomass does not always give us a true picture of what is happening as energy flows along a food chain. For example, Figure 14.6(a) shows a pyramid of biomass for the food chain:

cabbage plant ⟶ snails ⟶ birds ⟶ birds of prey

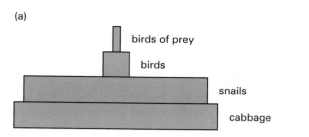

(a)

birds of prey

birds

snails

cabbage

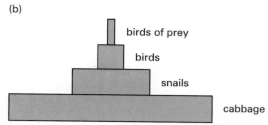

(b)

birds of prey

birds

snails

cabbage

▲ Figure 14.6
Pyramids of **(a)** biomass and **(b)** energy for the food chain: cabbage → snails → birds → birds of prey

You can see that the biomass of the snails is only a little less than the biomass of the cabbage plant on which they are feeding. Does this mean that an especially small amount of energy is lost between cabbages and snails?

In fact, it does not mean this. If we could find out the actual amount of energy in the cabbages, snails, birds and birds of prey, we would get a picture like Figure 14.6(b). This is a **pyramid of energy**. It gives a clear picture of how the amount of energy in each trophic level gets less and less as we go along the food chain.

This poses two questions. How can you find the amount of energy in an organism? And why do the pyramid of energy and the pyramid of biomass for this food chain have such different shapes?

You can find the amount of energy in an organism in the same way as you found the amount of energy in a peanut in Investigation 9.1 (page 125). You can burn it, and calculate how much energy it contains by measuring how much water can be heated by how many degrees Celsius. You would not want to do this with an animal! However, scientists *have* done this with dead animals of a few species.

The reason that the pyramids of biomass and pyramids of energy are not the same shape for this food chain is largely because of the snails. A lot of the mass of a snail is made up of its shell. The shell is made of calcium carbonate, and contains only a very small amount of energy compared with living cells. This makes the snail's biomass look almost as much as the biomass of the cabbage. However, when you work out its energy content, you can see that, as expected, a lot of energy has indeed been lost in the transfer between the cabbage and the snails.

▲ Figure 14.7
Soya growing.

Humans and food chains

Imagine one hectare of land, on which soya beans are growing. The soya plants capture some of the energy from the sunlight that falls onto the field, and convert it to chemical energy in the form of starch and protein.

People could then eat the soya beans. Quite a lot of the energy in the soya plants will be lost in the transfer between the plants and the people. The people can only eat part of the plants; the roots, stem and leaves cannot be eaten.

Another possibility is that the soya plants could be eaten by cattle. The cattle could be eaten by people. They might be killed and eaten as meat, or their milk might be drunk. Once again, a lot of energy will be lost in the transfer between cattle and people.

Figure 14.8 shows these two patterns of energy transfer as pyramids of energy. You can see that eating the soya directly provides more energy for people than eating the cattle. One hectare of land can support more people if they eat plants which grow on it, than if they feed on animals which eat the plants.

Figure 14.8 ▶
Pyramids of energy in agriculture.

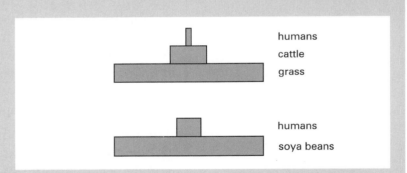

Is this always true? It very much depends on what the plants are. Soya beans contain a lot of protein and starch, and are quite easily digested. If grass was growing in the field, the picture would be very different. People cannot digest grass, because we do not have an enzyme which can break down cellulose. But cattle *can* digest grass and get energy from it, because they have bacteria in their stomachs that produce cellulase. If the only plant available is grass, then people need to let animals eat the grass and then feed on the animals. Grass is no use to humans as food.

In general, however, growing and eating plants is a much more efficient way of producing food than rearing animals. Crops such as sorghum, millet, maize, rice, wheat, potatoes, all types of nuts, beans and fruit all provide good energy sources for people. Where food is in short supply, it makes sense to concentrate on producing plants for people to eat, rather than feeding the plants to animals and then eating the animals. The nearer the beginning of a food chain we feed, the more efficient this is in terms of energy losses.

Question

14.5 a List the main crop plants grown in your area.

b List the main animals farmed in your area.

c If possible, find out what each of these kinds of animal feeds on.

d Imagine that the only food available in your country – including that fed to animals – has to be grown within your country. You cannot import any food from outside. In terms of the number of people that could be supported per hectare of land, does it make sense to farm animals, or would it be better to concentrate on plants?

Nutrient cycling in ecosystems ▶

Energy is not the only thing living organisms need. They also need a supply of the materials from which to build their bodies.

Animal and plant bodies are made out of just four main kinds of chemical substances. These are water, carbohydrates, proteins and fats. Molecules of these substances contain, between them, five kinds of atoms, or elements. These elements are hydrogen, carbon, oxygen, nitrogen and sulphur. Table 14.1 (overpage) shows just which elements are found in each substance.

The atoms from which these substances are made are passed from one organism to another, and back and forth from their environment. Each kind of atom moves around the ecosystem in a cycle, being reused over and over again by different organisms. We will look at how water molecules, carbon atoms and nitrogen atoms move round and round an ecosystem.

Type of substance	Elements it contains
Water	Hydrogen and oxygen
Carbohydrates	Carbon, hydrogen and oxygen
Fats	Carbon, hydrogen and oxygen
Proteins	Carbon, hydrogen, oxygen, nitrogen and sulphur

The water cycle

Figure 14.9 shows the water cycle. To describe it, we shall begin with water in a sea or lake.

▼ Figure 14.9
The water cycle.

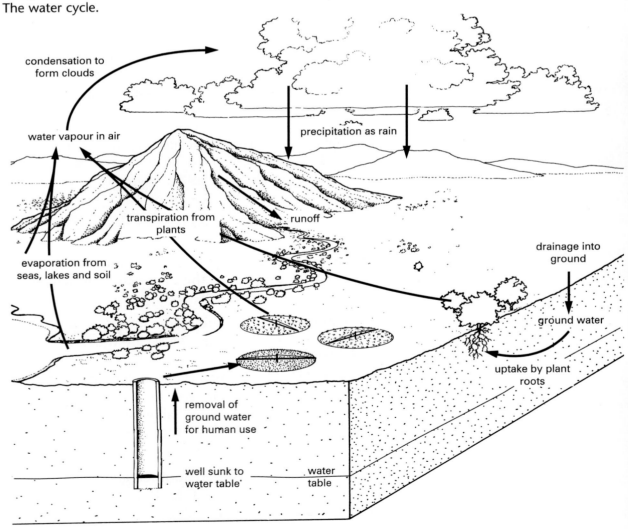

condensation to form clouds

water vapour in air

precipitation as rain

transpiration from plants

runoff

drainage into ground

evaporation from seas, lakes and soil

ground water

uptake by plant roots

removal of ground water for human use

well sunk to water table

water table

Some of the liquid water in seas and lakes **evaporates**, turning into **water vapour**. Water vapour is a colourless gas, which cannot be seen in the air. However, as the water vapour rises high into the atmosphere, it cools, and some of the water vapour **condenses** to form tiny water droplets. We can see these water droplets in the air – they form **clouds**.

The water droplets in the clouds may get bigger, so big that they cannot float in the air any more, and fall to the ground as **rain**, **hail** or **snow**. This is called **precipitation**. Some of this water soaks into the ground, and is taken up by plant roots. The plants use some of the water, but most of it evaporates out of their leaves, in the process called **transpiration**. Transpiration returns water vapour to the atmosphere.

Some of the water that falls to the ground is not taken up by plants. It may run over the surface of the ground, eventually forming **streams** and **rivers** that carry it into a lake or the sea. It may soak deep into the ground and remain there as **ground water**. Ground water may stay in the ground for hundreds or thousands of years; humans may sink deep wells into the ground to reach some of this water. Some of the ground water seeps into rivers, lakes and the sea.

Question

14.6 In some relatively dry areas of the world, it has been found that cutting down large areas of trees reduces the amount of rainfall in that area. Why might this be so?

The carbon cycle

Figure 14.10 (overpage) shows the carbon cycle. All of the carbon in any living organism's body was once part of a **carbon dioxide** molecule. Plants are able to take carbon dioxide from the air, and use it to make **carbohydrates**, **fats** and **proteins**.

Animals, however, are unable to make any use of carbon dioxide. To get a supply of carbon, animals must eat carbohydrates, fats or proteins, which have been made by plants. This is also true for decomposers, which get carbon from carbohydrates, fats and proteins in dead plants and animals, or from animal faeces.

Figure 14.10 ▶
The carbon cycle.

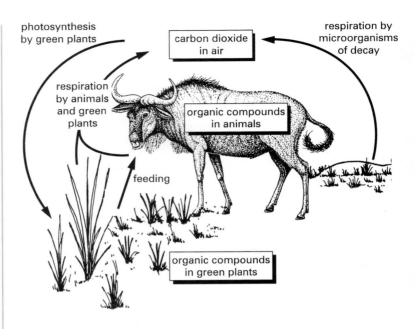

There is not very much carbon dioxide in the air – one litre of air contains only about $0.4\,cm^3$ of carbon dioxide. Despite the fact that green plants keep on taking carbon dioxide from the air, the amount in the air stays roughly constant. This is because all living things return carbon dioxide to the air when they respire.

Respiration takes place in every cell of every living thing – including plants. Respiration is the breakdown of carbohydrates, fats and proteins, in order to release the energy from them. In the process, carbon dioxide is produced and released into the air.

Overall, green plants take more carbon dioxide from the air than they put back into it. In other words, in plants, photosynthesis takes place at a faster rate than respiration. If this were not so, there would be no spare carbon-containing substances to be passed on from plants to animals.

▲ Figure 14.11
The atoms and molecules from this dead fur seal are gradually returned to the soil and air as it decays. Bacteria and other organisms feeding on it use its carbohydrates, fats and proteins for energy. They give out carbon dioxide to the air as they respire.

Supplement

Humans and the carbon cycle

As animals, humans fit in to the carbon cycle along with all other animals. We eat plants or animals to get our carbon. We break down these carbon-containing substances in the process of respiration, and breathe out the carbon dioxide we produce into the air. However, we also have other roles in the carbon cycle.

Combustion of fossil fuels Millions of years ago, many plants died and partly rotted in great swamps. Over many, many years, the plant remains gradually became compressed to form **coal**. A similar process, involving the death and partial decay of bacteria and other small organisms, produced **oil** and **natural gas**. All of these three substances are **fossil fuels**. They contain carbon, which was once part of the living organisms that formed the fuels.

When fossil fuels are burnt, the carbon in them combines with oxygen from the air, and forms carbon dioxide. This process is called **combustion**.

Combustion of fossil fuels is thought to be having an effect on the balance of the carbon cycle. The extra carbon dioxide may be causing the percentage of carbon dioxide in the air to increase, as Figure 14.12 shows.

Figure 14.12 ▶
Changes in atmospheric carbon dioxide concentration since 1750.

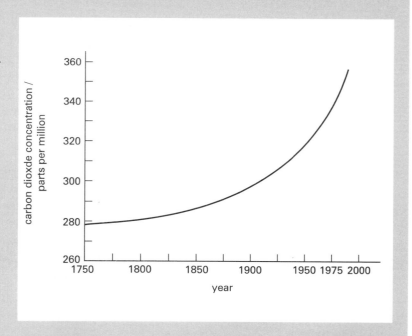

Question

14.7 On a copy of Figure 14.11, add a box to represent fossil fuels. Draw arrows to show how carbon passes into and out of this box. Label the appropriate arrow 'combustion'.

Cutting down forests All over the world, people have cut down forests. They do this to clear land for farming or building houses, and to use wood from the trees for building or making paper.

Initially, the loss of the trees may reduce the amount of photosynthesis taking place. This effect does not last long, because the trees are often quickly replaced by other plants. However, if the trees are burnt or allowed to rot, then the carbon from them will be returned to the air. This can cause a temporary increase in the amount of carbon dioxide in the air. (As you will see in Chapter 15, cutting down forests has other damaging effects, which are really far more significant than these possible changes in carbon dioxide levels.)

Does it matter if human activities lead to an increase in carbon dioxide concentration in the air? Perhaps it does not. There is a lot of evidence to show that carbon dioxide levels have fluctuated quite a lot in the past, long before humans were around to have any effect on them. It can therefore be argued that it is natural for there to be long-term changes in carbon dioxide levels. However, many people think that the currently rising carbon dioxide levels could be dangerous. This is because they may cause **global warming**.

Carbon dioxide in the air acts like a blanket around the Earth. The more carbon dioxide there is, the more of the Sun's heat is kept in, to warm the Earth. As carbon dioxide levels increase, it is expected that the average temperatures on Earth will also increase. This could have some very large effects on living organisms, including humans. For example, it could alter climatic patterns, so that some areas which now get plenty of rainfall could become deserts. It could alter sea levels, so that some areas which are now dry land could become flooded.

Question

14.8 Describe and explain the effect that combustion of fossil fuels, and cutting down forests, could have on the concentration of **oxygen** in the atmosphere.

The nitrogen cycle

Nitrogen gas is in abundant supply in the air. Almost 80% of the air is nitrogen. However, this gas is very unreactive, or **inert**. Animals and plants cannot use it. In order for this nitrogen to be able to become part of an organism's body, it must be changed into another, more reactive form, such as nitrate or ammonia. Changing nitrogen gas into nitrate or ammonia is called **nitrogen fixation**.

Figure 14.14 (overpage) shows three ways nitrogen gas from the air can be fixed. Two of these – fixation by lightning and by bacteria – occur naturally, and the third is done by humans.

- **Lightning** passing through the air provides enough energy to make nitrogen and oxygen react together to form nitrogen oxides. These are carried to the earth in rain, forming **nitrates** in the soil.

- **Nitrogen-fixing bacteria** live in the soil, or in little swellings on the roots of some kinds of plants. In particular, **leguminous** plants such as peas and beans contain these bacteria. Nitrogen-fixing bacteria change nitrogen from the air spaces in soil into ammonia.

- The **Haber process** is an industrial process in which nitrogen and hydrogen gas are made to react together to form ammonia. This is how many fertilisers are made.

The nitrates and ammonia made by these three processes can be taken up by plants through their roots. The plants use these substances to make **proteins**. Animals get their nitrogen, in the form of proteins, by eating plants or by eating each other.

When an animal or plant dies, the proteins in their bodies are gradually turned back to ammonia or nitrates by **decomposers** and **nitrifying bacteria**. The ammonia and nitrates can then be reused by plants, and go round the cycle again.

Another kind of bacteria, called **denitrifying bacteria**, turn ammonia and nitrates back into nitrogen gas again, so completing the nitrogen cycle. This happens most rapidly in very wet soil.

▲ **Figure 14.13**
Manure is spread onto a field from which maize has been harvested. Animal manure provides many nutrients for growing plants. It also helps to improve the texture and water-holding abilities of the soil.

Question

14.9 Why might farmers:

a put nitrogen-containing fertilisers onto their fields?

b grow a crop such as peas or beans in a field before planting a cereal crop such as wheat or maize?

c drain wet land?

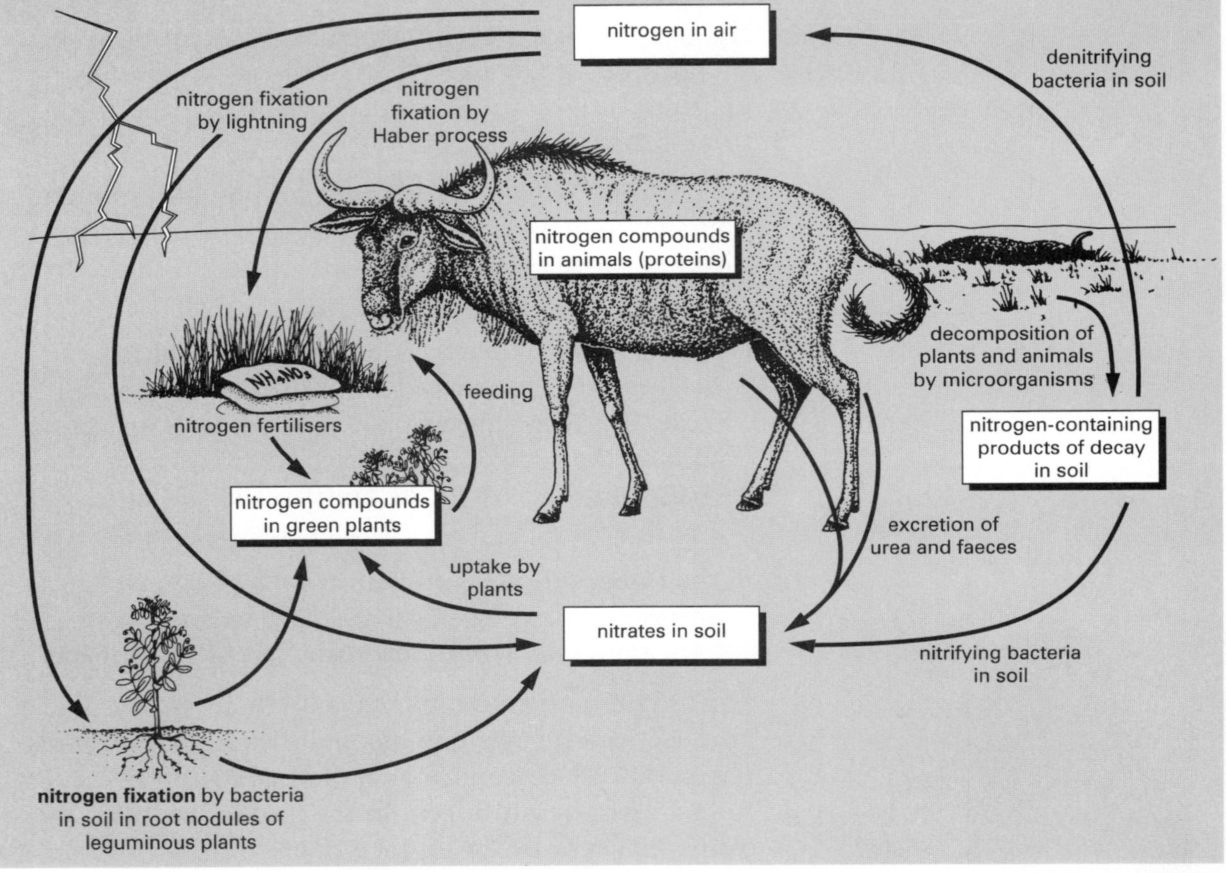

▼ **Figure 14.14**
The nitrogen cycle.

Population size ▶

A **population** is a group of organisms living in the same area, which can interbreed with one another.

If the number of organisms in a population is measured over a long period of time, it is usually found that this number goes up and down, or fluctuates. However, these fluctuations do not often result in a long-term decrease or increase in the population. The average population size stays about the same. Why is this so?

Many factors can affect the size of a population. Consider, for example, a zebra population. The number of zebras that can live in an area will largely depend on the supply of food and water. If the population size increases, then there may not be enough **food** for them to eat, and many will die of starvation. Large populations also increase the risk of **disease** striking, partly because it is easier for diseases to be transmitted from one organism to another when they are living closely bunched together, and partly because lack of food will make the animals weaker and less able to fight off disease. A very large population of zebras could also attract more **predators** to the area.

All of these three factors – food supply, disease and predators – could act to reduce the zebra population if it becomes larger than usual. Once the population has dropped, then food supply no longer becomes a problem, disease may die out, and predators may move away. Now the zebra population can begin to rise again. If it rises too far, then these factors will once again act to reduce it.

The sigmoid growth curve

We can get a picture of how different factors may limit population growth by studying populations of simple organisms in a laboratory. **Yeast** is a good subject for such investigations. Yeast is a single-celled fungus, which reproduces quickly, by budding, in suitable conditions. It can be grown in a flask containing a nutrient broth. The size of the yeast population can be measured by taking a sample from the broth, and counting the number of yeast cells per cubic centimetre.

Figure 14.15 shows the results of an experiment in which a few yeast cells were put into a flask containing nutrient broth, and left for a few days. To begin with, the yeast population did not grow (the lag phase). After a few hours, it began to grow very rapidly (the log phase). Eventually it slowed down and remained at a fairly constant level (the stationary phase). This kind of curve is called a **sigmoid curve**. 'Sigmoid' simply means 'S-shaped'.

When the yeast is first put into the broth, it takes a while to settle down and adjust to its new environment. This is why the population does not begin to increase straight away. Soon, however, the yeast cells begin to divide. There is plenty of food for them in the broth, so

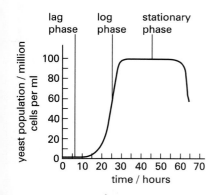

▲ **Figure 14.15**
Population growth of yeast in a flask of nutrient broth. In which part of the curve is population growth most rapid? In which part are the yeast cells dying?

there is nothing to stop the population growing. The only constraint on the rate of increase of the population is the rate of reproduction of the yeast cells.

This population increase cannot go on for ever, however. **Limiting factors** will eventually cause the population growth to slow down and then stop. In the flask, there are likely to be two important limiting factors. First, the yeast cells will begin to become short of food. Second, they produce alcohol as a waste product, which eventually builds up to such a concentration that it begins to poison the yeast.

Question

14.10 Imagine that six mice, three males and three females, are put onto an island on which no mice have lived before. The mice feed on grass roots and seeds. There is plenty of grass on the island, but there are several species of birds that feed on the seeds, and several species of insects that feed on grass roots. There are some predators on the island, which feed on a wide variety of small animals.

Suggest what might happen to the population of mice over a period of a few years. There are many possibilities, so feel free to make a wide variety of suggestions. However, for each suggestion you make, explain fully why you think this could happen.

Human populations

Figure 14.16 shows what has happened to the human population on Earth in the last 5000 years. Why is the curve this shape?

Figure 14.16 ▶
Human population growth in the last 6000 years. The shape of the curve from 2000 AD onwards is based on predictions by the United Nations.

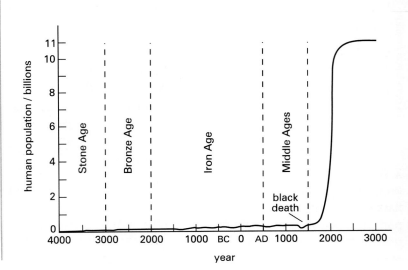

Until the last 1000 years or so, many factors stopped the human population from increasing by very much. For example, many people died from disease when they were very young. Food supply was often very limited, because farming – where it was carried out at all – was done using poor varieties of crops, and with few machines. Human populations, like the zebra population, were kept at a steady level by a combination of limited food supply and disease.

However, big changes have taken place in the way that people live. **Medicine** has enabled people in many parts of the world to live longer. As fewer people die young, more children are produced and more of these children survive. **Agriculture** has greatly increased the food supply in many parts of the world. Lack of food is no longer a factor limiting population size in developed countries, and is becoming less so in most developing countries. This has allowed the human population to increase at an alarming rate.

There is great concern, all over the world, about this increase in the human population. It obviously cannot go on increasing for ever. Some of the problems this population growth causes include:

- **more pollution.** More people mean more air and water pollution.

- **deforestation.** More people cut down more forests, to provide land for growing crops, and to build houses and roads.

- **loss of habitats for other species.** More people take over more land, damaging habitats of wildlife, and leading to the extinction of many species of animals and plants.

- **more soil erosion.** More people put more demands on the land, leading to more soil erosion (see page 259).

- **more demand for water.** More people need more water, which is already in short supply in some areas.

- **more disease.** People living very close together are more likely to pass on diseases from one to another, especially if food and water are in short supply.

14.11 Suggest and discuss some more problems which may be caused by a continuing increase in the human population.

Reducing human population growth

In most developed countries, populations are no longer growing. As death rates fell in the nineteenth and twentieth centuries, people gradually began to choose to have fewer children. This is also beginning to happen in most developing countries. However, at the moment, 95% of population growth is taking place in developing countries (Figure 14.17). Growth will continue in some countries, particularly in Africa, for at least another 20 years.

What can be done to decrease the rate of population growth? As has been seen in developed countries, improvements in living standards seem to lead naturally to a reduction in the number of children people have. Education can teach people about family planning, so that they can choose how many children to have. If

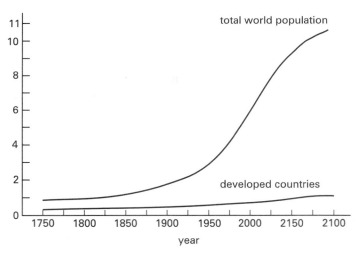

▲ **Figure 14.17**
Human population growth since 1750 in developed countries, compared with that of the whole world. Once again, the curves from the year 2000 onwards are based on UN predictions.

▲ **Figure 14.18**
Rapidly growing human populations often result in very poor living conditions. This family lives in a shanty town outside Rio de Janeiro, Brazil.

food is in adequate supply, medicine available, and living conditions good, then people choose to have fewer children. Where survival is a constant battle, on the other hand, people tend to have more children. This may be to help the family to grow crops or look after animals. People may want to have large families to make sure that there will be someone to look after them when they get old. Having a lot of children each earning a little money may make a poor family better off.

Thus, education, improved health care, access to family planning services, and care for the elderly and those unfit to work, can all help to reduce the number of children born. It is very much hoped that, in the first part of the twenty-first century, the size of the human population on Earth will begin to level out.

Questions

14.12 It is difficult to measure population growth in a country directly. It would mean counting how many people there were in the country each year, for many years. An easier way of getting a picture of population growth in a country is to count how many people there are in each age group. We can then draw a population pyramid.

Figure 14.19 shows a population pyramid. Each level in the pyramid represents the number of people of that age group, the number of men being shown on the left and number of women on the right.

a How many men aged between 30 and 40 are there in this population?

b How many people aged between 20 and 30 are there in this population?

c How many young people aged between 0 and 20 are there in this population?

d How many old people aged between 60 and 80 are there in this population?

e What would happen to the size of the population in this country if all the people in the 0–20 age group survived until they were in their 60s?

14.13 Figures 14.20 (a) and (b) (overpage) show population pyramids for Canada and Sierra Leone.

a Which country has a population that is decreasing? Explain your answer.

b Which country has a population that is increasing? Explain your answer.

14.14 Figure 14.21 shows the pattern of population change in different parts of the world which is expected to take

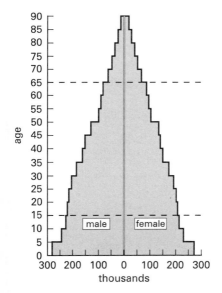

▲ **Figure 14.19**
A population pyramid.

Figure 14.20 ►
Population pyramids for
(a) Canada and
(b) Sierra Leone.

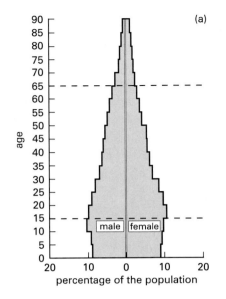

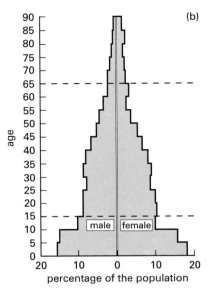

place up until the year 2020. These predictions were made by the United Nations in 1987.

a i What was the population of Africa in 1990?

ii What is expected to be the population of Africa by 2020?

iii What percentage population increase does this represent?

b In which part of the world is the population expected to increase by the *least* amount?

c In which part of the world is the population expected to increase by the *greatest* amount?

d Suggest reasons for the patterns shown by this graph.

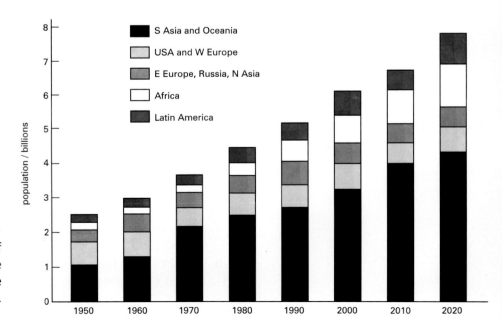

Figure 14.21 ►
Patterns of population change since 1950 in five world regions.

Summary

- An ecosystem is a group of living organisms and their environment. Energy enters an ecosystem as sunlight, and is converted by green plants to chemicals in their bodies. The energy is passed along from plants to animals as they eat each other. This is known as a food chain. Many food chains linked together form a food web.

- Energy is lost between each trophic level (feeding level) in a food chain. This means that there is not much energy for the last organism in the chain, so there tend to be fewer organisms, with less total body mass, at the end of a food chain than at the beginning. This can be shown by drawing pyramids of numbers, biomass or energy.

- The water cycle and carbon cycle are important to living organisms. Carbon dioxide from the air is converted into carbohydrates by photosynthesis, and then passed from animal to animal as they feed. Carbon dioxide is returned to the atmosphere as organisms respire.

- Nitrogen is needed to make proteins. Nitrogen-fixing bacteria, lightning and the Haber process convert unreactive nitrogen gas into compounds that a plant can use, such as nitrates. The plant makes proteins, and these can be eaten by animals.

- Human activities such as burning fossil fuels and deforestation are increasing the amount of carbon dioxide in the atmosphere, which may lead to global warming.

- The human population is growing rapidly, and will continue to do so for some time. Usually, a population's growth is slowed and stopped by limiting factors such as lack of food.

Human influences on ecosystems

Human activities may have harmful effects on ecosystems, for example by destroying habitats or polluting air, water or soil. Conservation can help to prevent and reverse such damage.

Food production ▶

Modern technology and agriculture

For thousands of years, people have been growing crops and keeping animals for food. At first, such agriculture was performed on a relatively small scale. As the human population has grown, and as the availability of machinery, fertilisers and pesticides continues to increase, people are able to produce more and more food from a given area of land.

This increase in agricultural production has brought great benefits to many people. In the developing countries of the world, general levels of nutrition have improved considerably in the last 40 years or so. For example, in 1961, the average daily energy intake of a person in a developing country was 8000 kJ. By 1983 this had increased to 10 000 kJ.

Nevertheless, the distribution of this improvement in agricultural technology around the world is very uneven. Figure 15.1 shows that although grain production has increased rapidly in Western Europe, it has not done so in Africa. This is partly because of

Figure 15.1 ▶
Changes in grain production since 1950 in Western Europe and Africa.

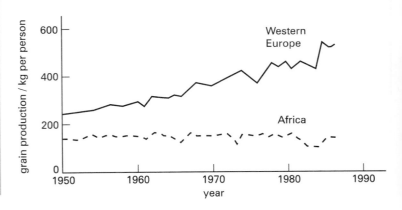

▲ **Figure 15.2**
In the USA, farming is done using sophisticated and powerful machinery. Here, wheat is harvested in California.

▲ **Figure 15.3**
In many parts of Africa, farmers are not able to use much machinery. This means that more people are needed to work the land, and they often have to work very hard. These farmers are ploughing in Ethiopia.

climatic problems such as lack of water in many parts of Africa, but is also because people do not have enough money to buy the machinery, fertilisers and pesticides which could help them to increase the yields of the crops they grow.

Moreover, although crop production may be increasing, so is the size of the human population. In Africa south of the Sahara, the human population is growing at a faster rate than the crop production. This means that the amount of food produced per person is actually getting less. This problem is not going to be solved simply by improvements in technology. Much of the problem lies in damage being done to the land, which results in soil erosion and loss of fertility.

Soil erosion

Soil is a precious material. A good, deep soil, suitable for growing crops, takes thousands of years to form. If it is lost, it cannot easily be replaced.

When there are plants growing in soil, it is very resistant to erosion. Rain falling onto the ground first hits the plants rather than the soil. The water soaks gently into the soil. A lot of the water is taken up by the plants. However, if all the plant cover has been removed, then the rain drops fall directly on the soil, loosening and moving the soil particles. There are no plants to absorb the water, so a lot of it runs off the land over the surface of the soil, carrying away the soil as it does so.

Country	Soil erosion / metric tonnes per hectare per year
USA	18
Jamaica	36
Nepal	50
Ethiopia	42
India	75

▲ **Table 15.1**
Rates of soil erosion in five countries.

Question

15.1 Use an atlas to find the five countries listed in Table 15.1. For each country, find out its average rainfall (this information should be in your atlas) and how mountainous it is. Use this information to suggest why some of these countries have higher rates of soil erosion than others.

When people **clear forests** to grow crops, they frequently open up the soil to this kind of erosion. The soil of tropical rainforests is especially thin, and easily eroded. Within a few years of cutting down the trees, the soil will probably be too thin and poor to grow crops.

▲ **Figure 15.4**
Removing trees can quickly lead to devastating soil erosion. Here you can see that, where the trees are growing, the soil has remained. Where they have been cut down, large amounts of soil have been washed away.

▲ **Figure 15.5**
Clearing forests on slopes allows more rainwater to run into rivers. This can cause flooding.

Another way plant cover can be removed from soil is by **overgrazing**. Animals such as cattle, sheep and goats may increase soil erosion by eating almost all the plants in an area, and trampling the soil.

Even deep, fertile soils are easily eroded. A farmer may leave his fields empty for part of the year. During this time, rainfall can easily wash away the soil.

As well as losing irreplaceable soil, this can cause damage to waterways. The eroded soil is carried into rivers. The rivers may silt up, reducing their navigability, and making use of the water for irrigation more difficult. When it rains heavily, the silted rivers cannot carry away the excess water, and flooding may result.

Reducing soil erosion

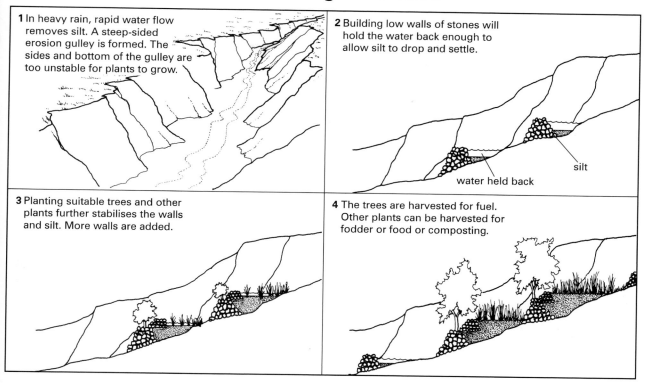

1 In heavy rain, rapid water flow removes silt. A steep-sided erosion gulley is formed. The sides and bottom of the gulley are too unstable for plants to grow.

2 Building low walls of stones will hold the water back enough to allow silt to drop and settle.

silt

water held back

3 Planting suitable trees and other plants further stabilises the walls and silt. More walls are added.

4 The trees are harvested for fuel. Other plants can be harvested for fodder or food or composting.

▲ **Figure 15.6**
Gulley erosion and reclamation. No expensive technology or materials are needed to stop this type of soil erosion – just stones, and people to carry them.

▲ **Figure 15.7**
Farmers on these hillsides in the Philippines have built terraces for growing rice. This stops too much soil being washed down the slope.

Figure 15.6 shows how erosion can lead to trenches or **gulleys** being formed in soil, and what can be done about this.

There are many other ways in which people can reduce soil erosion. These include:

- not cutting down trees in areas where the soil is most likely to erode, and planting trees to help to stabilise soil on open land

- not grazing too many animals on land where the soil is vulnerable to erosion

- making terraces where crops are grown on hillsides, so that water cannot wash soil down the slope

- adding humus, such as animal dung and rotted plant material, to the soil, to make it more likely to stick together and less easily washed away

- keeping a cover of plants on the soil, as their roots will help to hold the soil in place.

However, for people finding it difficult to get enough to eat, there may be little incentive to do any of these things. If your only concern is how to survive until tomorrow, or until next year, it is difficult to worry about what may happen to the soil in ten years' time. Problems of soil erosion in poor areas of developing countries can only be solved by improving people's standards of living, so that they do not need to make such heavy demands on the land.

Problems resulting from over-use of fertilisers

One of the main reasons for the increase in crop production in Western Europe shown in Figure 15.1 (page 258) is the increase in use of nitrogenous fertilisers. Adding fertilisers to the soil can greatly increase crop yields (Figure 15.8). Without fertilisers, there would be no hope of feeding the world's population.

Figure 15.8 ▶

Graph to show the relationship between application of nitrogen fertilisers and wheat yields in the UK, 1965–90.

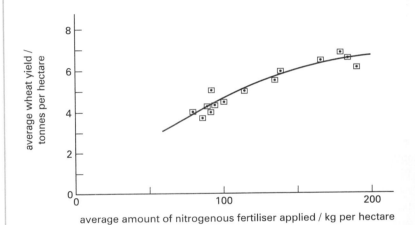

However, careless use of fertilisers can cause great damage to ecosystems. The nitrates contained in fertilisers are very soluble. Any nitrates put onto the soil and not immediately taken up by plants can be washed away when it rains. This is called **leaching**. The leached fertilisers may end up in streams, rivers and lakes.

The fertilisers provide nitrogen for plants and algae, which grow quickly. The algae may grow so much that the water looks thick and green. This blocks out light for the plants growing lower down in the water. These plants, and eventually the algae as well, die. This provides food for bacteria, so the populations of bacteria increase. The bacteria respire, using up oxygen in the water. Animals living in the water cannot breathe, and so they die.

This process is called **eutrophication**. It can happen whenever plant nutrients get into ponds, lakes, rivers or the sea. Fertilisers are not the only cause of eutrophication. Untreated sewage, and waste from factories producing foodstuffs can also cause this problem.

Question

15.2 Figure 15.9(b) shows how the amount of oxygen, numbers of bacteria and numbers of fish change as you go downstream from an outfall of untreated sewage. Suggest explanations for the shapes of each of these three curves.

no sewage added

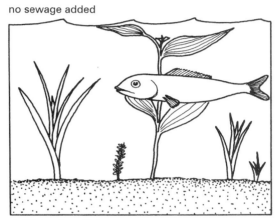

1 Water clear. Fish present.
   Water weeds growing.

sewage added

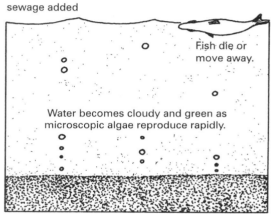

2 Water weeds die from lack of light.
   Bacteria grow quickly, using up oxygen.
   Foul-smelling gases escape from the mud.

(a) Eutrophication.

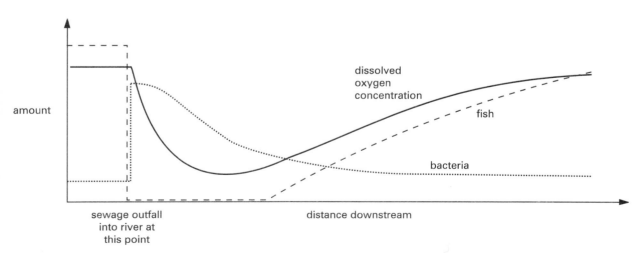

(b) Changes in dissolved oxygen, bacteria and fish, upstream and downstream of an outfall of untreated sewage.

▲ **Figure 15.9**

Preventing problems from over-use of fertilisers

To prevent these problems, people should:

- only apply fertilisers to land when plants are growing, so that they will immediately be taken up

- not apply too much fertiliser, so that it will all be taken up by plants

- not apply fertiliser when it is about to rain

- where possible, use manure or other organic fertilisers instead of fertilisers such as ammonium nitrate – manure is often cheaper, it breaks down slowly and releases the nitrogen to the plants over a long period of time, and adds humus to the soil, which can improve its texture and reduce erosion.

Pollution ▶

Pollution can be defined as *the addition of something to an ecosystem which can damage the living organisms within it.*

Water pollution

The effects of water pollution by **fertilisers** have just been described. Pollution by untreated **sewage** has a similar effect, causing eutrophication.

Pollution by sewage causes another problem, too. Sewage is waste water from houses and industries. It contains human urine and faeces, which may be contaminated with harmful viruses and bacteria. Many diseases, such as cholera, typhoid and poliomyelitis, can be transmitted in untreated sewage. A person may catch these diseases by swimming in or drinking contaminated water, or eating food that has come into contact with it.

Supplement

Sewage treatment

Figure 15.10 outlines how sewage may be treated to make it safe. After treatment, the effluent can be allowed to flow into a river, where it will not cause eutrophication, nor carry the risk of disease.

There are many different methods of sewage treatment, but all of them rely on microorganisms, such as

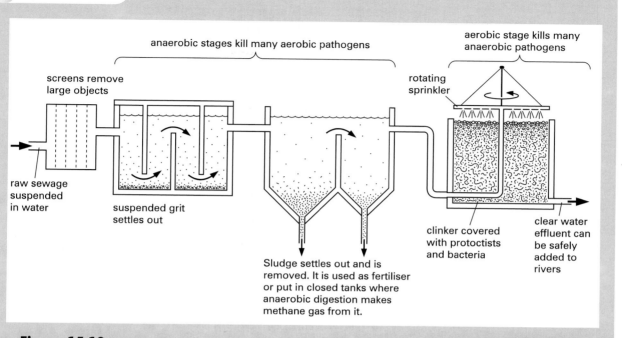

anaerobic stages kill many aerobic pathogens

aerobic stage kills many anaerobic pathogens

screens remove large objects

rotating sprinkler

raw sewage suspended in water

suspended grit settles out

Sludge settles out and is removed. It is used as fertiliser or put in closed tanks where anaerobic digestion makes methane gas from it.

clinker covered with protoctists and bacteria

clear water effluent can be safely added to rivers

▲ **Figure 15.10**
One method of sewage treatment.

bacteria and **protoctists**, to feed on the sewage. The microorganisms break down harmful substances in the sewage. In the example shown in Figure 15.10, this is partly done in **anaerobic**, or oxygen-free, conditions. This method has the advantage of producing methane, which can be used as a fuel.

Water pollution by inorganic waste

Inorganic substances are substances that have not been made by living things. They tend not to contain carbon in their molecules. One example is ammonium nitrate, which is widely used as a fertiliser. The effect of pollution by fertilisers has been described in this chapter.

Another important inorganic water pollutant is **mercury**. Mercury may get into water as a waste product from factories. It is highly toxic.

For example, in the 1950s a disease broke out in a Japanese fishing village. Some people died, others suffered from problems with their muscles and nervous systems, and many deformed babies were born. The problem was tracked down to mercury, which had got into the sea near the village from a factory making plastics. The factory was using mercuric sulphate as a catalyst. The mercury was getting into the bodies of fish, and then into people who ate the fish. Once the factory's discharge of waste into the sea was stopped, the disease disappeared.

Air pollution

We have already described, on page 247, how the burning of fossil fuels releases **carbon dioxide** into the atmosphere. Another gas produced when fossil fuels, especially coal, are burnt is **sulphur dioxide**. Most sulphur dioxide pollution is caused by coal-burning industries, such as power stations.

Sulphur dioxide is a very unpleasant gas. It is an **irritant**, which means that it causes discomfort when you breathe it in. In people who have a tendency towards bronchitis or asthma, it can trigger an attack. Sulphur dioxide gas can also get into plants, through the stomata in their leaves. It can kill cells in the leaf, eventually killing the whole plant if the pollution continues.

Figure 15.11 ▶
Sulphur dioxide pollution in Los Angeles comes from the huge number of cars which are used in the city.

Supplement

Acid rain

Sulphur dioxide, SO_2, in the atmosphere may be oxidised to sulphur trioxide, SO_3. The sulphur trioxide dissolves in water in the atmosphere to form sulphuric acid, which falls as acid rain or acid snow.

Sulphur dioxide is not the only gas that causes acid rain. **Nitrogen oxides** also do this. The major source of nitrogen oxides is car exhaust fumes. Figure 15.12 shows the formation and effects of acid rain.

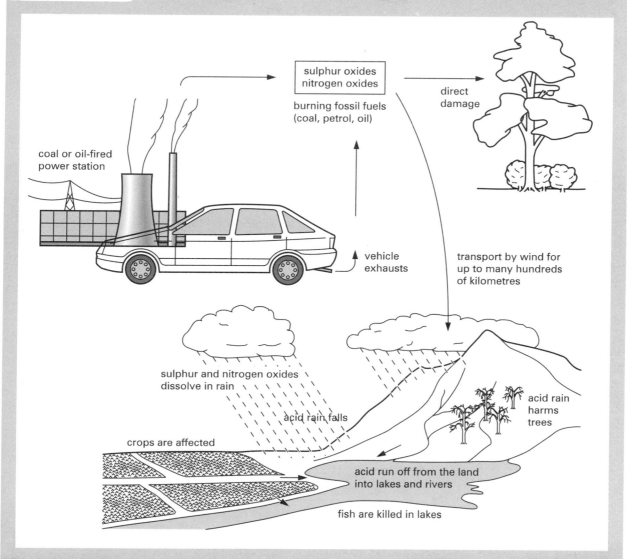

sulphur oxides
nitrogen oxides

burning fossil fuels
(coal, petrol, oil)

direct
damage

coal or oil-fired
power station

vehicle
exhausts

transport by wind for
up to many hundreds
of kilometres

sulphur and nitrogen oxides
dissolve in rain

acid rain falls

acid rain
harms
trees

crops are affected

acid run off from the land
into lakes and rivers

fish are killed in lakes

▲ **Figure 15.12**
Acid rain.

Acid rain may damage the leaves of trees directly, but these effects are relatively small. More importantly, it can dissolve and wash away important minerals, such as calcium and magnesium, as it soaks through the soil. On thin soils, such as those on mountainous areas of some parts of Europe (Figure 15.13 overpage), this can make the soil so poor that whole forests die.

The acid rain also washes out aluminium ions from the soil. The aluminium accumulates in rivers and lakes. Aluminium ions are toxic to fish, especially young ones, as they can stop the gills functioning properly. The fish in badly acidified lakes are often killed.

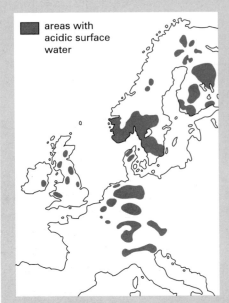

▲ **Figure 15.13**
Areas of Western Europe most affected by acid rain.

Acid rain can damage buildings. Some buildings are made of stone containing carbonates, such as calcium carbonate (limestone). The acid dissolves the carbonate, causing the stone to crumble away.

Reducing pollution from acid rain

Several steps are being taken in developed countries to reduce pollution by sulphur dioxide and nitrogen oxides. These include:

- Installing 'scrubbers' which remove almost all of the sulphur dioxide from the waste gases at coal-burning power stations. However, this is expensive, and means that the electricity produced by these power stations costs more.

- Using catalytic converters on car exhausts. These convert the nitrogen oxides into nitrogen. (However, although catalytic converters help reduce acid rain, they do nothing to reduce the amount of carbon dioxide emitted in the exhaust fumes.)

Pollution by pesticides and herbicides

Pesticides are chemicals used to kill pests, such as insects that eat crop plants. Herbicides are chemicals used to kill weeds.

Benefits of using pesticides Pesticides are used to reduce crop losses, and also to control the spread of diseases like malaria, which are spread by insect vectors.

Pesticides have been immensely valuable in increasing food production. In developing countries, it is estimated that at least a third of the crops grown are lost to pests. For cotton production, the figures are even worse – it has been calculated that, without the use of pesticides, almost half of the cotton produced in developing countries would be destroyed.

Pesticides also help to control diseases. Malaria is a devastating disease, which causes repeated and debilitating illness, and may kill. Without pesticides to control mosquitoes, many more people worldwide would suffer from malaria. A campaign run by the World Health Organisation since 1955, using pesticides and other methods to control mosquitoes and hence malaria, is estimated to have saved 15 million lives.

Problems with using pesticides Despite their benefits, pesticides must be used with great care. In the past, before the problems associated with pesticides were understood, a lot of damage was done to the environment.

For example, one of the first insecticides to be used was **DDT**. This was widely used in the 1950s and 1960s. However, it was discovered that DDT used to kill insects could enter food chains. It is a **persistent** pesticide – it does not break down, but remains in the environment. As it was passed along a food chain, it became more and more concentrated in each successive organism. Carnivores ended up with so much DDT in their bodies that they died. DDT has now been banned in most countries.

Persistent pesticides may end up in food intended for humans, as **pesticide residues**. This is particularly likely if food is harvested soon after it has been sprayed with pesticides. In most developed countries, there are strict regulations about how long food must be left between spraying and harvesting, but some developing countries do not follow these rules. Thus, people could be poisoned by eating food containing pesticide residues.

People using the pesticides can also be poisoned if they do not wear proper protective clothing. Many pesticides can be absorbed through the skin. In Britain, some farmers have become ill after using pesticides called organophosphates, to kill parasites on sheep.

Another problem is that insects and weeds may develop **resistance** to pesticides. This happens in a similar way to the development of resistance to antibiotics by bacteria, described on pages 229–230. This has happened, for example, with mosquitoes, which have built up resistance to the pesticides used to kill them. Mosquitoes, and the malaria they carry, are beginning to spread back into areas where they had been eradicated.

Insecticides (pesticides used to kill insects) often kill not only harmful insects, but also helpful ones. Such insecticides are said to be **non-specific**. Thus, a farmer spraying a crop with a pesticide to kill a pest may also kill all the natural predators, such as spiders, of that pest. In future, if he does not keep on spraying with the

▲ **Figure 15.14**
The amount of care taken over the use of pesticides in developed and some developing countries differs greatly. The first picture shows wheat being sprayed near Oxford, England, while in the second one a farmer sprays cotton plants with DDT in Nicaragua. What differences can you see in the way the pesticide is being used? What problems might the Nicaraguan farmer be causing?

pesticide, he will have an even worse problem with the pests than before.

How can all these problems be solved? Much more care is now taken when new pesticides are developed, to make sure that they are not persistent. However, it is now realised that it is in everyone's interest to find other ways of controlling pests. This may involve **biological control**, in which a natural predator of a pest is used to keep the pest's population low. This has the advantages that it is often cheaper, does not cause pollution, and only kills the pest and not other living organisms.

Question

15.3 The table shows the increase in use of pesticides on cotton crops in an area of Sudan between 1959 and 1979.

Year	Average number of times pesticide was sprayed in one year
1959	1.0
1964	2.5
1969	4.9
1974	6.0
1976	6.5
1977	8.1
1978	9.3

a Plot a graph to show these data. Take care with the x-axis!

b Describe what happened to the use of pesticides between 1959 and 1978.

c Suggest reasons for the changes you have described.

d Suggest what the cotton farmers of Sudan might have done to allow them to decrease their use of pesticides.

Pollution by nuclear fallout

Ionising radiation, such as alpha, beta and gamma radiation, damages DNA. This can lead to cancer or birth defects. Exposure to large amounts of radiation can also cause radiation sickness, when so many cells are damaged that the person becomes very ill, and may die.

There is ionising radiation all around, all the time. This is called **background radiation**, and it comes from rocks in the Earth, and from cosmic rays from the Sun. However, in most parts of the world, this background radiation is not great enough to cause any harm.

Nuclear reactions can produce large amounts of radiation. Nuclear reactions take place in nuclear power stations. If these are well designed, well built and well maintained, little or no radiation leaks from them. However, when accidents occur, such as at Chernobyl, large amounts of radioactive substances, emitting ionising radiation, can be released into the air. This is sometimes called nuclear fallout. Nuclear bombs also produce enormous quantities of nuclear fallout.

Some of the radioactive substances produced last for a very long time, and may be carried in the air over very large distances. In the Chernobyl accident, a radioactive form of iodine was produced, which fell to the ground in many countries, including Wales. The radioactive iodine was absorbed by grass, and eaten by sheep. Many years after the accident, it is still not safe to eat sheep which have grazed in some of these areas, because levels of radiation are still high.

Supplement

Pollution by non-biodegradable plastics

Substances such as sewage are **biodegradable**. Given time, bacteria and other microorganisms will break them down. Biodegradable substances cause only short-term pollution problems.

In the past, most of the waste substances produced by humans were biodegradable. However, many substances used in the manufacturing industry, such as metals, glass and plastics, are not biodegradable. If these materials are thrown away, they remain in the environment virtually for ever. They are an eyesore, and can be dangerous to small animals which may get trapped in them.

Disposal of non-biodegradable plastics is a problem. They can be buried, but they then remain in the soil for years. They can be burnt, but many of them release toxic gases.

Some plastics can be **recycled**. The plastic called PET, which is used for making bottles for soft drinks, can be reused. People save their empty PET bottles and take them to a collection point, from where they are taken to a recycling plant to be made into new plastic articles. This reduces plastic pollution. It would be better still if the bottles were cleaned and reused as they are, but this is expensive and difficult to do.

Question

15.4 One way of disposing of non-biodegradable plastics is to burn them in order to produce energy. The table shows the amount of energy released when 1 kg of different kinds of plastics are burnt.

Plastic	Energy released on combustion / kJ per kg
Polystyrene	38 000
Polyethylene	43 000
PVC	22 000
PET	22 000
Mixed plastic	37 000

a State one problem encountered when burning plastics.

b Suggest a use that could be made of the energy released from burning plastic waste.

c Suggest why sorting plastic waste before burning it could be useful.

d Assuming that all of these plastics could be recycled, and using only the information in the table, suggest which plastics would be better recycled than used as a fuel.

Conserving natural resources

Humans take and use a great many materials from the Earth. These are called **resources**. We shall consider just three examples – fossil fuels, water and trees used for paper.

Fossil fuels were produced millions of years ago. They are only forming very slowly, in just a few tiny areas, now. As we use up the fossil fuels in the Earth, they are not renewed. They are *non-renewable resources*.

Huge amounts of fossil fuels are being used all over the world, especially in developed countries, to provide energy. This causes several problems. Two such problems are:

- Burning fossil fuels causes pollution by carbon dioxide, sulphur dioxide and nitrogen oxides.

- Our supply of fossil fuels will soon run out.

Although some attempts have been made by some countries to cut down their energy consumption, and hence their rate of use of fossil fuels, there has been little success in this. Instead, we are beginning to turn to using **renewable resources** for energy production. These include solar power, wave and tidal power, hydroelectric power and wind power. By using these resources for generating electricity, we can not only reduce our rate of use of fossil fuels and ensure that we have energy supplies in the future, but can also reduce pollution.

Water is a vital substance which is in short supply in many countries. Although there is plenty of water on Earth to provide every person with more than enough for their needs, the distribution of water is very uneven. Thus, in parts of the world where population is very dense, or where rainfall is very low, water may be a resource that needs to be **conserved**.

Trees are used for many purposes, and the problems caused by deforestation have been described earlier. Many trees are cut down to produce **paper**.

Conservation of species and their environments

The impact of human activities on the environment, such as deforestation, farming and pollution, has caused

▲ Figure 15.15
When old forest trees are cut down, lasting damage is done, because it takes so long for such trees to be replaced. The environment is likely to be permanently damaged, destroying habitats for many different species of living organisms.

tremendous changes to the habitats of many organisms. This can destroy some species completely, making them extinct. Figure 15.16 shows some causes of threats to mammals and birds.

For example, the cutting down of tropical rainforest puts large numbers of species in danger of extinction. One hectare of tropical rainforest may contain 200 different species of trees, and thousands of species of other plants and animals. Many of these species have very small ranges, so that cutting down quite a small piece of forest may remove almost all of their habitat. It is very easy to make such a species extinct.

This is not a problem that has just begun to happen. Humans have been causing extinctions for a very long time. For example, it is thought that the first humans settled on the Pacific islands of Fiji, Tonga and Samoa about 3000 years ago. Their coming caused mass extinctions of animals living on the islands. Of the 25 species of flightless birds that lived there, only 8 survive today.

Similarly, Hawaii has suffered great losses of bird species. When European settlers first arrived there in 1778, there were 50 species of birds living there. Now there are only 34.

Why does it matter if a species becomes extinct? For many people, there is no question about this – it is obvious that the loss of a species is a loss to the whole

Figure 15.16 ▶
The relative importance of six types of environmental threat to mammals and birds.

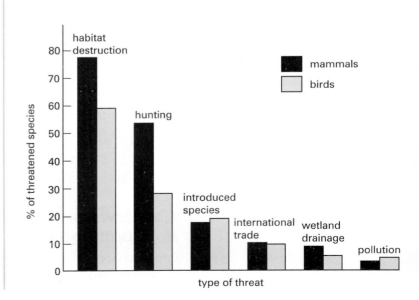

world. The fewer species there are on Earth, the less diverse and rich is our environment.

There are other arguments, too, directly related to the potential benefits to humans of conserving as many species as possible. The more different species there are in an ecosystem, the more stable the ecosystem is. This means that any changes which take place – such as a new disease evolving, or a climatic disaster – have less chance of causing lasting damage to the ecosystem than if only a few species live in it. Complex, rich ecosystems, with many different species living in them, help to stabilise the environment, making it more able to support not only the species that live in it but also humans as well. Rich ecosystems mean a healthy Earth.

You may be surprised to know that large numbers of new species are discovered each year. We still do not know all the different kinds of living things on the Earth. In 1993, the number of known species was about 1.4 million. Some biologists estimate that this is only one tenth of the number of species which live on Earth! Of course, these as yet undiscovered species will not be large animals, but mostly small ones such as insects (especially beetles), and small plants. When we destroy part of a tropical rainforest, we may be destroying many totally unknown species, for ever.

Some of these species may be directly useful to humans. For example, one small plant that comes from Madagascar, called the rosy periwinkle, was recently discovered to contain a chemical which can help to cure cancer. The use of this plant has saved the lives of hundreds of children suffering from leukemia. How many other useful, unknown, species exist?

Much can be done to reduce the likelihood of extinctions. The main focus must be on conservation of whole ecosystems. This means reducing the impact humans have on areas which are especially important for wildlife, such as tropical forests. However, this is not easy. Many of the countries in which tropical rainforests still grow are relatively poor. By cutting down their forests, people can temporarily increase their standard of living, by selling timber from the forest, or by increasing the amount of agricultural land. Such countries need help from richer ones, in order to be able to afford conservation measures. The developed

countries must not forget that they have already
destroyed many of their natural habitats.

Question

15.5 One strategy used to attempt to conserve species is to
preserve areas of their habitat.

For example, as rainforest in one part of the Amazon basin
was destroyed, areas of different sizes were left as
undisturbed habitat. Biologists counted the number of
species of birds in these areas before and after the removal
of the rainforest around them. They did this in areas of two
different sizes, one hectare and ten hectares. The results are
shown in Figure 15.17.

a Suggest why the number of bird species caught in the
area increased in the few weeks after the surrounding
forest was cut down compared with before.

b Suggest why the number of bird species caught in the
area gradually decreased to below the original levels.

c What do these results suggest about the usefulness of
such isolated patches of undisturbed habitat as wildlife
reserves?

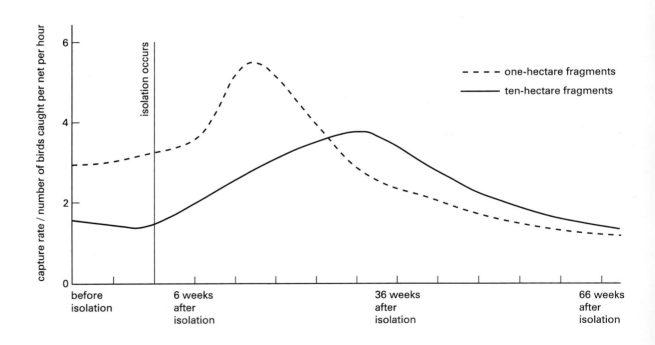

▲ **Figure 15.17**
The numbers of birds caught
before and after isolation of
fragments of forest.

Recycling

One way of conserving water is to reuse or **recycle** it. Water that has been used for washing, or in industry, or for any other purpose, can be treated to make it suitable for reuse. This can also apply to water that has been drunk! It is excreted from the body in urine, which can be treated in sewage plants to destroy any harmful organisms and produce a harmless effluent. The water will need further treatment before it is pure enough to drink.

We can reduce the number of trees that are cut down by recycling paper. Newspapers, magazines and cardboard wrapping can be collected and taken to recycling plants. Here, the print on the paper is removed using chemicals, and the paper mixed with water to make a slurry before being re-rolled into sheets. Recycled paper is not as pure white as 'first-time round' paper, nor can it be of such a fine texture. However, it is very suitable for making paper towels, paper bags, writing paper and packaging.

It should be realised, however, that in many parts of the world the trees cut down to make paper have been specially planted just for this purpose. When they are harvested, new trees are planted to take their place. Paper-making does most harm to the environment when the trees used are taken from mature forests, such as tropical rainforests, which are irreplaceable.

Summary

- Modern technology has greatly increased the output from farming. However, this technology is not always available to farmers in developing countries.
- Deforestation and overgrazing can cause soil erosion, which in turn can lead to flooding.
- Water pollution by fertilisers or untreated sewage can cause bacterial populations to increase rapidly. The bacteria use up oxygen in the water, so that animals such as fish cannot live there. This is called eutrophication.
- Sulphur dioxide is produced when coal or oil are burned. It combines with oxygen and water in the air to form acids, which fall as acid rain. This can damage trees and aquatic organisms.

- Nuclear fallout of radioactive substances can increase the likelihood of mutations occurring.
- Non-biodegradable substances, such as plastics, can cause pollution and may harm animals.
- Pesticides and herbicides that are not biodegradable can build up as they pass along a food chain, so that animals feeding at the end of the chain absorb large amounts of them and may be harmed.
- Conservation aims to maintain biodiversity and conserve natural resources. Recyling, for example of paper or water (sewage treatment) can reduce our use of natural resources and reduce pollution.

Investigations: apparatus and guidelines

Investigation 1.1 Looking at vertebrates
Skill C2

Apparatus list

Per student or group:
- living, dead or preserved specimens of one example of each of the five vertebrate classes, preferably organisms found locally.

Investigation 2.1 Looking at animal cells
Skills C1, C2

Apparatus list

Per class:
- a source of animal cells, for example some macerated liver or scrapings from the lining of the trachea from a set of sheep or other lungs (obtainable from a butcher).
- methylene blue, diluted but still strong enough to give a good blue colouring to cell nuclei – it is best to try this out first.

Per student or group:
- a clean microscope slide and coverslip
- a microscope with at least two objective lenses
- a piece of filter paper
- a dropper pipette.

Investigation 2.2 Looking at plant cells
Skills C1, C2

Apparatus list

Per class:
- a supply of filamentous pondweed, with strands made up of single cells joined end to end
- an onion, which can be cut into many pieces to provide each group of students with a small square containing some epidermis
- implements for handling and cutting specimens – forceps, tile, kitchen knife.

Per student or group:
- a microscope, two microscope slides, two coverslips
- filter paper
- a dropper pipette.

Teachers might also like to supply iodine in potassium iodide solution, which students could use to stain their plant specimens, to show up starch grains. This could be used instead of the drop of water, or could be introduced later by placing a drop at one edge of the coverslip, and then drawing it across the specimen by placing a piece of filter paper at the opposite edge.

Investigation 2.3 How quickly does ammonia diffuse?
Skills C2, C3 (both suitable for assessment) and part C4

Although this example of diffusion has no direct biological application, it does demonstrate diffusion quickly and vividly, and provides an opportunity for students to practise three Domain C skills.

The apparatus for this investigation is shown in Figure 2.9. The tube needs to be around 1 m long, as this allows several pieces of litmus paper to be arranged a reasonable distance apart. A longer tube gives better results, but it then becomes very difficult to place the pieces of litmus paper accurately. Even with a 1 m tube, the teacher will need to use a long thin implement to push the pieces of paper into place.

It is best to try out the concentration of ammonia solution beforehand. Bench strength ammonia solution will work, but more dramatic results are obtained with more concentrated solutions. However, these will produce unpleasant fumes, however quick you are at pushing the soaked cotton wool into the end of the tube and sealing it in with a rubber bung. If this is a problem, the experiment could be performed in a fume cupboard.

Investigation 2.4 Can iodine molecules or starch molecules get through Visking tubing?

Skills C1, C2, C3
Apparatus list

Per class:
- about 200 cm³ of starch suspension – the exact concentration does not matter
- about 500 cm³ of iodine in potassium iodide solution – again, the exact concentration does not matter, and it may be best to use a more dilute solution than normal, as students need relatively large quantities, and also need to be able to see through it.

Per group:
- a piece of Visking tubing about 150 mm long, and about 20 mm in diameter
- a dropper pipette
- a piece of cotton thread, long enough to tie around the tubing
- a small beaker or other container.

Investigation 2.5 Osmosis

Skills C1, C2, C3 (all suitable for assessment if done individually)
Apparatus list

Per student or group (see Figure 2.12):
- a piece of Visking tubing about 150 mm long – the exact length does not matter
- a dropper pipette
- some cotton thread
- some concentrated sugar solution
- a piece of glass tubing, at least 150 mm long
- a beaker
- a retort stand, boss and clamp
- a pen for marking on glass.

The exact concentration of the sugar solution is unimportant, but more rapid results will be obtained with a relatively concentrated solution.

Investigation 2.6 Osmosis and potato cells

Skills C1, C2, C3 (all suitable for assessment)
Apparatus list

Per class:
- distilled water
- four sucrose solutions, in the range 0.1 mol dm⁻³ to 0.8 mol dm⁻³, enough of each for each group to cover two pieces of potato in the containers provided.

Per group:
- one or two potatoes; these could be cleaned or peeled just beforehand, or the students could do this themselves
- a means of cutting equal sized pieces of potato, for example, a cork borer or kitchen knife
- paper towels
- five containers, large enough to take two pieces of potato
- a means of labelling these containers
- a ruler calibrated in millimetres.

Investigation 3.1 The effect of plant material on hydrogen peroxide

Skills C1, C2, C3 (not really sufficiently demanding for assessment purposes)

The experiment could be extended to investigate the effect of temperature on catalase in a more quantitative way. The living material could be exposed to different temperatures before being added to the hydrogen peroxide solution. The relative rates of reaction could be estimated by measuring the height of froth in the tubes, or by collecting the gas given off over water.

Apparatus list

Per class:
- a supply of one type of raw and cooked biological material, such as Irish potato, apple, celery, liver, or yeast suspension (one of these is sufficient)
- a supply of 20 volume hydrogen peroxide solution
- a supply of manganese(IV) oxide
- a flame in which a wooden splint can be lit.

Per student or group:
- three test tubes in a rack or beaker
- a dropper pipette
- a tile and knife on which to cut pieces of the biological material supplied
- a spatula or similar implement for handling this material
- a wooden splint
- safety glasses.

Investigation 3.2 The effect of temperature on the rate of breakdown of protein by trypsin

Skills C1, C2, C3 (all suitable for assessment, although not very demanding for Skill C2)

Like the catalase experiment, this is one in which the reaction produces a visible result, with no need for additional tests. Here, however, it is the disappearance of the substrate that can be observed, rather than the appearance of a product. The concentrations suggested should give results within 20 minutes or so.

Teachers might like to provide the students with a *reference tube*, in which the milk protein has been digested, so that they can see its appearance. This can be done by adding some $2\,mol\,dm^{-3}$ hydrochloric acid to some of the milk suspension, and keeping it warm for a few minutes.

Apparatus list

Per class:

- water baths at temperatures ranging from $0\,°C$ (crushed ice) or below ($-4\,°C$ in a freezer), through room temperature, to boiling, with thermometers for checking temperatures
- trypsin solution made by dissolving 0.5 g of trypsin in $100\,cm^3$ of distilled water – each group will need at least $25\,cm^3$ of this solution
- milk made by adding about 4 g of fat-free milk powder to $100\,cm^3$ of water – again, each group will need at least $25\,cm^3$ of this suspension
- a means of measuring $5\,cm^3$ accurately, such as small measuring cylinder or syringe
- method of timing
- means of labelling tubes (not with sticky paper labels, as these will wash off in the water baths).

Students who think carefully about this experiment will realise that it has no control. They cannot know whether it is the trypsin, or the different temperatures alone, that cause the changes in appearance of the milk suspension. This makes a good discussion point, and is something that should be included in an evaluation. If students realise this early on, then they could include control tubes in their investigation.

Investigation 3.3 The effect of pH on the breakdown of milk protein by trypsin

Skill C4 (suitable for assessment if planned and carried out individually)

This makes a relatively easy first chance for students to design an experiment for themselves. They will already have done Investigation 3.2, so will be familiar with the reaction. It is important to make sure that all students are familiar with the pH scale.

If this is the first time the students have been asked to plan an experiment, teachers may like to do this as a class activity. The design could be discussed by the teacher and students, with students providing the ideas rather than the teacher, whose role is to guide these ideas until they form a suitable plan. This should include a careful consideration of possible variables other than pH, which include temperature, volume and concentration of the substrate and enzyme, and total volume of reacting mixture.

One potential problem is that very low pHs will hydrolyse casein. In effect, this limits the possible range of pH to be tested from about 4 upwards. In practice, this is no problem, as the optimum pH for trypsin from most sources is around 8 or even 9.

Apparatus list

Students will ask for their apparatus, but are likely to require:

- trypsin solution and milk suspension, made up as in Investigation 3.2
- test tubes and rack
- buffer solutions ranging from 4 to 10 or over (these are easiest to make up from tablets, available from most suppliers)
- Universal Indicator solution or paper
- a water bath at around $37\,°C$
- a means of timing
- a means of measuring small volumes, such as a small measuring cylinder or syringe.

Investigation 4.1 Testing foods for carbohydrates

Skills C1, C2 (both suitable for assessment)
Apparatus list

Per class:
For both tests:
- at least five different foods, chosen so that some contain starch and/or sugar and some do not. Some foods of animal origin, such as fish, meat, eggs or milk, should be included, to enable students to answer question **4.3b**. It is best to avoid foods that the students will know contain sugar, but that do not contain *reducing* sugar, such as cakes and sweets. Raisins and sultanas can be guaranteed to give a good positive test for reducing sugar.

Per student or group:
For both tests:
- surface on which to put foods
- spatula or similar implement.

For starch test:
- iodine in potassium iodide solution
- dropper pipette.

For reducing sugar test:
- access to thermostatically controlled boiling water bath, or means of boiling water – Bunsen burner, heatproof mat, tripod, gauze, 250 cm³ beaker
- safety glasses
- five boiling tubes
- means of chopping or crushing food samples
- Benedict's solution
- dropper pipette.

Students should be able to design their own results tables, with help available to those who find this difficult. These should have separate columns for results and conclusions. The results should state the *colour* observed, not simply 'no change'. Students should be encouraged to record all relevant details of their observations, for example which parts of the food turned blue-black when iodine solution was added, or how long it took for the red-brown colour to appear when boiling with Benedict's solution.

If the same five foods are used for each test, then one results table could serve for both.

Investigation 4.2 Testing foods for protein

Skills C1, C2
Apparatus list

Per class:
- at least five foods, chosen so that some contain protein and some do not. Those that do contain protein should include some of animal origin, and some of plant origin, such as lentils or other legume seeds.

Per student or group:
- surface on which to put foods
- means of chopping or crushing food samples
- spatula or similar
- five test tubes
- 20% potassium hydroxide solution and 1% copper sulphate (or biuret reagent) and dropper pipette
- safety glasses.

The purple colour indicating the presence of protein is not always easy to distinguish from blue. It is recommended that a test is first done on water, which gives a blue colour, and then on albumen solution, which gives a good strong purple. These two tubes can then be put on display as references against which students can compare the colours they obtain.

The biuret test identifies the presence of peptide bonds, and only gives clear results for soluble proteins. Some foods may therefore not give good positive results, even if they are known to contain protein. Foods which give a good purple colour include cheese, milk and crushed pulses. Bread also gives a positive test.

Care should be taken with potassium hydroxide, as it is a strong alkali. This feels soapy on the skin, and students should be alerted to watch out for this feeling, and to rinse their skin if they think they may have some reagent on it.

Investigation 4.3 Testing foods for fats

As the ethanol test uses absolute alcohol, teachers may prefer to demonstrate it rather than allow students to perform the test.

Apparatus list

Per class:
- at least five foods, some of which should contain fat and some not. This test works best with fats which are not too solid at room temperature.

Per student or group:
- surface on which to put foods
- means of chopping or crushing food samples
- ten very clean and dry tubes and test tube rack
- absolute ethanol and dropper pipette
- access to distilled water.

Investigation 4.4 Which milk makes the best yoghurt?

Skills C2, C3 (both suitable for assessment)
Apparatus list

Per class
- one or two small pots of natural yoghurt containing live bacteria (read the label carefully to ensure that the yoghurt has not been heat-treated to kill the bacteria – yoghurt containing live bacteria is sometimes labelled 'live yoghurt')
- a warm place, or a water bath set at about 40 °C
- a pH meter if available, or Universal Indicator solution
- a small roll of clingfilm.

Per student or group:

- about 10 cm³ of two types of milk – possible types include: cow's milk; goat's milk; sheep's milk; pasteurised, raw or sterilised, skimmed or whole milk; milk made up from milk powder
- two clean boiling tubes or other small containers and a rack or beaker
- a clean syringe, pipette, measuring cylinder or other method of measuring 10 cm³
- a method of labelling the boiling tubes or other containers.

As the bacteria work on the milk, two noticeable changes will occur. The milk will become thicker, and its pH will drop as lactose in the milk is converted to lactic acid. If students cannot taste the yoghurt, then they will have to rely on these two features to compare the yoghurts which they make.

Investigation 4.5 Making bread

Skill C4 (suitable for assessment, although limited as there is little opportunity for selection of techniques or apparatus)
Apparatus list

Per student or group:

- a little sugar (sucrose or glucose)
- a little yeast
- two 250 cm³ beakers
- about 75 g of flour
- at least one 100 cm³ measuring cylinder.

Other requirements will vary according to the hypothesis being tested. If ascorbic acid is being investigated, students could add about 1 g to the flour before mixing.

Times taken for rising vary considerably, and this must be allowed for; students should be able to measure the volume of their dough throughout the day, in case it rises only slowly. The measurement of the volume of the dough in a measuring cylinder is not ideal, and students should discuss this when writing up their investigation.

If this investigation can be done in a cookery room, then the risen dough can be baked and eaten. It is best to shape it into rolls, place these on a greased tray, and cook in a hot oven for about 10 to 15 minutes.

Investigation 5.1 Human teeth

This activity involves eating, and so should not be performed in a laboratory. As no apparatus apart from a mirror and a piece of food is required, this can easily be carried out at home.

Investigation 6.1 Oxygen production by a water plant

Skill C1 (suitable for assessment. If the experiment designed in question 4 is carried out, then Skills C2, C3 and C4 can also be assessed.)

The species most commonly used for this experiment is *Elodea canadensis* or other *Elodea* species. These have the advantage that bubbles of oxygen form on the cut ends of stems, which enables them to be trapped relatively easily. However, it is well worth experimenting with other water plants if *Elodea* is not available – and even if it is, as it can be unreliable.

Apparatus list

Per class:

- a supply of *Elodea* or other aquatic plant, as described above
- a supply of pond, stream, river or other water, as described below
- a Bunsen burner.

Per student or group:

- a glass beaker, about 250 cm³, or other transparent container
- a test tube
- a retort stand, boss and clamp
- a wooden splint.

The following procedures will maximise the chances of obtaining measurable oxygen production in a relatively short time.

- Obtain the plants a few days before you wish to use them, and keep them in a light, warm place, preferably in pond water, for several days before use. This gives them a chance to 'settle down' and photosynthesise. It also gives you the chance to see which pieces are performing well, and which are not.
- Just before use, make a slanting cut across the plant stem. This diagonal cut allows the oxygen bubbles to emerge and collect on the sloping surface before rising up from the plant.
- Use water from a relatively unpolluted pond, stream or river if at all possible – but do take care not to expose students to any potentially harmful organisms in this water. If this is not possible, then collect some tap water into a large, open container a few days before you wish to use it, to give time for at least some of the chemicals used in treatment, such as chlorine, to be lost.
- Add a little sodium hydrogencarbonate to the water before use, to ensure that the plant has an adequate 'carbon dioxide' supply.

- Provide water of a suitable temperature, neither too cold nor too hot; around 20–25 °C is ideal for *Elodea*, but this is worth experimenting with if other plants are used. The optimum temperature is likely to be close to that of the natural conditions in which the plant grows.
- Natural light is preferable to artificial light. In temperate countries, photosynthesis experiments are best carried out in spring or summer.

Investigation 6.2 Do leaves need light and chlorophyll to make starch?

Skills C1, C2, C3 (all suitable for assessment)

Teachers may prefer to separate this exercise into two, or even three – first testing a leaf for starch, then investigating the effects of light and chlorophyll separately.

Apparatus list

Per class:
- destarched variegated pot plants, with enough leaves for each student or group to have one, and still leave a few on the plants
- 70% ethanol.

Per student or group:
First session:
- black paper to wrap around a leaf
- scissors
- paperclips or access to a stapler.

Second session:
- a Bunsen burner, tripod, heat-proof mat and gauze
- a 250 cm³ beaker
- boiling tube
- forceps
- white tile
- iodine in potassium iodide and a dropper pipette.

Most variegated plants are suitable for this experiment, but those with very waxy leaves do not give such good results as those with dull leaves. *Pelargonium* is ideal. It is well worth trying the method out beforehand, so that students can be advised on the length of time for which to boil their leaf.

Ideally, the students should test the destarched plants before putting on the black paper, to check that there is no starch present before their experiment begins. In practice, this is time-consuming and could perhaps be done as a demonstration by the teacher.

Great care needs to be taken not to set fire to the ethanol. The best way to avoid this is to ensure that the Bunsen burner is turned out before the ethanol is given to the students. If the ethanol in the tube does begin to burn, a damp cloth placed gently over the top of the tube puts out the flame immediately.

This investigation tests for *starch*, whereas the equation given on page 83 indicates that *glucose* (sugar) is made by photosynthesis. It should be explained to students that some glucose is converted to starch for storage. Starch is likely to be present in larger quantities than is glucose, and is easier to test for.

Investigation 7.1 Listening to a heart beating

Skills C1, C2, C3 (not sufficiently demanding for assessment)
Apparatus list

- a stethoscope makes this exercise easier.

The sounds that can be heard are the valves shutting; you cannot hear any sound made by the muscles contracting. The sounds make a rhythm which can be represented as *lub-dup, lub-dup, lub-dup*. The first sound, *lub*, is made by the closure of the atrioventricular valves. It is followed by the *dup* sound, which is made by the closure of the semilunar valves in the aorta and pulmonary artery. The time interval between *lub* and *dup* is much shorter than between *dup* and *lub*. Some students may be able to use their own observations, and the information about time intervals on Figure 7.7, to work out what *lub* and *dup* represent, but most will need help.

It is not uncommon in young people for another sound to be audible, during diastole – this is quite normal.

During deep inspiration, the right ventricle takes slightly longer to fill and empty, so that it momentarily gets out of step with the left ventricle. This sometimes allows the closing of the valves on the left and right sides of the heart to be heard separately.

Investigation 7.2 The effect of exercise on heartbeat

Skills C2, C3 (suitable for assessment of C2, but not C3 until respiration has been fully covered)

A full interpretation of the results of this experiment is not possible until aerobic and anaerobic respiration have been covered in Chapter 9. Teachers may prefer to leave this investigation until then, when it could be combined with Investigation 9.5.

It is much easier to take someone else's pulse than your own, so that working with a partner is better than working individually. If a student has difficulty in finding a pulse in the wrist, an alternative point is just to one side of the trachea in the neck.

The line graph should have time in minutes on the x-axis, and pulse rate in beats per minute on the y-axis. Points should be joined with straight lines drawn with a ruler. Some method of indicating when sitting, standing and exercising took place should be used, such as vertical lines drawn on the graph.

Investigation 8.1 Measuring the rate of water uptake

Skills C1, C2, C3 (all suitable for assessment. If the experiment designed in step 7 is carried out, this can be used for assessment of Skill C4)
Apparatus list

Per student or group:
- a photometer
- graph paper, if the photometer tube is not calibrated
- one or more leafy shoots (see above)
- a stopclock, or sight of a clock with a second hand.

Students will ask for their own apparatus for step 7, but are likely to need some of the following:

- a fan
- access to a dark space (for example, a cupboard)
- access to a cold place (for example, a refrigerator)
- Vaseline (to cover leaf surfaces).

Investigation 8.2 Adaptations of plants to their environment

Skills C2, C3 (both suitable for assessment)

In question **8.4**, students have the opportunity to look at pictures of plants from a variety of countries, and to consider how they are adapted for their environments. In this investigation, the emphasis should be on plants that grow locally.

While it is very desirable for students to look at living plants, great care must be taken not to damage habitats. By far the best way of observing plants is to go out into the environment, and see them growing *in situ*, and it is strongly recommended that this should be done. As a last resort, plant material could be brought into the laboratory for examination.

Plants from at least two contrasting environments should be studied. The choices will depend on the situation of the school.

Investigation 9.1 Releasing energy from a peanut

Skills C1, C2, C3 (all suitable for assessment)

This classic investigation is of great value in helping students to understand the way energy can be released from food. It is presented as a quantitative exercise, but could easily be adapted to be merely qualitative if desired. Peanuts (groundnuts) are specified because they are cheap, but any type of nut can be used. You may need to avoid peanuts if anyone in your class has an allergy to them – check this first. Students might like to compare the energy content of different types of nut, which ranges between about 2000 and 2700 kJ/100 g. In practice, however, these differences are so small as to be quite lost in the unavoidable errors in this investigation. A rather messy, but interesting, alternative is to use cubes of dry bread and bread soaked in oil. A large heatproof mat (to catch the burning, dripping oil) will then be needed, as well as safety goggles.

Apparatus list

Per class:
- balance to weigh to at least 0.1 g and preferably to 0.01 g.

Per student or group:
- Bunsen burner and heat-proof mat
- one peanut
- a mounted needle (preferably with a wooden handle)
- a retort stand, clamp and boss
- a boiling tube
- means of measuring 40 cm³ of water
- a thermometer 0–110 °C.

It is important that the water does not reach

boiling point, or the amount of energy cannot be calculated. One peanut will normally cause a suitable temperature rise in 40 cm^3 of water, but teachers should be prepared to adapt this volume if necessary.

Questions

The opportunity is provided for students to work out for themselves how to do the calculations. Some may need considerable help.

1 Energy that went into the water
= temperature rise/°C × volume of water/cm^3
× 4.2 joules

2 Energy in 1 g of peanut
$$= \frac{\text{answer to question 1/joules}}{\text{mass of peanut}}$$

3 and 4 There are very many reasons. The two most important groups include:

- Incomplete combustion of the peanut – this includes the probability that some of the 'peanut molecules' did not completely oxidise, which could be improved by burning in pure oxygen; and also that some of the peanut did not burn at all, which could be partly taken into account by subtracting the mass of the peanut that remained after burning from the original mass, to find the mass that actually burned.
- Heat loss to surroundings – to air, through the walls of the boiling tube, through the mounted needle; this could be partly remedied by insulating the tube, or by enclosing the whole apparatus, as in a calorimeter.
- Students may also suggest inaccurate measurement of the water volume, or inaccurate measurement of temperature; these should not be important factors, and are not good answers to this type of question.

Investigation 9.2 Comparing inspired and expired air

Skills C1, C3, C3 (not sufficiently demanding for assessment)
Apparatus list

Per student or group:

- the apparatus shown in Figure 9.5; any transparent container will do in place of the boiling tubes
- some hydrogencarbonate indicator solution or limewater
- a thermometer
- some dry cobalt chloride paper.

Investigation 9.3 How the diaphragm helps with breathing

Skills C2, C3 (neither suitable for assessment)
Apparatus list

See Figure 9.13. This apparatus can be made from any transparent airtight container, across whose base an air-impermeable barrier can be stretched.

1 Lungs – the balloons.
Ribs and body wall – the container (the bell jar in the photograph).
Diaphragm – the rubber sheet.
Trachea and bronchi – the tubes leading from the air to the balloons.

2 The balloons inflate. This is because you have increased the volume inside the bell jar, thus reducing the air pressure there so that it is lower than the air pressure outside the bell jar. Air moves in down this pressure gradient. The only way in is through the glass tubes, so the air goes into the balloons.

3 The pulling down of the rubber sheet is like the downward movement of the diaphragm as its muscles contract when you breathe in. When you let go of the sheet, it springs back up, just as the diaphragm does as its muscles relax when you breathe out.

4 The intercostal muscles (students may also suggest others, such as skin).

Investigation 9.4 Anaerobic respiration in yeast

Skills C1, C2, C3 (not sufficiently demanding for assessment)

This is a standard experiment, and may have been carried out by students in Chemistry lessons. If not carefully prepared, very little may happen. To ensure success:

- Ensure that the yeast used is alive and active; if dried yeast is used, test some before the practical session to make sure that it will be activated by immersion in warm water and sugar – if not, obtain a new supply.
- Keep everything warm, but not hot. The water used should be around 20–30 °C – in a warm room, no heating will be required, but in cold temperatures a water bath could be used both for activating the yeast and for the experimental apparatus.
- Ensure that the amounts of yeast suspension used in the apparatus are reasonably large,

so that there is not a large air space in which the carbon dioxide can accumulate rather than affecting the carbon dioxide concentration in the indicator.

Apparatus list

Per student or group:
- about 40–50 cm^3 of activated yeast suspension, made by mixing about 1–2 g of dried yeast into boiled, warm water
- a small quantity of sucrose solution, concentration unimportant
- glassware, bungs and tubing shown in Figure 9.15
- limewater
- a small amount of oil such as olive oil
- a dropper pipette.

Investigation 9.5 The effect of exercise on breathing rate

Skill C4 (suitable for assessment; could also be used for assessment of Skills C2 and C3)

No apparatus is required.

This investigation gives students an opportunity to think carefully about controlling variables – not an easy task in this context. A good plan will either involve repeat measurements on one person, or measurements on several different people, rather than a 'one-off' experiment. Testing of the third hypothesis needs at least one week, whereas the other two can be done in a single session. The investigations can either be done individually, or with students working in pairs; this latter arrangement can, however, make assessment very difficult.

Investigation 10.1 Investigating factors that affect the rate of heat loss from the body

Skills C2, C3, C4 (all suitable for assessment)

Students will probably have drawn cooling curves before, and most should be able to record, interpret and evaluate their results with little if any assistance. These investigations give ample opportunity for controlling variables. It is best if each student tests just one hypothesis; class results can then be pooled and discussed.

Water at a temperature of around 80 °C makes a good starting point. The easiest way to provide this is to boil a kettle; by the time the water is transferred to the test tubes, its temperature will have dropped to around 80 °C.

Apparatus list

Students will ask for their own apparatus, but are likely to require some of:
- several test tubes, perhaps with holes through which thermometers can be inserted
- corks or bungs to fit the tubes, perhaps with holes through which thermometers can be inserted
- access to a supply of hot water
- retort stands, bosses and clamps
- beakers
- a means of measuring water volumes, e.g. a measuring cylinder
- thermometers
- rubber bands
- various types of material for insulating
- bowls or other large containers which can be filled with water
- stopclocks or sight of a clock with a second hand.

Investigation 11.1 The structure of the human eye

Skill C2 (suitable for assessment)

This is a straightforward task of observation and recording. No apparatus is required, except mirrors if students wish to draw their own eye rather than someone else's.

Investigation 11.2 Looking at a sheep's eye

Skills C1, C2 (both suitable for assessment if done individually)

There is no doubt that this exercise does give great pleasure to some students, but it can also cause distress to others. The decision about whether or not to carry it out should be made carefully, and no student should be forced to take part if they are unhappy to do so.

Apparatus list
- eyes from a sheep or other animal – these may have been previously frozen
- dishes or boards
- newspaper
- dissecting scissors, forceps and scalpel
- disposable gloves.

Investigation 11.3 Investigating phototaxis in maggots

Skills C2, C3 (suitable for assessment)

Maggots are often available from pet shops, where they are sold as food for some kinds of birds or lizards, and in shops that sell fishing equipment. If maggots are not available, then alternative invertebrates can be used. They should be small, move slowly enough for records to be easily kept of their movements, and show a clear taxic response to a stimulus.

Apparatus list

Per student or group:
- at least five active, clean maggots
- a large sheet of paper, at least A2 size, preferably larger, ruled into squares (this could be done by the students)
- a source of bright light, for example a lamp or a window
- a means of shading the paper from all directions except one
- a stopclock or sight of a clock with a second hand.

No help is given to the students in writing up the investigation, thus giving them the opportunity to demonstrate achievement at the highest levels of *Skills C2* and *C3*.

Investigation 11.4 The response of cress seedlings to light

Skill C2 (suitable for assessment)
Apparatus list

Per class:
- three cardboard boxes.

Per student or group:
- some cress seeds, or small seeds of any quickly germinating plant
- three Petri dishes with lids, or other small containers that can be covered to prevent desiccation
- absorbent material on which to sow seeds, for example cotton wool or filter paper (soil is not appropriate, as it can introduce uncontrolled variables).

Cress seedlings will germinate very rapidly, and, depending on environmental temperature, may provide results within three or four days. Germination rates should not vary in the three conditions. Subsequent growth, however, will

show marked differences. The seedlings grown in complete darkness will become **etiolated**; they will be taller and thinner than the others, with long internodes and yellow stems and leaves, indicating absence of chlorophyll. Those in light from all sides will be short and strong, with short internodes and large green leaves. Those in unidirectional light will be similar, though perhaps a little etiolated, leaning towards the direction from which light came.

Investigation 12.1 Investigating a flower

Skills C2, C3 (suitable for assessment of C2)

Students will probably already know a little about flowers. This investigation gives them the opportunity to look closely at one flower, and to work out the functions of each part. It is suggested that this practical should be done *before* they have covered this work in theory.

Apparatus list

Per student or group:
- one or more insect-pollinated flowers from a named locally-growing plant
- a hand lens – or, preferably, a microscope and glass slides
- a sharp knife or scalpel
- a white tile or other suitable surface on which to work.

Investigation 12.2 The structure of a seed

Skills C2, C3 (both suitable for assessment – extra tasks such as measurement could be added)

There is no better way of understanding how a flower eventually produces seeds inside a fruit than looking carefully at the different stages in this process. In this investigation, bean or pea pods are suggested, but there may be many other possibilities available. Simply adapt these ideas to fit whatever plant material you can find. If students have not previously drawn annotated diagrams, they could refer to Figure 2.6 to give them an idea of what they should do. You may need to remind them to give a scale with each drawing.

If the micropyle is difficult to find, immerse the soaked seed in water and squeeze gently – small bubbles should appear from the micropyle.

Apparatus list

Per student or group:
- a fresh pea or bean pod, containing developing seeds

- a soaked bean seed
- a tile or other surface on which to work.

Investigation 12.3 Fruits

Skills C2, C3 (both suitable for assessment)

The fruits to be provided will depend on what is available locally. It is well worth keeping a collection of dry fruits, which can be used for many years.

Apparatus list

Per student or group:
- a variety of locally-obtained fruits, to show different methods of dispersal, if possible with flowers also – but take care – consider conservation!

There are many other possibilities for investigations related to seed and fruit dispersal. For example:

- The pattern of dispersal of winged seeds or fruits around a tree could be investigated. Samples can be taken using quadrats. The distribution could be related to factors such as wind direction or shelter.
- The length of time fruits with wings of different surface areas, or with different numbers of wings, spend in the air can be investigated. This can be done by making 'model fruits' out of paper – this is the easiest way to vary wing length while keeping all other factors constant. Students could be asked to design their own investigation, which would probably entail dropping the 'fruits' from a standard height, and timing the fall. Alternatively, real fruits could be investigated. There are several types of trees that naturally produce fruits with different wing sizes or numbers; their dispersal could be investigated either in the field, by measuring the distance from the tree of fruits found on the ground, or in the laboratory in the same way as the 'model fruits' described above.
- The success of germination and subsequent growth of seeds planted near to the parent tree could be investigated. Competition between seedlings can also be measured by growing different numbers of seedlings together in small containers, and keeping records of height, number of leaves, etc.

Investigation 12.4 What conditions are needed for seed germination?

Skill C4 (suitable for assessment so long as the teacher is certain that students have not done this investigation before, and have not used reference books to produce their design)

In producing a design for this investigation, care will be needed to keep all variables constant except the one under consideration. Thus, a tube to test whether light is needed should be supplied with all other factors suspected to be necessary, except light.

Light and soil are included because many students believe these to be needed for germination. No seeds need soil, but some do need light. These tend to be very small seeds, which germinate on the surface of recently disturbed soil; some varieties of lettuce have this requirement.

Students should find that seeds need moisture, a suitable temperature and air for germination.

Apparatus list

Per student or group:
- viable seeds, preferably small, and of a variety that germinates rapidly, such as mustard
- several test tubes, boiling tubes or other small transparent containers
- black paper
- scissors and glue or sticky tape
- boiled cooled water
- oil
- cotton wool or other material that will soak up and hold water.

Investigation 12.5 How a bean seed germinates

Skill C2 (suitable for assessment)

Students may well have done this exercise before, but this gives them an opportunity to interpret what they see in the light of new knowledge they have acquired during their IGCSE Biology course. Beans are suggested as they are large and easy to see, but any sizeable seed would be suitable.

Apparatus list

Per student or group:
- two or three large seeds, such as beans
- a glass jar, such as a jam jar or gas jar
- some absorbent paper, such as blotting paper.

Investigation 13.1 Human variation

Skills C2, C3 (both suitable for assessment)

Although it is suggested that variation should be measured in humans, this exercise could also be carried out with other organisms, such as leaves or seeds, which are available in large quantities.

Students should choose a suitable degree of accuracy of measurement. Height, for example, could be measured to the nearest centimetre, while it is more sensible to measure wrist circumference to the nearest 0.5 cm, and length of big toe to the nearest millimetre.

Apparatus list

If tape measures are not available, lengths of string or cotton can be used to measure circumferences; they can then be measured against a ruler.

Investigation 14.1 Investigating an ecosystem

Although it is very time consuming to make any measurements of energy flow in ecosystems, it is extremely valuable for students to get out of the classroom and investigate an ecosystem directly. This could be combined with the work on classification covered in Chapter 1. Seeing living organisms in their environment is a much more memorable experience than looking at pictures and preserved specimens.

The amount and type of field work that can be done will vary tremendously from school to school and from country to country. Although a visit to a special area some distance from the school can be very stimulating, a lot can be done by investigating living organisms in the school grounds. A tree, a pond or an area of rough ground can provide plenty of opportunity to find living things in their natural environment, and to begin to get an idea of how they interact with each other. Because of the wide range of possibilities, it is not possible to give an apparatus list for this investigation.

Some means of identification of the organisms likely to be found will be needed. Illustrated guide books are always an appealing method of identification for students. Teachers could also draw up dichotomous identification keys for the species they know to be present. This can be time consuming, but once produced such keys can be

used year after year, and added to as new species are found by especially observant students. It is also quite valid for students simply to ask their teacher to identify plants and animals for them – but this can be very demanding!

Index

contraction, muscles 20
convergence, light rays 154–5
cornea 154
coronary arteries 96, 100
cortex 114
cotton production 268
cotyledons 9, 208
cross-pollination 206, 212
crowns 70
crustaceans 6
cuticle 84, 115
cuttings 175
cytoplasm 16, 17, 55, 159–60

DDT 269
deamination 139
decomposers 239, 245, 249
deficiency diseases 54, 55, 59
deforestation 248, 253, 260,
    261, 274–6
denatured enzymes 37
dendrites 160
denitrifying bacteria 249
dentine 70
deoxygenated blood 95, 125
depressants 164
detergents 40
development
    human 202–3
dialysis 141–3
diaphragm 132
diastole 97
dichotomous keys 13–14
dicotyledons 9
diffusion 22–6, 85, 101, 104,
    106, 112, 125
    see also osmosis
digestive system 22, 52, 56–7,
    68–82
diploid cells 180, 181, 207,
    218
discontinuous variation
    224–5
disease 251, 253, 264, 265–6,
    268–9
    see also individual disease
    names
dispersal, seeds 207, 209
divergence, light rays 155,
    156
DNA 11, 17–18, 129, 177,
    178, 214, 228
dominant alleles 216, 221,
    223
dormancy 208
Down's syndrome 227, 228
drugs 129, 130, 164–6, 191,
    201, 229–30
duodenum 68
dust 130

ears 153
ecosystems 234–5
    conservation 274–6
    energy flow 234–43
    nutrient cycles 243–50
education 254–5
effectors 149, 159
effluent 264–5
egestion 80, 138
ejaculation 186
electricity 268, 273

embryos
    animals 187
    plants 208
emphysema 130
emulsification 75, 79
emulsion test 51
enamel 70
endocrine glands 169–71
energy 43, 48, 50, 52, 57–8,
    122, 123, 133, 134
    conservation 273
    in food chains 235–43
environment 225–6, 274–6
enzymes 34–41, 50
    digestive system 70, 73–9
    genetics 214–15
    plants 41, 207
epidermis 22, 84, 86
epididymis 185
erector muscles 146
erosion, soil 253, 259–61, 264
ethanol 133
ethanol test 51
eutrophication 263
evaporation 56, 115, 244, 245
evolution 229
excretion 2, 139–42
exercise 134, 135, 192
exhaust fumes 267, 268
expired air 126–7
extensor muscles 169
extinctions 274–6
eyes 153, 154–9
    infections 200

faeces 80, 264
Fallopian tubes 182, 198
family planning 194–8, 254–5
farming see agriculture
fat 48, 81, 190–91
fats 42, 43, 51–2, 141, 244,
    245, 246
    digestive process 75, 76, 79
fatty acids 51, 75, 76, 108
feedback 149–50
femidom 197
fermentation 133
fertilisation
    animals 180, 186, 218
    in vitro 198–9
    plants 207
fertilisation membrane 186
fertilisers 92–3, 249
    over-use 262–4
fertility 198–9
fetus 187–9
fibre 56–7
fibrin 108
fibrinogen 108, 138
filaments 204
fish 3, 126, 263, 266, 267
flaccidity 30
flavourings, food 62
flexor muscles 169
flowers 9, 203–7
fluoride 72
focusing 154–6
food
    additives 62–4
    distribution worldwide
    60–62

production 235, 242–3,
    258–64, 268–70
food chains 42, 235–43, 269,
    271
food poisoning 63
food webs 238–9
fossil fuels 247, 266, 273
fruits 207–208, 209
fungi 10, 239
    reproduction 177, 178
    see also mycoproteins

galactose 41
gall bladder 68, 79
gametes
    animals 180, 217–19
    plants 203, 204–5, 207, 212
gas, natural 247
gaseous exchange 22, 124–32
    see also respiration
gases 23, 25–6
gastric juice 74, 78
genes 178
    see also genetics
genetic diagrams 218–19
genetics 214–33
genotypes 215–23, 231
genuses 12
geotaxis 166
geotropism 174
German measles 192
germination 41, 207, 210–11
gibberellin 175
gills 126, 267
global warming 248
glucagon 149, 171
glucose 41, 44, 73, 81, 95–6,
    122, 133, 134
    regulation 148–50
glycerol 51, 75, 76, 79, 108
glycogen 44, 81, 148, 149
goblet cells 128, 129
gonorrhoea 199–200
ground water 244, 245
growth 2
    humans 202–3
    plants 91, 173, 174–5
guard cells 84

Haber process 249
habitats 234
    loss of 253
haemoglobin 20, 50, 54–5,
    104, 125, 214, 231
haploid cells 180, 182, 207,
    218
hay fever 130
health care 255
heart 94, 95–101
heart attacks 100
heart disease 129
heartbeats 97–9
heat 43, 52, 56, 153, 236–7
    see also temperature
    regulation
hepatic portal vein 81, 138
herbicides 268
herbivores 236
    see also food chains
hermaphrodites 203
heterotrophic nutrition 43

heterozygous organisms 217,
    220–22, 231, 232
hilum 208
HIV (human
    immunodeficiency virus)
    11, 12, 196, 200
homeostasis 137, 143–50
homologous chromosomes
    215–16
homozygous organisms 217,
    220–21
hormones 50, 148, 169–72,
    184, 185, 189, 195, 198,
    199, 203
    see also plants, growth
    hormones
human immunodeficiency
    virus (HIV) 11, 12, 196,
    200
humerus 168
hydrochloric acid 39, 78
hydroelectric power 273
hydrogen 43, 44, 51, 92, 243,
    244
hydrogen peroxide 34–5, 36
hyphae 10, 177
hypothalamus 144–5

ileum 68
immune system 109–10, 194
immuno-suppressant drugs
    110
implantation 187
in vitro fertilisation 198–9
incisors 70
inert gases 249
ingestion 76
inheritance, genetic 217–26,
    229
inorganic substances 42–3,
    83, 265
insect pollination 205, 206
insecticides 269–70
insects 6, 268–9
inspired air 126–7
insulation 52
    see also temperature
    regulation
insulin 50, 148–50, 170
intestine
    large 68, 69, 80
    small 68, 69, 73, 74, 75,
    79–80
intra-uterine device (IUD)
    197
invertebrates 6, 166
involuntary actions 161–2
iodine, radioactive 271
iodine tests 26–7, 46–7
ionising radiation 228,
    270–71
ions 22–3
    inorganic 42, 43, 54, 83,
    191
iris 154, 163
iron 54–5, 59, 190, 191
irritants 266
IUD (intra-uterine device)
    197

Answers to questions

1.1 **a** A car could be said to show nutrition, respiration, movement and excretion.

b Cars do not grow, reproduce or show irritability.

1.2 Possible reasons include: to produce some order from chaos, to make it easier to study organisms – if you already know something about others in its group, you will also know a lot about any new organism that is discovered, if you can decide to which group it belongs.

1.3 The answers to be filled in in the table can all be found in the text and figures on pages 3–4.

1.4 See Table A1.4 below.

1.5 **a** Arthropods 235 degrees; other invertebrates 20 degrees; vertebrates 9–10 degrees; protista 15 degrees; fungi 20 degrees; plants 60 degrees.

b The arthropod sector should be divided into insects (200 degrees) and other arthropods (35 degrees).

1.6 Both annelids and arthropods have bodies made up of many segments.

Arthropods have jointed legs, but annelids do not.

Arthropods have an exoskeleton, but annelids do not.

1.7 **a** monocot **b** monocot **c** dicot **d** dicot

1.8 *Homo sapiens*

2.1 See Table A2.1 on page 295.

2.2 Annotated diagrams are a very useful and efficient way of presenting a considerable amount of information relatively quickly. Students may already have drawn such diagrams in Investigation 1.1. This exercise gives them a relatively gentle opportunity to learn how to do this, as the diagram is already provided, and all the information for the annotations is available in the text.

Students should be advised that, if they use annotated diagrams when answering examination questions, it is a waste of time to repeat any of the information given on the diagram and annotations by writing it all out in sentences as well.

2.3 Nervous system: brain, spinal cord, nerves, eye, ear.
Gaseous exchange system: trachea, bronchi, bronchioles, lungs.
Digestive system: oesophagus, stomach, small intestine, large intestine, liver, pancreas.

2.4 Having had the situation and events in Figure 2.14 explained to them, students are now asked to extend these ideas to the reverse

Group of arthropods	Number of legs	How body is divided up	Number of antennae	Other special features
Myriapods	Many pairs	Many segments, no obvious head, thorax or abdomen	One pair	
Insects	Three pairs	Head, thorax and abdomen, each made up of several segments	One pair	Many insects have two pairs of wings
Crustaceans	More than three pairs	Cephalothorax and abdomen, each made up of several segments	Two pairs	Exoskeleton is very hard, as it contains calcium carbonate
Arachnids	Four pairs	Cephalothorax and abdomen, each made up of several segments	None	

Table A1.4

Structure	Is it found in animal cells?	Is it found in plant cells?	Comment
Cytoplasm	Yes	Yes	This is where many metabolic reactions take place
Nucleus	Yes (except in red blood cells)	Yes	This contains the chromosomes, made of DNA, that contain inherited information about what proteins the cell should make
Cell wall	No	Yes	It is made of cellulose, and it helps to support the plant cell and hold it in shape; it also stops the cell bursting if it takes up a lot of water
Chloroplasts	No	Yes	They contain chlorophyll, and are the site for photosynthesis
Vacuole	Small ones are sometimes present	A large vacuole is almost always present	Plant cell vacuoles contain cell sap

Table A2.1

situation. Part **c** is very important. Students often state that *solutions* move in and out of cells, and they should be encouraged always to think of each type of molecule separately.
a The cytoplasm.
b From the cytoplasm to the salt solution.
c They are unable to cross the cell surface membrane. (This is not strictly true, but is the expected answer at this level.)
d The cell will get smaller, as its volume decreases with the net loss of water.

2.5 This is a more difficult question, full answers involving several steps which some students may find difficult to hold together. Parts **a** and **b** should help to lead them into the realisation that haemoglobin is held inside the cells by the cell surface membrane, and therefore may help them towards the idea of water moving either into or out of the cells by osmosis. In **d**, a full explanation should include a mention of this partially permeable membrane, not just a statement that water moved either into or out of the cells.
a Haemoglobin.
b The haemoglobin is all inside the red cells, not in the plasma. It is kept inside the red cells because its molecules are too large to get through the cell surface membrane.
c The cells in tube A burst, but those in tubes B and C did not.
d In tube A, water entered the cells by osmosis, moving down a water potential gradient from the high water potential

outside the cell to the lower water potential inside it. This made the cells swell and burst. The liquid became clear, because now there were no cells floating about in it, only haemoglobin. Haemoglobin is soluble, and a true solution is always clear.

This did not happen in the other two tubes. In tube B, the water potential inside and outside the cell was about the same so there was no net water movement. In tube C, the water potential inside the cells was higher than that outside, so net water movement was out of the cells.

If you looked at these liquids under the microscope, you would not be able to see anything in tube A. In tube B, you would see normal red blood cells. In tube C, you would see shrunken red blood cells.

2.6 The cell wall is fully permeable, and therefore space X contains whatever is outside the cell wall – in this case, concentrated sugar solution.

3.1 a i To speed up a reaction, without the catalyst itself undergoing any change.
   ii A biological catalyst, a protein.
   b 37 °C. Amylase is an enzyme found in humans, and works fastest at human body temperature. (Note, however, that the amylase supplied to schools is usually of bacterial or fungal origin, and is stable up to quite high temperatures.)
   c At higher temperatures, both the starch . . . .

molecules and amylase molecules are moving faster, and are therefore likely to bump into each other more often.

    d At 80 °C, the amylase molecules lose their shape, becoming denatured. The starch molecules no longer fit the active sites, and so are not broken down to maltose.

3.2 **a** At high temperatures, up to 100 °C.

    b At temperatures around the optimum for enzymes – often at around 40 °C.

    c A washing powder may contain both detergents and enzymes; the best temperature for one is not the best temperature for the other.

    d These bacteria must contain enzymes that can function at temperatures above 40 °C. Perhaps some of these enzymes could be used in washing powders.

4.1 Sugar, wood, paper, alcohol and leather are organic substances. Iron, water, oxygen, glass and copper sulphate are inorganic substances.

4.2 'Carbo' because they contain carbon. 'Hydrate' because they contain hydrogen and oxygen in the same proportions as in water.

4.3 **a** The answer will depend on the results of the investigation.

    b Students should find that all the foods containing significant amounts of carbohydrate are of plant origin. The exception is milk, which contains lactose, and so gives a positive test for reducing sugar.

    c This could be a point of discussion, especially valuable if the class contains students from different countries. The idea of 'staple foods' could be brought out.

4.4 **a** This will depend on the foods used in the investigation.

    b Protein-rich foods come from both animals and plants.

    c Grains and pulses.

4.5 **a** The answer will depend on the results of the investigation.

    b Foods rich in fat come from both plants and animals.

4.6 See Table A4.6 below.

4.7 See Table A4.7 opposite.

4.8 **a** All the functions listed apply to plants as well as to animals. Although plants do not have blood, they do use water as a solvent for transport in xylem and phloem tissue. Evaporation of water from leaves, i.e. transpiration, is important in cooling plants growing in hot climates.

    b Photosynthesis.

4.9 **a** Beef, like most of the other foods, contains a high proportion of water.

    b Butter is almost pure fat, and has a very low water content.

    c Chicken contains less fat than beef.

4.10 **a** A 14-year-old has a larger body, and therefore requires more heat energy to keep him or her warm, more energy for movement and so on.

    b A 14-year-old is growing, whereas the man is not. Energy is needed for building new materials from the materials we eat.

    c A woman with an active job requires a considerable amount of energy to do work (in the sense in which this term is used in Physics); a pregnant woman also has to do extra work in moving her heavier body, and

Nutrient	Elements contained in its molecules	Name of the smaller molecules from which it is made	Use in body	Foods that contain a lot of it	How to test for it
Carbohydrate	C, H, O	Sugars	For energy	(As appropriate)	Iodine test for starch, Benedict's test for reducing sugars
Protein	C, H, O, N, S	Amino acids	(Examples on p. 50)	(As appropriate)	Biuret test
Fat	C, H, O	Fatty acids and glycerol	(Examples on p. 52)	(As appropriate)	Ethanol test

Table A4.6

Nutrient	Use in body	Deficiency symptoms	Food that contains it
Vitamin C	Making collagen, so helps to keep the skin and the walls of blood vessels healthy	Scurvy – skin ulcers, bleeding gums	Citrus fruits, blackcurrants, fresh vegetables
Vitamin D	Helps in the absorption and use of calcium in making bones and teeth	Rickets – bent leg bones	Fish oil, egg yolks, milk; also made in the skin in sunlight
Iron	Making haemoglobin	Anaemia – insufficient haemoglobin in the blood, so lighter coloured skin and feeling of tiredness	Red meat, especially liver and kidney; green leafy vegetables
Calcium	For building bones and teeth, and for blood clotting	Weak bones and crumbling teeth	Milk and other dairy products, hard water

Table A4.7

in building her baby's body. The extra demands on both women are roughly equal.

  d In both a pregnant woman and one who is breast feeding, extra energy is needed for building the baby's body. However, the breast-feeding baby is larger and more active than the unborn one. It also needs to produce a considerable amount of heat energy from its food, more of which will be lost from its body than before it was born.

4.12 There are no 'right' answers to each of these statements; they are intended for discussion, to enable student to consider different views carefully before making up their own minds about how they feel on this important issue.

4.14 The food can be made using waste which would otherwise have to be disposed of, possibly causing pollution. The food can therefore be made more cheaply than meat – meat involves a three-level food chain, with consequent inefficiency of energy transfer from plant to human. The food is high in protein, but low in fat, which may help to reduce the risk of heart disease. The food can be eaten by vegetarians.

5.1 **a** An increase in fluoride concentration produces a decrease in percentage of tooth decay up to a level of 2.0 parts per million, after which there is no further effect.

  b No – natural fluoride levels may already be high; in some parts of the world, tooth decay is not an important problem.

  c People like to think their drinking water is 'pure' and do not like the idea that it contains 'additives'; high fluoride levels may produce dark coloration on teeth.

  d Brushing with toothpaste containing fluoride. Some students may also know that dentists can 'paint' teeth with fluoride, or that fluoride tablets are available.

5.2 **a** Gastric juice contains hydrochloric acid; hydrochloric acid kills bacteria; food poisoning is caused by bacteria; less acid provides more opportunity for large numbers of such bacteria to survive in the alimentary canal.

  b Stress increases gastric juice secretion, therefore increasing the amount of hydrochloric acid and pepsin in the stomach; this may damage the cells lining the stomach.

5.3 See Table A5.3 on page 298.

6.1 A large surface area makes contact with more carbon dioxide than a small area would do; a thin leaf minimises the distance for diffusion from air to mesophyll cells; stomata allow entry into the leaf; air spaces between cells allow diffusion within the leaf.

6.2 A large surface area to intercept most sunlight; thin leaf to allow light to penetrate to all parts of the leaf; epidermis cells are thin with no chloroplasts, to allow maximum light through to the mesophyll; only a few cell layers, so not too many cell walls for the sunlight to travel through; chloroplasts can move; on the whole plant, leaves are often arranged so that they do not shade one another.

6.3 Water (or temperature). Increase the amount of water (or the temperature) while keeping other factors constant. If the rate of photosynthesis increases, then water (or temperature) was a limiting factor.

6.4 **a** Carbon dioxide. As carbon dioxide concentration is increased, the rate of photosynthesis increases, so the amount of carbon dioxide must have been limiting the rate.

b Probably light. Repeat the experiment at higher light intensities (or just measure the rate of photosynthesis at these high carbon dioxide levels at a higher light intensity); if the rate of photosynthesis increases, then light was the limiting factor.

c Up to a point, higher temperatures increase the rate of reaction, so keeping the plants at reasonably high temperatures should increase the rate of photosynthesis. Very high temperatures, however, may damage enzymes and so slow photosynthesis. (Another correct answer is that tomatoes could be damaged by frost in temperate countries. Yet another is that photo-respiration may occur at high temperatures, but this is well beyond IGCSE level.)

d The rate of photosynthesis (or growth) of tomatoes at different light intensities and carbon dioxide levels should be investigated, to find out the optimum levels for each –

there is no point in providing extra light if carbon dioxide is the limiting factor, and vice versa. Cost then needs to be considered; there is no point in providing extra lighting or carbon dioxide if the increased yields do not provide extra profit in excess of the extra costs.

7.1 The left-hand side of the heart, the aorta and the pulmonary vein red; the right-hand side of the heart, the vena cava and the pulmonary artery blue.

7.2 **a** The left atrium and left ventricle contain oxygenated blood; the right atrium and right ventricle contain deoxygenated blood.

b Blood flows into the atria.

c Bloods flows out of the ventricles.

7.3 **a** 0.6 seconds.

b 100 beats per minute.

c **i** The pressure rises in the ventricles as the muscle in their walls contract, squeezing in on the blood. As they relax it drops rapidly. It rises slowly from 0.4 s onwards because blood is trickling into the ventricles from the atria.

ii The pressure rises in the atria as they contract. However, the muscle is not very thick, so the pressure does not rise as high as in the ventricles. The pressure

Table A5.3

Part of alimentary canal	Juices secreted	What the juices contain	What is digested	Any other points
Mouth	Saliva	Mucus, amylase	Starch to maltose	Chewing increases surface area of food
Stomach	Gastric juice	Mucus, hydrochloric acid, pepsin	Proteins to polypeptides	Muscles of stomach wall contract to mix food with gastric juice
Small intestine	Pancreatic juice Bile Maltase is secreted by villi	Pancreatic juice contains sodium hydrogencarbonate, trypsin, amylase, lipase Bile contains bile salts	Starch to maltose, proteins to polypeptides and amino acids, fats to fatty acids and glycerol Maltase digests maltose to glucose	Bile salts help to emulsify fats so that they are easier for lipase to digest Absorption of glucose, amino acids, fatty acids, glycerol, water, mineral salts and vitamins takes place here
Large intestine: Colon Rectum	None None		Nothing Nothing	Water is absorbed here Faeces are stored here before being passed out through the anus

in the atria rises from 0.2 s to 0.4 s because more blood is flowing into the atria from the veins.

7.4 **a i** The atria only have to push the blood down into the ventricles; the ventricles have to provide enough force to push the blood out of the heart and through the arteries.

ii The left ventricle has to push the blood through the aorta and then all around the body; the right ventricle has to push it only to the lungs.

b When the ventricles contract, some of the blood will flow back up into the atria. Not as much blood will be pushed out of the heart with each beat, so less oxygen will be collected at the lungs and less delivered to the tissues. The person will lack energy.

7.5 It carries deoxygenated blood.

7.6 See Table A7.6 below.

7.7 **a** Blood in arteries has just left the heart, where the contraction of the ventricles increased the pressure of the blood. As it moves further away from the heart, the pressure slowly drops. This happens especially as it passes into the capillaries, as it spreads out into myriads of small vessels. (The total cross-sectional area of the capillaries branching from one artery is considerably greater than the cross-sectional area of the artery itself.)

b The blood pressure in an artery increases as the ventricles contract (systole) and decreases as they relax (diastole). The recoil of the stretched arteriole walls helps to smooth the blood flow. By the time the blood reaches the veins, it is a long way from the heart, so blood flows steadily and smoothly.

7.8 **a** blue
b red
c pulmonary artery and pulmonary vein

7.9 **a** The biconcave shape increases their surface area to volume ratio, so increasing the rate at which oxygen can diffuse into or out of the cell.

b The smaller they are, the greater their surface area to volume ratio – see **a** above. Also, their small size allows capillaries to be very small, so bringing red cells and their oxygen very close to individual cells in tissues.

c Shortage of iron means shortage of haemoglobin, which means shortage of oxygen. Lack of oxygen reduces respiration, through which energy is released.

7.10 **a** Lymph is very like blood plasma.
b Lymph does not contain red blood cells.

7.11 **a** An antigen is a molecule on the outside of a cell – different organisms have different antigens. (Viruses also carry antigens, although they are not cellular.) An antibody

Feature	Arteries	Veins	Capillaries
What is their function?	Carry blood away from the heart	Carry blood back to the heart	Deliver and collect substances from cells
How thick are their walls?	Quite thick, to withstand high pressures	Quite thin, as blood is at low pressure	Very thin, usually only one cell thick, so that substances can easily move in and out
Do the walls contain elastic fibres?	Yes – a lot, so that they can 'give' as the blood pulses through	Only a few, as the blood flows through smoothly	No
How wide are the vessels?	Fairly wide, to transport a lot of blood quickly	A little wider than arteries, so that blood can flow through easily	Very narrow, so that the blood is taken very close to the body cells
Do they contain valves?	No – blood is forced through by the heart	Yes – to make sure blood keeps flowing back towards the heart	No

Table A7.6

is a molecule made by a lymphocyte, which is specific to a particular antigen, and can help to destroy the cells that carry it.

b Exposure to a particular antigen stimulates the lymphocytes that make the appropriate antibody to divide. This relatively large population of lymphocytes will be able to respond rapidly if the same antigen appears again. (Details of different types of lymphocytes, cloning and memory cells are not needed at this level.)

c Although immunity may have been built up against one virus as explained in **b**, a virus with a different antigen cannot be destroyed by the same antibody as the first one.

d In a healthy person, the lymphocytes will be able to produce antibodies to destroy the tuberculosis bacteria.

e In the disease AIDS, the lymphocytes do not make sufficient antibodies to control the population of tuberculosis bacteria, which multiply and cause disease.

f The weakened bacteria cause the appropriate lymphocytes to divide and to produce antibodies. If live tuberculosis bacteria with the same antigen later enter the body, this population of lymphocytes will destroy them.

8.1 High concentrations of ammonium nitrate dissolved in the soil water will reduce its water potential. Water will therefore not enter the root hairs by osmosis – it may even be drawn *out* of the roots. The plant may die from dehydration.

8.2 **a** Some would soak into the soil, some would run off the surface of the soil, some would evaporate back into the air.

b Less water would evaporate into the air than if trees were present. The air would become less humid.

8.3 **a** Hot weather – the higher the temperature, the faster molecules move, so diffusion of water vapour out of the leaf will take place faster.

b A dry atmosphere – the water potential of the atmosphere will be lower, so a steeper water potential gradient will exist between leaf and air.

c A windy day – the moving air will take away the moisture-laden air next to the leaf, so maintaining a steep water potential gradient.

d Bright sunshine – the plant will open its stomata to allow entry of carbon dioxide for photosynthesis; open stomata allow diffusion of water vapour from the leaf.

8.4 **a** Sisal is a succulent, with swollen leaves which store water. The leaves are covered with a thick layer of wax, which cuts down transpiration. The leaves are stiff, thick and narrow, with a relatively small surface area.

b The barrel cactus is made up of a swollen stem, which stores water. This shape minimises the surface area in contact with the air. The leaves are reduced to spines, so that there is virtually no transpiration from them. The ground-hugging growth for reduces exposure to the air.

c The baobab has a thick trunk and branches, in which water can be stored. There are few leaves on this tree, which reduces the leaf surface from which transpiration can take place.

8.5 **a** To make proteins; students may also state particular uses of proteins.

b If a complete ring of phloem is removed, sucrose cannot travel to the roots from the leaves. The roots will live for some time, using up their stored reserves, but will eventually die. Once the roots die, the whole tree will die.

9.1 **a** From the right ventricle of the heart; it is deoxygenated because it has passed around the body, giving up its oxygen to respiring cells.

b To the left atrium of the heart.

9.2 See Table A9.2 on page 301.

Note that the surface does *not* need to be moist to allow gaseous exchange to occur – oxygen will, in fact, diffuse more quickly through a dry surface than a wet one. Gaseous exchange surfaces are kept moist to prevent the cells from which they are made from drying out when in contact with dry air.

9.3 • Oxygen – oxygen from inspired air diffuses into the blood and is carried to body cells, where it is used in respiration.

• Carbon dioxide – this is produced by cells in respiration, and transported in the blood to the lungs, where it diffuses into the air in the alveoli.

• Nitrogen – this is not used by the body. Some diffuses into the blood, but simply passes round the circulation – the same

a	b
Large surface area	To increase the rate of oxygen and carbon dioxide diffusion into and out of the blood
Good blood supply	To carry away oxygen and bring carbon dioxide to the exchange surface, so maintaining a diffusion gradient
Thin	To minimise the diffusion distance for oxygen and carbon dioxide, so speeding the rate of gaseous exchange

Table A9.2

amount diffuses into the blood as diffuses out. (In fact, the percentage concentration of nitrogen in expired air is slightly lower than that in inspired air, not because the amount of nitrogen has changed, but because the amounts of other gases change. This is too difficult a concept for students at this level.)

- Moisture – water from the lining of the respiratory passages, including the alveoli, evaporates into the air as it passes over these tissues. Small droplets of liquid water will also be present in the expired air.

9.4
- An increase in the blood supply to the muscles means an increased rate of supply of oxygen; muscles can therefore respire aerobically for longer, so increasing both the possible rate of muscle activity and the duration for which muscles can be active – the athlete should be able to run faster and for longer.
- An increase in myoglobin has a similar effect.
- An increase in tolerance to lactic acid allows anaerobic respiration to continue for longer; this will allow high level activity, such as sprinting, to carry on for longer and at greater speed.

10.1 Students should be able to suggest fats. They may also suggest carbohydrates (as glycogen), iron and vitamins, which are stored in the liver.

10.2 Proteins students should have met include: antibodies, made in white cells (lymphocytes); keratin, made in skin cells; haemoglobin, made in (precursors of) red blood cells; various enzymes, such as amylase made in cells in salivary glands. They may also know insulin, made by cells in the pancreas.

10.3 Some proteins are eaten. Proteins are digested into amino acids. Amino acids are absorbed into the blood. Amino acids travel along the hepatic portal vein. Amino acids enter liver cells. The liver delaminates excess amino acids. Urea is produced. Urea passes into the blood. Urea is carried to the kidneys. The kidneys remove urea from the blood. Urine is produced. Urine flows along the ureters. Urine is stored in the bladder. Urine flows along the urethra.

10.4 a Excretion is the removal of (perhaps toxic) waste products of metabolism, and of substances that are in excess of the body's needs. Egestion is the removal of undigested waste material from the alimentary canal.
b Urine is a liquid produced by the kidneys, which contains urea dissolved in water.
c The ureter leads from the kidneys to the bladder. The urethra leads from the bladder to the outside.

10.5 a Salty food will raise the concentrations of sodium and chloride in the blood, which could cause harm, as the kidneys cannot bring levels back down to normal. While on dialysis, sodium and chloride ions can diffuse from the blood into the dialysis fluid, so reducing their concentrations to that of the dialysis fluid.
b Protein.

10.6 a Muscular activity produces heat, which raises the internal body temperature; this is sensed by the hypothalamus, which causes sweat glands to secrete more sweat; evaporation of this sweat from the skin produces cooling.
b Vasoconstriction of arterioles carrying blood to the surface is a response to a drop in body temperature, in order to reduce heat loss from the skin. Very cold conditions may cause an extreme response, entirely cutting off blood flow to extremities.

c Food, especially carbohydrate and fat, is used as fuel for metabolic reactions such as respiration, which are used for heat generation.

d Several layers of thin clothes trap more air than one layer. Air is an excellent insulator, thus reducing heat loss from the body.

e Water in clothing will evaporate. Latent heat of vaporisation will be removed from the body, cooling it. This cooling effect will be greater than the insulating effect of the clothing, which is unlikely to be trapping air any more. The person should have their wet clothing removed, and then be wrapped in something dry.

f Evaporation of sweat, which cools the body, can only take place if there is 'room' for more water vapour in the air. If the air is already fully saturated with water vapour, then sweat will simply lie on the skin, producing no cooling effect.

g In hot weather, a large amount of water vapour is lost from sweat. This water needs to be replaced by drinking.

h The evaporation of water from the tongue and lining of the mouth produces the same cooling effect as sweating. Panting also increases the rate of evaporation of water from the moist surfaces of the respiratory passages, again producing a cooling effect.

10.7 2.5% of 80 kg = 2 kg, so the man's liver would weigh about 2 kg. Thus the liver could store about 50 × 2 = 100 g of glycogen.

10.8 See Table A10.8 below.

11.1 See Table A11.1 opposite.

11.2 The brain senses poor focus of the image; messages are sent along nerves to the ciliary muscles; the ciliary muscles relax; therefore the muscle ring becomes wide; this increases the tension on the suspensory ligaments; the lens pulled is wide and thin; light is refracted less; light rays are brought to a focus on the retina.

11.3 This question asks students to add functions to the levels on a diagram of an eye. It is suggested that this is done as an overlay, to avoid crowding of labels. Many of these functions have been related to structures in the text, but some will have to be worked out by the students.

- contains receptor cells – retina
- refracts the light rays – cornea
- responsible for fine adjustments – lens
- strong fibres – suspensory ligaments
- a ring of muscles – ciliary muscles
- the coloured part – iris
- a thin, transparent, protective covering – conjunctiva
- a tough, outer covering – sclera
- a dark layer – choroid

11.4 a These animals use their eyes only in dim light; cones are therefore of no use as they only function in bright light.

b Cones do not function in the dark; rods do, but are not sensitive to colour.

c Looking directly at an object focuses its image on the yellow spot, where there are only cones. Looking to one side of it focuses light

Stimulus to which receptor cells are sensitive	Sense organ in which receptor cells are found
Light	Eye
Temperature	Skin
Sound	Ear
Touch	Skin
Taste	Mouth and nose

Table A11.1

Table A10.8

	Temperature	Blood glucose
Sensor	Hypothalamus	Pancreas
Effector(s)	Muscles, especially erector muscles and muscles in the wall of arterioles in the skin; sweat glands	Liver
How the effectors respond to a rise in the level	Erector muscles relax, thus increasing heat loss from skin; sweat glands produce more sweat	Takes up more glucose from the blood
How the effectors respond to a drop in the level	Erector muscles contract, thus reducing heat loss from the skin	Breaks down glycogen stores and releases glucose into blood

elsewhere on the retina, where rods, sensitive to dim light, are found.

11.5 This question is designed to help students to analyse the components of a response to a stimulus. There are very many possible answers.

11.6 **a** An increase in the heart rate speeds the blood supply to muscles, so increasing the supply of oxygen, allowing faster respiration and greater energy production; muscles can therefore work harder.
Breakdown of glycogen in the liver increases glucose supply to muscles, with the same effect.
Dilation of blood vessels supplying muscles has the same effect.
Widening bronchioles can increase the rate of oxygenation of the blood, with the same effect.

b If this did not happen, you would go on feeling frightened, with all the accompanying physiological changes, for a very long time. As it is, the length of time for which the changes last can be controlled by regulating the length of time over which adrenaline is released.

11.7 See Table A11.7 below.

12.1 Each length of DNA (each chromatid) will have to make a copy of itself, to form a chromosome with two chromatids again.

12.2 The information for this is in the text. The table should include a comparison between number of parents (look out for the common mistake of thinking that sexual reproduction must involve two parents), type of cell division involved, involvement of gametes, fertilisation, formation of zygote, presence or absence of variation in offspring.

12.3 **a** ovary, testis   **b** testis
c ovary   **d** prostate gland
e oviduct/Fallopian tube
f uterus

12.4 Both are adapted for absorption. They both have a large surface area. They both have a good blood supply.

12.6 The information for this is in the text. Tables will vary, but should include comparisons between flower size, colour and size of petals, and position and shape of anthers and stigmas. Many wind-pollinated flowers also have very flexible filaments, which may be noticed if a wind-pollinated flower can be investigated. Students could also include a comparison between the quantities and shapes of pollen grains in insect- and wind-pollinated flowers.

12.7 To allow colonisation of new areas. To reduce competition for water, light or nutrients between the parent and the offspring, and between offspring. To ensure that at least some seeds will land in a suitable environment.

13.1 **a** A gene is a length of DNA on a chromosome, which is a recipe for making a protein, or which produces a certain characteristic. An allele is a variety of a gene. For example, the gene for eye colour might have an allele for brown eyes and an allele for blue eyes.

b The genotype of an organism is the alleles it has. The phenotype of an organism is a characteristic which it shows. (Later, students should realise that, in may instances, phenotype is produced by an interaction between the genotype and the environment.)

c Homozygous means possessing two identical alleles of a gene.
Heterozygous means possessing two different alleles of a gene.

13.2 **a** For example, **A** = allele for long legs,
a = allele for short legs.

Nervous system	Hormonal system
Message carried as electrical impulses	Message carried as chemical
Message carried along nerves	Message carried in blood
Very rapid response	Slower response
Usually short-term response	Response may be long term
Usually very localised response	Response may be widespread

Table A11.7

b

genotype	phenotype
AA	long legs
Aa	long legs
aa	short legs

13.3 a tall
b **t**, the allele for short.

13.4 a Horns is the dominant allele.
b For example, **H** = allele for horns, **h** = allele for no horns.
c hh
d horned

13.5

Parents' phenotypes	Red spines	Brown spines
Parents' genotypes	**Rr**	**rr**
Gametes	Ⓡ and ⓡ	ⓡ

Offspring genotypes

Gametes	ⓡ
Ⓡ	Rr
ⓡ	rr

Offspring phenotypes: **Rr** = red, **rr** = brown

Ratios: 1 red : 1 brown

13.6 As a new colour appears in the offspring, the allele for this colour must have been hidden in parents. It must therefore be a recessive allele. For the colour to appear in the offspring, some must be homozygous for this recessive allele. Therefore they must get the allele from each parent. Each parent is therefore heterozygous.

Suitable symbols could be, for example, **Y** = allele for yellow flowers, **y** = allele for white flowers.

Parents' phenotypes	Yellow flowers	Yellow flowers
Parents' genotypes	**Yy**	**Yy**
Gametes	Ⓨ and ⓨ	Ⓨ and ⓨ

Offspring genotypes

Gametes	Ⓨ	ⓨ
Ⓨ	YY	Yy
ⓨ	Yy	yy

Offspring phenotypes: **YY, Yy** = yellow, **yy** = white

Ratios: 3 yellow : 1 white

13.7 a The small number of offspring means that the ratio is not exact, but it is very close to a 1 : 1 ratio. These results could be obtained if either the allele for long hair, or the allele for short hair, is dominant. One parent must be heterozygous, and the other homozygous for the recessive characteristic.
b Interbreed goats with long hair with each other, and also goats with short hair with each other. Whichever group always produces young with hair like themselves (i.e. is pure breeding) has the recessive characteristic.

13.8 a **EE** and **Ee**
b ee
c

Parents' phenotypes	Brown eyes	Blue eyes
Parents' genotypes	**BB**	**bb**
Gametes	Ⓑ	ⓑ
Offspring genotypes	**Bb**	
Offspring phenotypes	All with brown eyes	

d

Parents' phenotypes	Brown eyes	Blue eyes
Parents' genotypes	**Bb**	**bb**
Gametes	Ⓑ and ⓑ	ⓑ

Offspring genotypes

Gametes	ⓑ
Ⓑ	Bb
ⓑ	bb

Offspring phenotypes: **Bb** = brown eyes, **bb** = blue eyes

Ratios: 1 brown eyes : 1 blue eyes

e Bb
f The daughter. With small numbers of offspring, it is possible that, just by chance, no blue-eyed rabbits were produced, even though the parent had an allele for blue eyes. She should repeat the cross to produce enough offspring to be sure.

Note that, if you get even *one* blue-eyed rabbit in the offspring from a test cross, this proves the genotype of the unknown parent to be **Bb**. However, *not* getting a blue-eyed offspring does not quite so conclusively prove the genotype to be **BB**.

13.9 **a** For example, H^R = red hair, H^W = white hair.

b

Genotype	Phenotype
$H^R H^R$	Red coat
$H^R H^W$	Roan coat
$H^W H^W$	White coat

c

Parents' phenotypes	Roan	Roan
Parents' genotypes	$H^R H^W$	$H^R H^W$
Gametes	H^R and H^W	H^R and H^W

Offspring genotypes

Gametes	H^R	H^W
H^R	$H^R H^R$	$H^R H^W$
H^W	$H^R H^W$	$H^W H^W$

Offspring phenotypes $H^R H^R$ = red, $H^R H^W$ = roan, $H^W H^W$ = white

Ratios 1 red : 2 roan : 1 white

13.10 **a** For example, L^G = allele for green leaves, L^W = allele for white leaves.

b The ratio 20 : 46 : 21 is close to 1 : 2 : 1, as in question 13.9.

Parents' phenotypes	Green	Green
Parents' genotypes	$L^G L^W$	$L^G L^W$
Gametes	L^G and L^W	L^G and L^W

Offspring genotypes

Gametes	L^G	L^W
L^G	$L^G L^G$	$L^G L^W$
L^W	$L^G L^W$	$L^W L^W$

Offspring phenotypes $L^G L^G$ = green, $L^G L^W$ = variegated, $L^W L^W$ = white

Ratios 1 green : 2 variegated : 1 white

The white plants would die as soon as they had used up the food reserves in the seeds. With no chlorophyll, they would not be able to photosynthesise.

13.11

Parents' phenotypes	Blood group O	Blood group AB
Parents' genotypes	$I^O I^O$	$I^A I^B$
Gametes	I^O	I^A and I^B

Offspring genotypes

Gametes	I^O
I^A	$I^A I^O$
I^B	$I^B I^O$

Offspring phenotypes $I^A I^O$ = blood group A, $I^B I^O$ = blood group B

Ratios 1 group A : 1 group B

13.12 For a child to have group O, it must receive allele I^O from each parent. Thus the only possibilities for the parents' genotypes are as follows.

Parents' phenotypes	Blood group A	Blood group B
Parents' genotypes	$I^A I^O$	$I^B I^O$
Gametes	I^A and I^O	I^B and I^O

Offspring genotypes

Gametes	I^A	I^O
I^B	$I^A I^B$	$I^B I^O$
I^O	$I^A I^O$	$I^O I^O$

Offspring phenotypes $I^A I^B$ = group AB, $I^B I^O$ = group B, $I^A I^O$ = group A, $I^O I^O$ = group O

Ratios 1 group AB : 1 group B : 1 group A : 1 group O

13.13 The baby with blood group O has inherited allele I^O from each parent. Thus, Mr Y cannot be the father of this baby, as his genotype must be $I^A I^B$.

Both sets of parents could have a child with blood group A, but as Baby P must belong to Mr and Mrs Y, then Baby Q must belong to Mr and Mrs X.

13.14 sperm

13.15 a There are few such characteristics which are likely to come to a student's mind. One possibility is sex. Others include various genetic diseases, such as cystic fibrosis, sickle cell anaemia and so on. Albinism is another example. In some groups of people, there are variations in hair and eye colour.

b A wide range of possibilities would be correct here.

c In general, the characteristics listed in **a** are more likely to show discontinuous variation than those in **c**.

13.16 Answers cannot be provided, as they will depend on the students' research.

13.17 These questions are intended for discussion or suggestions, and there are not absolutely correct answers. Possible effects include:

a This will increase the number of **h** alleles being passed on into each generation, and so you might expect to see an increase in the incidence of sickle cell anaemia.

b People with sickle cell anaemia in their family may choose to be tested, and couples who know they are both heterozygous may choose not to have children. This would decrease the number of children born with sickle cell anaemia. On the other side of the argument, many couples will not be tested, and, of those that are tested and are found to be heterozygous, many may still choose to have children.

c The distribution of sickle cell anaemia will spread from those areas shown in the map in Figure 13.14. This has already happened; there are large numbers of people in the USA and other countries with sickle cell anaemia.

d Malaria may become an even more dangerous disease in many parts of the world, increasing the selection against people with the genotype **HH**, and increasing the advantage of people with the genotype **Hh**. Thus, the incidence of sickle cell anaemia could increase.

14.1 a A community is all the living organisms in a habitat (or ecosystem). A population is all the living organisms of one species in a habitat (or ecosystem).

b A habitat is a place where an organism lives. An ecosystem is an interacting group of organisms and their environment.

14.2 There is such a wide range of possibilities that no answers are suggested here. Students are likely to find it very difficult to think of a sensible food chain with five links in it; aquatic food chains involving fish are the easiest. Discourage students from suggesting very unusual food chains, such as tigers eating humans.

14.3 Energy is lost as it passes along a food chain. The further up a food chain an organism feeds, the less energy is available to it. There is simply not enough energy left by the time it reaches the fifth or sixth link.

14.4 This is a very difficult task, and requires a knowledge of what each kind of animal found in the investigation feeds on. It is best to limit the web to just a few organisms at each trophic level. Books are the best source of information on feeding habits; other methods of discovering these are really too time-consuming for students at this level.

14.5 It is not possible to provide answers to this question, as these will vary widely. The purpose of the question is to ask students to apply their theoretical knowledge of energy flow along food chains to the production of food for humans in their country. In **d**, the obvious answer that it would be more economical to concentrate on growing plants rather than farming animals may not be the only one, and reasons for farming animals should be considered carefully.

14.6 This would reduce transpiration. More water would seep into the ground, rather than being taken up by plant roots. Thus the levels of water vapour in the air would decrease, which could lead to reduced rainfall.

14.7 An arrow should be drawn to the box from the plants. An arrow labelled 'combustion' should be drawn from the box to carbon dioxide in the air.

14.8 Both will reduce the amount of oxygen in the air. Combustion uses oxygen. Cutting down forests may (but see argument above) reduce the level of photosynthesis, which returns oxygen to the air.

14.9 a To increase crop growth, as nitrogen is needed by plants to make proteins.

b To increase growth of the subsequent (wheat) crop; peas and beans are legumes, and have nitrogen-fixing bacteria in nodules on their roots. These fix nitrogen, some of which will be left in the soil in a form available to plants after the peas and beans have been harvested. To increase the benefits from this, it is best to leave the pea and bean roots in the soil.

c This can decrease the activities of denitrifying bacteria, so allowing nitrates to build up in the soil.

14.10 Having seen how a yeast population grows in a closed environment, students are asked to project their ideas into a more complex situation. The scenario given includes competitors for food, and also predators, neither of which are present in the yeast's culture flask.

It is impossible to make firm predictions about what will happen to the mice, but students should be able to put forward a range of suggestions, supported by arguments. For example, it might be expected that the mice would not breed for a while (as in phase A of the yeast curve) as they settled in to their new environment. They might all be eaten rapidly by the predators, in which case that is the end of the answer! Alternatively, they might begin to breed rapidly, their rate of increase limited only by their own maximum rate of reproduction, if food and space were in ample supply. As their population increases, so competition for food would increase, both within the mouse population and between the mice and the other grass-eating species which could limit population growth – it might then oscillate at this level for a while. Predators could also be considered.

14.11 There is a huge number of possibilities here. Two examples include problems with lack of available jobs, leading to unemployment, which can then lead on to increase in crime, illness and poverty; and increased tension amongst crowded populations competing for inadequate resources, leading to wars and other conflicts.

14.12 a 30–35 = about 180 000; 35–40 = about 150 000. Therefore the answer is about 330 000.
 b About 800 000.
 c About 1 880 000.
 d About 600 000.
 e It would increase.

14.13 a Canada. There are fewer young people in the age range 0–10 than in older age groups.

b Sierra Leone. There is a very high population of young people compared with older ones. As these grow up, they will swell the population, especially if they all have children of their own.

14.14 a i About 0.6 billion.
 ii About 1.3 billion.
 iii Increase = 1.3–0.6 = 0.7 billion.

Therefore percentage increase
$$= \frac{0.7}{0.6} \times 100\% = 117\%$$

b USA and Western Europe.
c S. Asia and Oceania.
d Answers should point out that the greatest increase in population since 1950, and predicted into the beginning of the twenty-first century, has been in developing countries. Population growth in developed countries has slowed and even stopped. Reasons for this are varied; students will find some ideas in the section **Reducing human population growth**, but may have other ideas of their own to add.

15.1 In general, there is a correlation between amount of rainfall, the amount of high land and the rate of soil erosion. This is not absolute, as many other factors will also affect soil erosion. It tends to be worst in places where rainfall occurs most intensively; if rainfall is spread evenly throughout the year, there is likely to be less erosion than if it falls very heavily over a short period. The amount of land without plant cover when the rain falls is also extremely important.

15.2 The high level of nutrients entering the river provides food for bacteria, both directly, and by increasing the rate of plant growth – the bacteria feed on the plants as they die. Thus the bacterial population increases just below the sewage outlet, and then decreases downstream, as the level of nutrients lessens.

The oxygen level is directly related to the bacterial population. High numbers of bacteria consume large amounts of oxygen in respiration, so lowering the oxygen concentration in the water. Oxygen levels rise downstream, as oxygen from the air dissolves in the river water, and as the demand on it from bacteria becomes less.

The number of fish is directly related to the oxygen levels. They cannot live just below the sewage outfall, as there is insufficient oxygen for them. As oxygen levels increase, so the fish become able to survive.

15.3 This is a classic case of the 'pesticide treadmill'. The use of pesticides has killed predators which used to control pest populations; the pests have also become resistant to many of the pesticides used. Thus pest populations have actually *increased* over the years, and more and more pesticides have to be used to control them.

  a Students may have problems with the *x*-axis, as the years given in the table do not follow a simple progression. They should draw a line graph, in which each point is joined to the next by a ruled, straight line.

  b The use of pesticides has increased nine-fold. It more than doubled in the first five years of this time period. The rate of increase was especially high in the last few years.

  c As explained above – probably development of resistance by pests, and the loss of their natural predators.

  d There are many possible suggestions, and this could provide an interesting discussion. Teachers could introduce students to the idea of integrated pest control systems; in this case, it might involve a reduction in the use of pesticides and the introduction of natural predators of the pests, the growth of a crop other than cotton on at least some of the land for at least part of the time, and the development of crop varieties resistant to the pest.

15.4 a Toxic fumes are produced.

  b Heating; generating electricity.

  c If plastics were sorted into those that produce a large amount of heating energy and those that do not, then only the former could be used. This would generate more heat per kilogram than a mixture. Students could quote figures from the table.

  d PVC and PET, as they produce least heat energy per kilogram.

15.5 a Birds that had been living in the forest which was cut down moved into the conserved patches.

  b The forest patches were not large enough to support this number of birds – perhaps food or nesting sites were insufficient. Some of the birds therefore died or moved to other areas.

  c The numbers of birds in the isolated patches never quite returned to their levels before the surrounding forest was cut down. The results suggest that the patches of forest remaining should be as large as possible, in order to offer genuine chances of conserving the number of birds at its original level.